Mometrix
TEST PREPARATION

Praxis

School Counselor (5422)
Secrets Study Guide

Dear Future Exam Success Story

First of all, **THANK YOU** for purchasing Mometrix study materials!

Second, congratulations! You are one of the few determined test-takers who are committed to doing whatever it takes to excel on your exam. **You have come to the right place.** We developed these study materials with one goal in mind: to deliver you the information you need in a format that's concise and easy to use.

In addition to optimizing your guide for the content of the test, we've outlined our recommended steps for breaking down the preparation process into small, attainable goals so you can make sure you stay on track.

We've also analyzed the entire test-taking process, identifying the most common pitfalls and showing how you can overcome them and be ready for any curveball the test throws you.

Standardized testing is one of the biggest obstacles on your road to success, which only increases the importance of doing well in the high-pressure, high-stakes environment of test day. Your results on this test could have a significant impact on your future, and this guide provides the information and practical advice to help you achieve your full potential on test day.

Your success is our success

We would love to hear from you! If you would like to share the story of your exam success or if you have any questions or comments in regard to our products, please contact us at **800-673-8175** or **support@mometrix.com**.

Thanks again for your business and we wish you continued success!

Sincerely,
The Mometrix Test Preparation Team

> **Need more help? Check out our flashcards at:**
> **http://mometrixflashcards.com/Praxisii**

TABLE OF CONTENTS

INTRODUCTION _____ 1

SECRET KEY #1 – PLAN BIG, STUDY SMALL _____ 2

SECRET KEY #2 – MAKE YOUR STUDYING COUNT _____ 3

SECRET KEY #3 – PRACTICE THE RIGHT WAY _____ 4

SECRET KEY #4 – PACE YOURSELF _____ 6

SECRET KEY #5 – HAVE A PLAN FOR GUESSING _____ 7

TEST-TAKING STRATEGIES _____ 10

DEFINE _____ 15
   ROLES OF THE SCHOOL COUNSELOR _____ 15
   HUMAN GROWTH AND DEVELOPMENT _____ 20
   STUDENT DIVERSITY _____ 25
   ETHICS AND LEGAL ISSUES _____ 39
   CHAPTER QUIZ _____ 48

DELIVER _____ 49
   GUIDANCE AND COUNSELING _____ 49
   ADDRESSING SPECIFIC CONCERNS _____ 59
   ACADEMIC ADVISEMENT AND CAREER PLANNING _____ 73
   PROMOTING A HEALTHY SCHOOL ENVIRONMENT _____ 75
   CONSULTATION, COLLABORATION, AND COORDINATION _____ 82
   CHAPTER QUIZ _____ 95

MANAGE _____ 96
   COUNSELING AND SCHOOL GUIDANCE PROGRAM DESIGN _____ 96
   DEVELOPING INSTRUCTION AND ASSESSMENT _____ 105
   TECHNOLOGY AND COUNSELING _____ 108
   CHAPTER QUIZ _____ 109

ASSESS _____ 110
   RESEARCH-BASED PRACTICE _____ 110
   STUDENT ASSESSMENT _____ 120
   CHAPTER QUIZ _____ 126

PRAXIS PRACTICE TEST #1 _____ 127

ANSWER KEY AND EXPLANATIONS _____ 151

PRAXIS PRACTICE TESTS #2 AND #3 _____ 172

HOW TO OVERCOME TEST ANXIETY _____ 173

ADDITIONAL BONUS MATERIAL _____ 179

Introduction

Thank you for purchasing this resource! You have made the choice to prepare yourself for a test that could have a huge impact on your future, and this guide is designed to help you be fully ready for test day. Obviously, it's important to have a solid understanding of the test material, but you also need to be prepared for the unique environment and stressors of the test, so that you can perform to the best of your abilities.

For this purpose, the first section that appears in this guide is the **Secret Keys**. We've devoted countless hours to meticulously researching what works and what doesn't, and we've boiled down our findings to the five most impactful steps you can take to improve your performance on the test. We start at the beginning with study planning and move through the preparation process, all the way to the testing strategies that will help you get the most out of what you know when you're finally sitting in front of the test.

We recommend that you start preparing for your test as far in advance as possible. However, if you've bought this guide as a last-minute study resource and only have a few days before your test, we recommend that you skip over the first two Secret Keys since they address a long-term study plan.

If you struggle with **test anxiety**, we strongly encourage you to check out our recommendations for how you can overcome it. Test anxiety is a formidable foe, but it can be beaten, and we want to make sure you have the tools you need to defeat it.

1

Secret Key #1 – Plan Big, Study Small

There's a lot riding on your performance. If you want to ace this test, you're going to need to keep your skills sharp and the material fresh in your mind. You need a plan that lets you review everything you need to know while still fitting in your schedule. We'll break this strategy down into three categories.

Information Organization

Start with the information you already have: the official test outline. From this, you can make a complete list of all the concepts you need to cover before the test. Organize these concepts into groups that can be studied together, and create a list of any related vocabulary you need to learn so you can brush up on any difficult terms. You'll want to keep this vocabulary list handy once you actually start studying since you may need to add to it along the way.

Time Management

Once you have your set of study concepts, decide how to spread them out over the time you have left before the test. Break your study plan into small, clear goals so you have a manageable task for each day and know exactly what you're doing. Then just focus on one small step at a time. When you manage your time this way, you don't need to spend hours at a time studying. Studying a small block of content for a short period each day helps you retain information better and avoid stressing over how much you have left to do. You can relax knowing that you have a plan to cover everything in time. In order for this strategy to be effective though, you have to start studying early and stick to your schedule. Avoid the exhaustion and futility that comes from last-minute cramming!

Study Environment

The environment you study in has a big impact on your learning. Studying in a coffee shop, while probably more enjoyable, is not likely to be as fruitful as studying in a quiet room. It's important to keep distractions to a minimum. You're only planning to study for a short block of time, so make the most of it. Don't pause to check your phone or get up to find a snack. It's also important to **avoid multitasking**. Research has consistently shown that multitasking will make your studying dramatically less effective. Your study area should also be comfortable and well-lit so you don't have the distraction of straining your eyes or sitting on an uncomfortable chair.

 The time of day you study is also important. You want to be rested and alert. Don't wait until just before bedtime. Study when you'll be most likely to comprehend and remember. Even better, if you know what time of day your test will be, set that time aside for study. That way your brain will be used to working on that subject at that specific time and you'll have a better chance of recalling information.

Finally, it can be helpful to team up with others who are studying for the same test. Your actual studying should be done in as isolated an environment as possible, but the work of organizing the information and setting up the study plan can be divided up. In between study sessions, you can discuss with your teammates the concepts that you're all studying and quiz each other on the details. Just be sure that your teammates are as serious about the test as you are. If you find that your study time is being replaced with social time, you might need to find a new team.

Secret Key #2 – Make Your Studying Count

You're devoting a lot of time and effort to preparing for this test, so you want to be absolutely certain it will pay off. This means doing more than just reading the content and hoping you can remember it on test day. It's important to make every minute of study count. There are two main areas you can focus on to make your studying count.

Retention

It doesn't matter how much time you study if you can't remember the material. You need to make sure you are retaining the concepts. To check your retention of the information you're learning, try recalling it at later times with minimal prompting. Try carrying around flashcards and glance at one or two from time to time or ask a friend who's also studying for the test to quiz you.

To enhance your retention, look for ways to put the information into practice so that you can apply it rather than simply recalling it. If you're using the information in practical ways, it will be much easier to remember. Similarly, it helps to solidify a concept in your mind if you're not only reading it to yourself but also explaining it to someone else. Ask a friend to let you teach them about a concept you're a little shaky on (or speak aloud to an imaginary audience if necessary). As you try to summarize, define, give examples, and answer your friend's questions, you'll understand the concepts better and they will stay with you longer. Finally, step back for a big picture view and ask yourself how each piece of information fits with the whole subject. When you link the different concepts together and see them working together as a whole, it's easier to remember the individual components.

Finally, practice showing your work on any multi-step problems, even if you're just studying. Writing out each step you take to solve a problem will help solidify the process in your mind, and you'll be more likely to remember it during the test.

Modality

Modality simply refers to the means or method by which you study. Choosing a study modality that fits your own individual learning style is crucial. No two people learn best in exactly the same way, so it's important to know your strengths and use them to your advantage.

For example, if you learn best by visualization, focus on visualizing a concept in your mind and draw an image or a diagram. Try color-coding your notes, illustrating them, or creating symbols that will trigger your mind to recall a learned concept. If you learn best by hearing or discussing information, find a study partner who learns the same way or read aloud to yourself. Think about how to put the information in your own words. Imagine that you are giving a lecture on the topic and record yourself so you can listen to it later.

For any learning style, flashcards can be helpful. Organize the information so you can take advantage of spare moments to review. Underline key words or phrases. Use different colors for different categories. Mnemonic devices (such as creating a short list in which every item starts with the same letter) can also help with retention. Find what works best for you and use it to store the information in your mind most effectively and easily.

3

Secret Key #3 – Practice the Right Way

Your success on test day depends not only on how many hours you put into preparing, but also on whether you prepared the right way. It's good to check along the way to see if your studying is paying off. One of the most effective ways to do this is by taking practice tests to evaluate your progress. Practice tests are useful because they show exactly where you need to improve. Every time you take a practice test, pay special attention to these three groups of questions:

- The questions you got wrong
- The questions you had to guess on, even if you guessed right
- The questions you found difficult or slow to work through

This will show you exactly what your weak areas are, and where you need to devote more study time. Ask yourself why each of these questions gave you trouble. Was it because you didn't understand the material? Was it because you didn't remember the vocabulary? Do you need more repetitions on this type of question to build speed and confidence? Dig into those questions and figure out how you can strengthen your weak areas as you go back to review the material.

Additionally, many practice tests have a section explaining the answer choices. It can be tempting to read the explanation and think that you now have a good understanding of the concept. However, an explanation likely only covers part of the question's broader context. Even if the explanation makes perfect sense, **go back and investigate** every concept related to the question until you're positive you have a thorough understanding.

As you go along, keep in mind that the practice test is just that: practice. Memorizing these questions and answers will not be very helpful on the actual test because it is unlikely to have any of the same exact questions. If you only know the right answers to the sample questions, you won't be prepared for the real thing. **Study the concepts** until you understand them fully, and then you'll be able to answer any question that shows up on the test.

It's important to wait on the practice tests until you're ready. If you take a test on your first day of study, you may be overwhelmed by the amount of material covered and how much you need to learn. Work up to it gradually.

On test day, you'll need to be prepared for answering questions, managing your time, and using the test-taking strategies you've learned. It's a lot to balance, like a mental marathon that will have a big impact on your future. Like training for a marathon, you'll need to start slowly and work your way up. When test day arrives, you'll be ready.

Start with the strategies you've read in the first two Secret Keys—plan your course and study in the way that works best for you. If you have time, consider using multiple study resources to get different approaches to the same concepts. It can be helpful to see difficult concepts from more than one angle. Then find a good source for practice tests. Many times, the test website will suggest potential study resources or provide sample tests.

Practice Test Strategy

If you're able to find at least three practice tests, we recommend this strategy:

UNTIMED AND OPEN-BOOK PRACTICE

Take the first test with no time constraints and with your notes and study guide handy. Take your time and focus on applying the strategies you've learned.

TIMED AND OPEN-BOOK PRACTICE

Take the second practice test open-book as well, but set a timer and practice pacing yourself to finish in time.

TIMED AND CLOSED-BOOK PRACTICE

Take any other practice tests as if it were test day. Set a timer and put away your study materials. Sit at a table or desk in a quiet room, imagine yourself at the testing center, and answer questions as quickly and accurately as possible.

Keep repeating timed and closed-book tests on a regular basis until you run out of practice tests or it's time for the actual test. Your mind will be ready for the schedule and stress of test day, and you'll be able to focus on recalling the material you've learned.

5

Secret Key #4 – Pace Yourself

Once you're fully prepared for the material on the test, your biggest challenge on test day will be managing your time. Just knowing that the clock is ticking can make you panic even if you have plenty of time left. Work on pacing yourself so you can build confidence against the time constraints of the exam. Pacing is a difficult skill to master, especially in a high-pressure environment, so **practice is vital**.

Set time expectations for your pace based on how much time is available. For example, if a section has 60 questions and the time limit is 30 minutes, you know you have to average 30 seconds or less per question in order to answer them all. Although 30 seconds is the hard limit, set 25 seconds per question as your goal, so you reserve extra time to spend on harder questions. When you budget extra time for the harder questions, you no longer have any reason to stress when those questions take longer to answer.

Don't let this time expectation distract you from working through the test at a calm, steady pace, but keep it in mind so you don't spend too much time on any one question. Recognize that taking extra time on one question you don't understand may keep you from answering two that you do understand later in the test. If your time limit for a question is up and you're still not sure of the answer, mark it and move on, and come back to it later if the time and the test format allow. If the testing format doesn't allow you to return to earlier questions, just make an educated guess; then put it out of your mind and move on.

On the easier questions, be careful not to rush. It may seem wise to hurry through them so you have more time for the challenging ones, but it's not worth missing one if you know the concept and just didn't take the time to read the question fully. Work efficiently but make sure you understand the question and have looked at all of the answer choices, since more than one may seem right at first.

Even if you're paying attention to the time, you may find yourself a little behind at some point. You should speed up to get back on track, but do so wisely. Don't panic; just take a few seconds less on each question until you're caught up. Don't guess without thinking, but do look through the answer choices and eliminate any you know are wrong. If you can get down to two choices, it is often worthwhile to guess from those. Once you've chosen an answer, move on and don't dwell on any that you skipped or had to hurry through. If a question was taking too long, chances are it was one of the harder ones, so you weren't as likely to get it right anyway.

On the other hand, if you find yourself getting ahead of schedule, it may be beneficial to slow down a little. The more quickly you work, the more likely you are to make a careless mistake that will affect your score. You've budgeted time for each question, so don't be afraid to spend that time. Practice an efficient but careful pace to get the most out of the time you have.

6

Secret Key #5 – Have a Plan for Guessing

When you're taking the test, you may find yourself stuck on a question. Some of the answer choices seem better than others, but you don't see the one answer choice that is obviously correct. What do you do?

The scenario described above is very common, yet most test takers have not effectively prepared for it. Developing and practicing a plan for guessing may be one of the single most effective uses of your time as you get ready for the exam.

In developing your plan for guessing, there are three questions to address:

- When should you start the guessing process?
- How should you narrow down the choices?
- Which answer should you choose?

When to Start the Guessing Process

Unless your plan for guessing is to select C every time (which, despite its merits, is not what we recommend), you need to leave yourself enough time to apply your answer elimination strategies. Since you have a limited amount of time for each question, that means that if you're going to give yourself the best shot at guessing correctly, you have to decide quickly whether or not you will guess.

Of course, the best-case scenario is that you don't have to guess at all, so first, see if you can answer the question based on your knowledge of the subject and basic reasoning skills. Focus on the key words in the question and try to jog your memory of related topics. Give yourself a chance to bring the knowledge to mind, but once you realize that you don't have (or you can't access) the knowledge you need to answer the question, it's time to start the guessing process.

It's almost always better to start the guessing process too early than too late. It only takes a few seconds to remember something and answer the question from knowledge. Carefully eliminating wrong answer choices takes longer. Plus, going through the process of eliminating answer choices can actually help jog your memory.

Summary: Start the guessing process as soon as you decide that you can't answer the question based on your knowledge.

7

How to Narrow Down the Choices

The next chapter in this book (**Test-Taking Strategies**) includes a wide range of strategies for how to approach questions and how to look for answer choices to eliminate. You will definitely want to read those carefully, practice them, and figure out which ones work best for you. Here though, we're going to address a mindset rather than a particular strategy.

Your odds of guessing an answer correctly depend on how many options you are choosing from.

Number of options left	5	4	3	2	1
Odds of guessing correctly	20%	25%	33%	50%	100%

You can see from this chart just how valuable it is to be able to eliminate incorrect answers and make an educated guess, but there are two things that many test takers do that cause them to miss out on the benefits of guessing:

- Accidentally eliminating the correct answer
- Selecting an answer based on an impression

We'll look at the first one here, and the second one in the next section.

To avoid accidentally eliminating the correct answer, we recommend a thought exercise called **the $5 challenge**. In this challenge, you only eliminate an answer choice from contention if you are willing to bet $5 on it being wrong. Why $5? Five dollars is a small but not insignificant amount of money. It's an amount you could afford to lose but wouldn't want to throw away. And while losing

$5 once might not hurt too much, doing it twenty times will set you back $100. In the same way, each small decision you make—eliminating a choice here, guessing on a question there—won't by itself impact your score very much, but when you put them all together, they can make a big difference. By holding each answer choice elimination decision to a higher standard, you can reduce the risk of accidentally eliminating the correct answer.

The $5 challenge can also be applied in a positive sense: If you are willing to bet $5 that an answer choice *is* correct, go ahead and mark it as correct.

Summary: Only eliminate an answer choice if you are willing to bet $5 that it is wrong.

Which Answer to Choose

You're taking the test. You've run into a hard question and decided you'll have to guess. You've eliminated all the answer choices you're willing to bet $5 on. Now you have to pick an answer. Why do we even need to talk about this? Why can't you just pick whichever one you feel like when the time comes?

The answer to these questions is that if you don't come into the test with a plan, you'll rely on your impression to select an answer choice, and if you do that, you risk falling into a trap. The test writers know that everyone who takes their test will be guessing on some of the questions, so they intentionally write wrong answer choices to seem plausible. You still have to pick an answer though, and if the wrong answer choices are designed to look right, how can you ever be sure that you're not falling for their trap? The best solution we've found to this dilemma is to take the decision out of your hands entirely. Here is the process we recommend:

Once you've eliminated any choices that you are confident (willing to bet $5) are wrong, select the first remaining choice as your answer.

Whether you choose to select the first remaining choice, the second, or the last, the important thing is that you use some preselected standard. Using this approach guarantees that you will not be enticed into selecting an answer choice that looks right, because you are not basing your decision on how the answer choices look.

This is not meant to make you question your knowledge. Instead, it is to help you recognize the difference between your knowledge and your impressions. There's a huge difference between thinking an answer is right because of what you know, and thinking an answer is right because it looks or sounds like it should be right.

Summary: To ensure that your selection is appropriately random, make a predetermined selection from among all answer choices you have not eliminated.

Test-Taking Strategies

This section contains a list of test-taking strategies that you may find helpful as you work through the test. By taking what you know and applying logical thought, you can maximize your chances of answering any question correctly!

It is very important to realize that every question is different and every person is different: no single strategy will work on every question, and no single strategy will work for every person. That's why we've included all of them here, so you can try them out and determine which ones work best for different types of questions and which ones work best for you.

Question Strategies

⊘ READ CAREFULLY

Read the question and the answer choices carefully. Don't miss the question because you misread the terms. You have plenty of time to read each question thoroughly and make sure you understand what is being asked. Yet a happy medium must be attained, so don't waste too much time. You must read carefully and efficiently.

⊘ CONTEXTUAL CLUES

Look for contextual clues. If the question includes a word you are not familiar with, look at the immediate context for some indication of what the word might mean. Contextual clues can often give you all the information you need to decipher the meaning of an unfamiliar word. Even if you can't determine the meaning, you may be able to narrow down the possibilities enough to make a solid guess at the answer to the question.

⊘ PREFIXES

If you're having trouble with a word in the question or answer choices, try dissecting it. Take advantage of every clue that the word might include. Prefixes can be a huge help. Usually, they allow you to determine a basic meaning. *Pre-* means before, *post-* means after, *pro-* is positive, *de-* is negative. From prefixes, you can get an idea of the general meaning of the word and try to put it into context.

⊘ HEDGE WORDS

Watch out for critical hedge words, such as *likely, may, can, sometimes, often, almost, mostly, usually, generally, rarely,* and *sometimes.* Question writers insert these hedge phrases to cover every possibility. Often an answer choice will be wrong simply because it leaves no room for exception. Be on guard for answer choices that have definitive words such as *exactly* and *always.*

⊘ SWITCHBACK WORDS

Stay alert for *switchbacks.* These are the words and phrases frequently used to alert you to shifts in thought. The most common switchback words are *but, although,* and *however.* Others include *nevertheless, on the other hand, even though, while, in spite of, despite,* and *regardless of.* Switchback words are important to catch because they can change the direction of the question or an answer choice.

10

⊘ Face Value

When in doubt, use common sense. Accept the situation in the problem at face value. Don't read too much into it. These problems will not require you to make wild assumptions. If you have to go beyond creativity and warp time or space in order to have an answer choice fit the question, then you should move on and consider the other answer choices. These are normal problems rooted in reality. The applicable relationship or explanation may not be readily apparent, but it is there for you to figure out. Use your common sense to interpret anything that isn't clear.

Answer Choice Strategies

⊘ Answer Selection

The most thorough way to pick an answer choice is to identify and eliminate wrong answers until only one is left, then confirm it is the correct answer. Sometimes an answer choice may immediately seem right, but be careful. The test writers will usually put more than one reasonable answer choice on each question, so take a second to read all of them and make sure that the other choices are not equally obvious. As long as you have time left, it is better to read every answer choice than to pick the first one that looks right without checking the others.

⊘ Answer Choice Families

An answer choice family consists of two (in rare cases, three) answer choices that are very similar in construction and cannot all be true at the same time. If you see two answer choices that are direct opposites or parallels, one of them is usually the correct answer. For instance, if one answer choice says that quantity x increases and another either says that quantity x decreases (opposite) or says that quantity y increases (parallel), then those answer choices would fall into the same family. An answer choice that doesn't match the construction of the answer choice family is more likely to be incorrect. Most questions will not have answer choice families, but when they do appear, you should be prepared to recognize them.

⊘ Eliminate Answers

Eliminate answer choices as soon as you realize they are wrong, but make sure you consider all possibilities. If you are eliminating answer choices and realize that the last one you are left with is also wrong, don't panic. Start over and consider each choice again. There may be something you missed the first time that you will realize on the second pass.

⊘ Avoid Fact Traps

Don't be distracted by an answer choice that is factually true but doesn't answer the question. You are looking for the choice that answers the question. Stay focused on what the question is asking for so you don't accidentally pick an answer that is true but incorrect. Always go back to the question and make sure the answer choice you've selected actually answers the question and is not merely a true statement.

⊘ Extreme Statements

In general, you should avoid answers that put forth extreme actions as standard practice or proclaim controversial ideas as established fact. An answer choice that states the "process should be used in certain situations, if…" is much more likely to be correct than one that states the "process should be discontinued completely." The first is a calm rational statement and doesn't even make a definitive, uncompromising stance, using a hedge word *if* to provide wiggle room, whereas the second choice is far more extreme.

11

⌀ Benchmark

As you read through the answer choices and you come across one that seems to answer the question well, mentally select that answer choice. This is not your final answer, but it's the one that will help you evaluate the other answer choices. The one that you selected is your benchmark or standard for judging each of the other answer choices. Every other answer choice must be compared to your benchmark. That choice is correct until proven otherwise by another answer choice beating it. If you find a better answer, then that one becomes your new benchmark. Once you've decided that no other choice answers the question as well as your benchmark, you have your final answer.

⌀ Predict the Answer

Before you even start looking at the answer choices, it is often best to try to predict the answer. When you come up with the answer on your own, it is easier to avoid distractions and traps because you will know exactly what to look for. The right answer choice is unlikely to be word-for-word what you came up with, but it should be a close match. Even if you are confident that you have the right answer, you should still take the time to read each option before moving on.

General Strategies

⌀ Tough Questions

If you are stumped on a problem or it appears too hard or too difficult, don't waste time. Move on! Remember though, if you can quickly check for obviously incorrect answer choices, your chances of guessing correctly are greatly improved. Before you completely give up, at least try to knock out a couple of possible answers. Eliminate what you can and then guess at the remaining answer choices before moving on.

⌀ Check Your Work

Since you will probably not know every term listed and the answer to every question, it is important that you get credit for the ones that you do know. Don't miss any questions through careless mistakes. If at all possible, try to take a second to look back over your answer selection and make sure you've selected the correct answer choice and haven't made a costly careless mistake (such as marking an answer choice that you didn't mean to mark). This quick double check should more than pay for itself in caught mistakes for the time it costs.

⌀ Pace Yourself

It's easy to be overwhelmed when you're looking at a page full of questions; your mind is confused and full of random thoughts, and the clock is ticking down faster than you would like. Calm down and maintain the pace that you have set for yourself. Especially as you get down to the last few minutes of the test, don't let the small numbers on the clock make you panic. As long as you are on track by monitoring your pace, you are guaranteed to have time for each question.

⌀ Don't Rush

It is very easy to make errors when you are in a hurry. Maintaining a fast pace in answering questions is pointless if it makes you miss questions that you would have gotten right otherwise. Test writers like to include distracting information and wrong answers that seem right. Taking a little extra time to avoid careless mistakes can make all the difference in your test score. Find a pace that allows you to be confident in the answers that you select.

⊘ Keep Moving

Panicking will not help you pass the test, so do your best to stay calm and keep moving. Taking deep breaths and going through the answer elimination steps you practiced can help to break through a stress barrier and keep your pace.

Final Notes

The combination of a solid foundation of content knowledge and the confidence that comes from practicing your plan for applying that knowledge is the key to maximizing your performance on test day. As your foundation of content knowledge is built up and strengthened, you'll find that the strategies included in this chapter become more and more effective in helping you quickly sift through the distractions and traps of the test to isolate the correct answer.

Now that you're preparing to move forward into the test content chapters of this book, be sure to keep your goal in mind. As you read, think about how you will be able to apply this information on the test. If you've already seen sample questions for the test and you have an idea of the question format and style, try to come up with questions of your own that you can answer based on what you're reading. This will give you valuable practice applying your knowledge in the same ways you can expect to on test day.

Good luck and good studying!

Define

Transform passive reading into active learning! After immersing yourself in this chapter, put your comprehension to the test by taking a quiz. The insights you gained will stay with you longer this way. Scan the QR code to go directly to the chapter quiz interface for this study guide. If you're using a computer, simply visit the bonus page at **mometrix.com/bonus948/praxsccoun5422** and click the Chapter Quizzes link.

Roles of the School Counselor

TRANSFORMED ROLE OF THE SCHOOL COUNSELOR

The **role of the school counselor** has broadened and integrated, so that the goals and delivery of the counseling program dovetail with those of the **school as a whole**. School counselors as educators recognize that school curriculum delivery and achievement standards are quantifiable media to address the access, attainment, and achievement goals of each individual student as well as the student body as a whole. Counselors also frame their approach with a basic premise that students who are given rigorous curricula and good support are capable of realizing their potential. Besides leading individual sessions and group workshops, counselors can participate in academic program planning. By **integrating educational and counseling goals**, counselors can provide the bridge between personal success and academic achievement. The counseling program can provide immediate assessment that describes the holistic achievement of the students.

DEVELOPMENT OF SCHOOL COUNSELING

Until the 1940s, school guidance counseling was primarily focused on **helping students choose vocations** suited to their personality traits. In the 1940's, Carl Rogers instigated a change in the professional focus from vocational to **individual counseling**. In the 1950s, professional organizations appeared, setting standards for school counseling training and the profession. The **National Defense Education Act**, a reaction to the start of the Cold War, changed the focus back to vocation as the US government provided funding to increase the number of scientists and mathematicians in the arms race. In the 1960s and 1970s, the focus again shifted to **individual support and developmental guidance**. In 1987, a journal article defining the perception of school counseling as unnecessary prompted the profession to take on a holistic focus and to create national standards for training school counselors and for the professional activities of school counselors, in effect saving itself from becoming obsolete by both increasing its professional scope and taking an active interest in promoting and advocating for the profession.

PROMOTING PARENTAL INVOLVEMENT

Parents are often hesitant about getting involved in school functions because they often feel that they are not important and that their opinions do not count. In some cases parents may have had a negative experience involving a principal or other school official. It is the responsibility of the counselor to **make parents feel valued and important** before discussing any type of involvement. An effective counselor knows the **value of parental involvement** and realizes that they must invite, recruit, and motivate all parents to get involved. When these efforts do not work, a counselor may have to offer incentives or rewards in order to get parents to take the first step toward involvement. Involving a parent does not mean they have to speak in public or put on a carnival; it could be as simple as donating time to repair something in the school.

CHARACTERISTICS TO PROMOTE WHEN BUILDING A SCHOOL CULTURE

When a counselor is striving to **build a school culture**, it is important to promote certain characteristics. School culture consists of everyone: teachers, students, parents, and other staff members. One of the important traits is attention to the values of the members. One sign of an effective culture is the behavior of the members: that is, whether or not they are positive and upbeat. Another sign is whether teachers, students, and parents are interacting in a positive and effective way. A strong culture also respects the written and unwritten policies and procedures. In order for the counselor to truly understand the school's culture, they should take the time to perform group interviews, in order to accurately understand the issues of the school.

RESPONDING TO NEGATIVE REACTIONS TO AUTHORITY

When a counselor is faced with a **negative reaction to authority**, his or her first reaction may be to become defensive or upset. However, the appropriate way to handle this situation is to **investigate** and **examine** the reasons why others are responding this way. This may be a difficult reaction to have for many counselors. The feelings of hurt and anger are normal: however, an effective counselor knows how to put those feelings away and move on to the problem-solving stage. The challenge to authority can be a positive situation, especially if the causes are understood. The key to diagnosing the reasons for the negative reaction is to have a **discussion with the parties involved**. Every effort should be made to avoid putting anyone on the defensive, and every attempt should be made to understand the person's point of view.

EXERCISING AUTHORITY SUCCESSFULLY

There are numerous reasons why people **question and challenge authority**. However, if a counselor follows certain guidelines, then this issue can be overcome. Counselors are obviously going to have to make some very difficult decisions and give directives to others. One consideration a counselor should decide on is how and in what style the directive will be given. It is important for a counselor to remember that regardless of how professional the directive was given, if the person who received it does not feel that it is in their best interest, there is going to be an issue of resistance. A counselor should also consider the strengths and weaknesses of the person before giving a directive. Issuing an order for someone who is not motivated will result in failure. They should also explain the rationale behind the directive and remember that not everyone may understand the value in it.

IMPORTANCE OF SELF-NURTURING

Counselors have an extremely difficult job: they must motivate, coach, lead, attend meetings, and maintain the mission and goals of the school. These job duties can be rewarding; they can also be emotionally draining. Many times, this can cause **burn-out** among counselors, which can have a negative impact on the rest of the school. In order for a counselor to perform their responsibilities effectively, they must remember that they are individuals too, and take care of themselves. It is important for counselors to find a **healthy balance** between work and personal life. Sleep, relaxation, fitness, and a healthy diet will enable a counselor to be a well-adjusted person. When a counselor has found a way to balance their responsibilities, they become a healthier individual and a better role model for staff members, students, and parents.

BARRIERS TO EFFECTIVE COMMUNICATION

Every message a counselor sends out will be interpreted in different ways by every person who receives it. Many times, the message will not be successfully communicated simply because of factors outside the control of the counselor. Often, a counselor will send out a message they believe is extremely important, only to find that the recipients do not share the same opinion. Sometimes, the person receiving the message lacks the background knowledge needed to understand the message. Certain phrases or words require a base of knowledge to be understood. Understanding the group who will be receiving the message can help the counselor determine how the message should be written in order to help reduce the misunderstanding.

ENHANCING SCHOOL CULTURE

Before a counselor can **enhance a school culture**, he or she must first achieve a good understanding and full knowledge of what the organizational culture is. After this has been achieved, the counselor can move on to enhancing the culture. If the school culture is not an effective one, it will be a challenge for the counselor to change it. The counselor must envision the future of the school: what is the goal that will make the school improve? A counselor must also make it a priority to meet the needs of the teachers and students. Enhancing the school culture will more likely be achieved if the counselor views a problem as an opportunity to find solutions rather than as a burden. It will also be enhanced if teachers are encouraged to use creative practices and are given opportunities to share their ideas and made to feel they are a vital part of the improvement of the school. The most important factor that will enhance school culture is a relentless focus on student achievement.

SCOPE OF PRACTICE OF A SCHOOL COUNSELOR

School counselors are not expected to engage in either diagnosis or long-term therapy with students. A student demonstrating out-of-the-ordinary behavioral problems of a complex nature is beyond the expertise level and **scope of practice** of a school counselor. Speaking to the parents will help give more context to the behavior and possibly shed light on potential causes and conditions: physical, social, or emotional. It is one of the ethical duties of a school counselor to inform and partner with parents in the care of children, and it's a practical first step in understanding familial conditions that may contribute to or potentially help solve the student's problem.

Referral to a psychologist for assessment and diagnosis is a logical next step, and having the child's physical health checked by a doctor helps rule out medical conditions that might be contributing to or causing the behavioral problems. Seeing that the student's problems are beyond his or her ethical remit, the obligation is to facilitate. Primarily, the school counselor, rather than attempting diagnosis or treatment him/herself, becomes the person who **liaises** with family, teachers, and other professionals, assembling a treatment team that takes over the continuing care of the student.

HANDLING CONFLICT BETWEEN FORMAL AND INFORMAL LEADERS

When a school has a number of different leaders, there is a strong potential for **conflict**. There could be a disagreement on a wide variety of topics, and any type of conflict could make it harder for the counselor to build a unified organizational culture. The most important habit a counselor needs to cultivate is listening to both sides in order to understand the main issue of the conflict. There should be an opportunity for both the **formal and informal leaders** to voice their opinions and feel they are contributing. A counselor can use their influence to persuade one party of the direction that is more suitable to the overall school organizational culture. There is no one correct way of handling a situation like this; however, a counselor with strong conflict resolution skills can change a difficult situation.

ADOLESCENT RISK BEHAVIORS AND HIV AND AIDS

The Center for Disease Control asserts that a tendency to have unprotected sex and multiple sex partners places adolescents at a greater risk of contracting HIV and the AIDS virus. The risk seems to be especially high for minority adolescents. Individuals are considered to be at special risk of contracting HIV if they are regular substance abusers, do not have much awareness of the risks of

17

HIV, come from a poor and/or uneducated background, or have dropped out of school. In order to combat this problem, the CDC has developed a number of programs to continue providing education to students in both classrooms and community centers. Many of these programs specifically target minorities.

ADOLESCENT RISK BEHAVIORS AND SEXUALLY TRANSMITTED INFECTIONS

Because they are more likely to engage in **risky sexual activity** with multiple partners, adolescents are more likely to contract a sexually transmitted infection. The CDC believes that **adolescents are particularly at risk** if they are frequent drug users and if they do not have access to contraceptives or to sex education. In order to meet the ongoing needs, the CDC has developed programs to present important information to adolescents so that they can protect themselves, as well as so that they can seek treatment if they do contract an STI. Part of the CDC's mission is to increase the level of parental involvement in the lives of adolescents. The CDC has published a number of statistics indicating that when parents actively supervise their children's lives, the children are less likely to engage in dangerous sexual behavior.

ADDRESSING CHILD ABUSE

Counselors are required by federal mandate to report any cases of **child abuse or neglect**. This is mandated by the Keeping Children and Families Safe Act of 2003. If a counselor or other professional has reason to believe that abuse or neglect has occurred within 24 to 72 hours, she or he is obligated to call **Child Protective Services (CPS)** and report orally and in writing their suspicions within a time frame specified by the state. Note that if a report proves false, the counselor/professional is not liable unless the report was made with malicious intent. Child abuse can include physical abuse, mental injury, sexual abuse or exploitation, maltreatment of a child under 18 or the age specified by the state child protection law, and negligent treatment. Counselors should be knowledgeable of state and other mandates regarding the report of child abuse.

HIPAA AND FERPA REGULATIONS

There are three key federal acts governing the disclosure of student records. The most significant is the **Family Educational Rights and Privacy Act (FERPA)** of 1974, which limits the disclosure of student records. The Privacy Rule of 2001 established national rights for privacy and security regarding health information, and these rights were in concert with FERPA. The **Health Insurance Portability and Accountability Act (HIPAA)** of 1996 generated national standards regarding the privacy of individually identified health information, set criteria for health records, and delineated patients' rights. Any school records, including health records, that are protected under FERPA are not subject to HIPAA regulations, however, educators in special education may be required to obtain the services of outside professionals whose services are governed by HIPAA. Counselors should be knowledgeable and aware of regulations regarding the exchange of student information and when exceptions to FERPA are warranted by HIPAA or other law.

DEVELOPING TEACHING PLANS

A teacher cannot be effective without **properly planning every aspect of class**. Good plans give a teacher confidence, security, and a definite direction in class. Teachers that are successful planners typically follow four steps when they plan an activity. First, they have a total understanding of the activity: what it will involve, what it is designed to teach, and what potential problems it might have. Next, the teacher imagines its implementation in the classroom, and makes whatever modifications to the environment are necessary. Then, the teacher evaluates the strengths and weaknesses of his or her class, and alters the activity to suit them. Finally, an effective teacher will create a mental image of the finished activity, and imagine exactly how it will be accomplished.

18

CASE STUDIES

Teachers can effectively use **case studies** to solidify conceptual knowledge that has been taught in a particular unit. In a case study, the teacher provides specific information, and students are required to analyze and evaluate the information. For example, students might be presented with a business plan and asked to describe its strengths and weaknesses. When developing case studies, a teacher should make sure that the information is comprehensible to all the members of the class and that no untaught concepts are required to perform an adequate analysis. It is also important to limit the amount of information given: too much data may confuse students and detract from the power of the exercise. Finally, teachers should ensure that there are some areas of the assignment that require creative thought, rather than simply recitation of the course material.

SYLLABUS

A **syllabus** is essential for effectively organizing and administrating a class. Preparing a clear and detailed syllabus before the start of the school year allows teachers to be sure that all of the essential areas will be covered, that there will be enough variety among assignments to hold the interest of the class, and that all the students will understand the program and the expectations. A proper syllabus should include a defined aim for the course, clear assessment objectives, an outline of the assessment structure (that is, how students will be examined), the content of the curriculum, and a grading scale. The grading scale should include a sufficient description of the quality of work that merits each letter grade.

GENERAL COURSE STRUCTURE

Although there is no one way to order the material of a course, some ways seem to make more sense than others. For instance, most teachers will want to begin the course with an overview of the general themes of the course, so that students will have an idea of the **structure of the course** and will be prepared for its various transitions. This process is enacted in miniature at the beginning of each lesson, as the teacher describes the rough elements of the material that will be covered during the class period. In most courses, there is a sequential order that must be followed; for instance, some elements of geometry cannot be taught until algebra has been learned. In other subjects, however, as for instance literature, a teacher will have more freedom to arrange course material according to improvised themes or narratives.

DIFFERENTIATION

In classes that consist of students with varying abilities, it is crucial for a teacher to practice **differentiation**: that is, distinguishing between students and adjusting the class material to engage all of them. This of course is a great responsibility for a teacher: more time must be spent planning, and teachers must guard against settling for lessons that appeal strictly to the middle level of the class. Besides differentiating between students, teachers must also differentiate between classes. Some classes may have a different "character" than others, depending on the time of day when they are held and their composition. Differentiation is especially important in classes, because they are frequently available to all students, regardless of aptitude.

TIPS CONCERNING ASSIGNMENTS IN CLASS

Teachers will typically assign students a task or series of tasks to solidify and assess learning. **Class assignments** encourage students to manipulate and analyze course material. When making assignments, teachers should make sure to have a clear idea of what knowledge they are seeking to reinforce. Assignments should have varying degrees of difficulty, such that the least able students can attempt everything and the most able students will feel challenged. If research is required to complete the assignment, the teacher should have established the means for the students to perform this research. Finally, teachers should always grade every particular part of an assignment separately, so that students will have a better idea of what is expected of them, and in what areas they need to improve.

FACTORS INDICATING EFFECTIVE USE OF AFFECTIVE SKILLS

Some of the factors that can be used to measure how well-developed an individual's **affective skills** are include determining how well the individual receives emotional stimuli and how well the individual responds to those stimuli. It is also important to determine how easy it is for the individual to acknowledge the worth of a particular situation, relationship, or individual and whether the individual has an organized and well-conceived value system. An individual's ability to receive and respond to emotional stimuli can be measured by how aware the individual is of a particular stimulus, how willing the individual is to acknowledge that particular stimulus, and how focused the individual is on that stimulus. An individual's ability to assign value to a situation and uphold a value system can be measured by how motivated the individual is, how the individual behaves, and how consistent that individual's behavior is. For example, a student that always comes to class and clearly always pays attention may have well-developed affective skills.

WORKING COOPERATIVELY WITH OTHER EDUCATORS AND MENTAL HEALTH PROFESSIONALS

School districts may employ or call upon numerous **professionals** in the endeavor to provide **mental health services** to students. These may include psychologists, school nurses, social workers, crisis intervention counselors, as well as staff educators and administrators. School counselors often form a part of this larger network of mental health professionals on the school campus, working with the same population of students. It is in the counselor's and program's best interest that school counselors develop and maintain a spirit of cooperation when working with these diverse groups of mental health professionals. It is not advisable, nor is it generally successful, to generate an attitude of superiority or a hierarchical stance when working with other professionals. Remember that all of the groups and individuals involved are striving for the same goal: the mental health of the students. By working cooperatively and inclusively, counselors can benefit from the support and expertise of those in peripheral professional positions.

EXPECTATIONS WHEN REPORTING SUSPECTED CHILD ABUSE

It is important to remember that the counselor is obligated to **report suspicion of child abuse**. Counselors who suspect child abuse and do not report it could lose their license or certification, face disciplinary action, and/or have their employment terminated. It is also significant to remember that an individual who reports reasonable suspicion of child abuse is not required to prove the abuse, but rather just to report suspicion. The law protects the individual who **reasonably suspects child abuse**. Also notable is that parents and guardians are not granted rights to information during this process, and should not be informed regarding the report. The department of social services and/or law enforcement agencies will contact the parents as appropriate and will conduct the investigation. Counselors should be knowledgeable about laws regarding child abuse, as well as school, district and other applicable procedures.

Human Growth and Development

PIAGET'S THEORIES OF DEVELOPMENT OF STUDENTS IN EARLY CHILDHOOD

According to **Piaget**, students in early childhood (the years between 2 and 6, spanning preschool to kindergarten) generally are incapable of grasping **abstract concepts**, such as those dealing with time and space. They are developing **motor skills**, usually through play, as well as language skills and the ability to imitate events. These skills will grow and develop during the early childhood years, which will be reflected in improved use of language, increased motor skills, and the appearance of more concreteness in their drawings. During this time, children are egocentric; however, they are also **developing social skills** as well as the ability to regulate some of their own emotional responses. Counselors will be well served to engage a child's imaginative skills in the session, as well as to consider some of the theoretical concepts of childhood experts like Piaget.

Carl Rogers's Contribution to Counseling

Rogerian therapy assumes that counseling clients become healthier when therapists provide them with human acceptance rather than "expert" guidance. Earlier psychotherapy saw the client as someone to be acted upon: Rogers used the therapeutic relationship to create a medium of **unconditional positive regard**. Therapists use empathy (or empathic understanding) to reach out to and nurture clients and teach self-acceptance.

Rogers believed that therapists should be as transparent or genuine as possible; a departure from earlier ideas of therapy that positioned the therapist as unknowable, unflappable, and an expert on the client's "problem." Rogerian therapy takes the client as the expert on him/herself, and counselors are careful not to provide interpretation, advice, or didactic training but to simply be there with the client, attending to the growing relationship, considered the central place of healing in client-centered therapy.

In Rogerian counseling, therapists teach clients to lead the process, asking perhaps for the first time in their lives, "What do *I* want? What matters to *me*?" Rogerian therapists model genuineness and congruence in their relationships with clients, who, it may be argued, suffered from a lack of congruence in early family life that perpetuates mental suffering in adult life.

Erik Erikson's Stages of Early Childhood Development

In **Erikson's** theoretical paradigm, the years of early childhood development are defined by a **series of crises** which result in **positive or maladaptive behaviors**. Each developmental stage is preceded by a crisis that ideally is resolved through positive development of skills and behaviors. For instance, ego development may be prompted by the crisis of self-promotion being perceived as counter to the obligation to others: that is, the drive to grow and develop being tempered by a sense of guilt. Refining the balance between these two directives (incorporating self-worth, imagination and sometimes gender) contributes to the child's self-discovery. Counselors should encourage students to explore positive behaviors or actions that may be out of the student's normal realm, in the interest of developing new skills. In addition, increases in language and motor skills tends to encourage self-promotion and self-discovery. Opportunities for developing these skills should be seized in the counseling setting.

Play-Time Setting

For children between the ages of 2 and 6, play is an integral part of development. Children often **express emotions, describe events, and project their desires in a play setting**. In the counseling session, a good strategy is for the counselor to interact with the child in play-time settings, using such manipulatives as dolls, toys, puppets, art projects, or other favorites. The play-time setting can be a wonderful opportunity for children to explore not only their environment, but also their own capabilities and skills. The counseling session will be best served if the child is allowed sufficient and reasonable latitude for exploring the boundaries of self-discovery, self-confidence, and emotional self-regulation. The play setting provides an environment for developing and regulating skills and behaviors. Counselors can provide such media as dolls, animals, art supplies, and animals, through which children can express themselves.

DEVELOPMENTAL STAGE OF MIDDLE CHILDHOOD

Middle childhood, generally associated with the ages between 7 and 11, is most easily distinguished by the ability to **think logically, read and write more skillfully, and mentally reverse actions**. While they are still unable to grasp many abstract ideas, students in this age group are nonetheless increasingly able to manipulate concrete information. They are able to generalize about their actions or their environment based on this information. The development of logical thinking allows children in this age group to interact more cooperatively, in part because they are more able to recognize intentionality and are becoming less egocentric. Counselors working with this age group can use such strategies as exploration, manipulation of information, and action. Sessions are best served if the counselor remains aware that students in this age group are generally able to reason logically, based on concrete information. For this reason, middle childhood is often called the concrete operational stage.

ERIK ERIKSON'S 8 STAGES OF PSYCHOSOCIAL DEVELOPMENT

Each of **Erik Erikson's eight developmental stages** contains a psychosocial crisis, the positive resolution of which results in attainment of a basic virtue. Erikson's theory posits that people move through stages in order, with each stage being resolved positively or negatively. The more stages whose outcomes are healthy, the healthier the personality.

The school ages (between 5 and 12 and 12 and 18) are stages of Industry versus Inferiority and Identity versus Role Confusion. Adolescence is characterized by the identity crisis, in which students explore and create a unique self.

Although some developmental stages may not be positively resolved the first time around, Eriksonian theory says that they can be returned to later in life and successfully worked through.

Psychosocial Crisis	Basic Virtue	Age
Trust vs. Mistrust	Hope	0-1.5 years old
Autonomy vs. Shame	Will	1.5-3 years old
Initiative vs. Guilt	Purpose	3-5 years old
Industry vs. Inferiority	Competency	5-12 years old
Identity vs. Role Confusion	Fidelity	12-18 years old
Intimacy vs. Isolation	Love	18-40 years old
Generativity vs. Stagnation	Care	40-65 years old
Ego Integrity vs. Despair	Wisdom	65+ years old

B. F. SKINNER'S BEHAVIOR MODIFICATION THEORY

Skinner believed that behavior was **created and reinforced by the environment**. In his theory of operant conditioning, a stimulus generates a response, and behavior is learned by experiencing the outcome of one's behavior as positive or negative. Behaviors that create an unpleasant outcome (punishment) are avoided, and those creating a pleasant outcome (reward) are repeated. Behavior can be reinforced or extinguished by applying different outcomes, and the challenge is to discover why an outcome that one person might find rewarding (recognition by the teacher in front of the whole class) might be a punishment for someone else.

In **behavior modification**, reinforcements may be positive or negative, meaning that the reinforcement may occur after the response (positive reinforcement) or may be taken away after the response (negative reinforcement). For example, if a child misbehaves while playing a game, he/she may be put in time-out. Removing the child from the game is a negative reinforcement and should diminish the misbehavior. On the other hand, if the misbehavior goes unchallenged and the

22

child wins the game, the misbehavior would be positively reinforced by winning. Skinner's model also posits that behaviors can be increased or decreased by planned repetition, or schedules of reinforcement.

ROBERT HAVIGHURST'S THEORY OF PSYCHOSOCIAL DEVELOPMENT

Like Erikson, **Robert Havighurst** identified stages of development based on chronological age and the resolution of specific developmental tasks throughout the life span. Havighurst proposed a six-stage model of human development:

Tasks:

- **Infancy/early childhood, age birth to 6 years**—learning to crawl, talk, and walk; being potty trained, knowing gender
- **Middle childhood, age 6 to 12**—learning social roles, values, morality, and relational skills; learning about one's self; becoming independent.
- **Adolescence, age 13 to 18**—growing independence, handling physical changes of puberty and sexuality, and beginning to work
- **Early adulthood, age 19 to 30**—becoming a mate, a spouse, and/or a parent; finding an occupation; becoming socially responsible
- **Middle age, age 30 to 60**—finding satisfaction at work, exploring outside interests (hobbies), experiencing the start of aging, and caring for parents
- **Later maturity, age 60+**—changing living situations, experiencing and coping with the physical changes of aging, and retiring and handling the changes of income and social life that retirement brings

SIGMUND FREUD'S THEORY OF PSYCHOSEXUAL DEVELOPMENT

Freud's three parts of the personality, which drive behavior, he labeled id, ego, and superego. The id, or pleasure principle, is primitive and unconcerned with morality or rationality. The ego, logical and stable, is concerned with higher thought processes. The superego contains or inhibits antisocial behavior.

Stages of Psychosexual Development:

- **Oral, birth to 1 year**—Everything goes into the mouth! The child gets primary satisfaction from biting, chewing, and sucking. Frustration at this stage may cause overeating or smoking habits, nail biting, or talking too much.
- **Anal, age 1 to 3 years**—The primary focus is on potty training. Harsh parental attitudes around toileting may cause children to grow up overinhibited and obsessed with cleanliness: permissive parenting can create messy, sloppy, "over-expressive" adults.
- **Phallic, age 3 to 6 years**—Freud identified two complexes that he believed accompanied children's growing awareness of the opposite sex and sexual feelings. The Oedipus Complex and the Electra Complex, he thought, defined the attraction children felt for the other-gendered parent.
- **Latent, age 6 to 11 years**—The superego reigns: children learn to delay gratification. Friendships and peer groups gain importance. Sexuality temporarily recedes.
- **Genital, age 11 to 18**—With puberty, sexuality reassumes its importance in the life cycle and people begin to engage in mature sexual relationships.

POSITIVE FEEDBACK FOR STUDENTS IN MIDDLE CHILDHOOD

Middle childhood is distinguished by a developing, yet often fragile **sense of competency**. This sense of competency is particularly dependent on external feedback, from friends, family, and authority figures. A sense of competency is also encouraged by the student's own success in accomplishing increasingly challenging tasks, though it can also be discouraged by failure. Counselors working with this age group need to be sensitive to this fragility, and respond by providing manageable tasks that the student is more likely to succeed in. Positive, encouraging feedback is also very beneficial to students in this age group. Both **positive feedback** and opportunities for success provide valuable buffers against the development of feelings of inadequacy in students in middle childhood, including self-fulfilling behaviors that validate a sense of incompetence and failure.

ENCOURAGING PEER RELATIONSHIPS FOR MIDDLE CHILDHOOD STUDENTS

During this time of competency development, peer interaction is particularly important for the student in middle childhood for a number of reasons. Not only is peer feedback important, but peer interaction provides an opportunity for students to see their peers in a similar balance of success and failure, which validates their position and allows for the development of empathy for others' positions. Likewise, students in this age group develop a sense of understanding and tolerance for differing appearances and behaviors through healthy peer interaction. A counselor can provide opportunities for peer interaction by holding group counseling sessions, as well as by encouraging healthy friendships for students in this age group. Often, significant friendships are formed. These friendships can be pivotal to the development of a student's sense of self-competency and significance among their peers.

CHARACTERISTICS OF THE STAGES OF ADOLESCENCE

Adolescence is a time of breakthrough transition between childhood and adulthood, and is generally divided into three sub-stages. Although the stages are very individualized, the years between ages 11 to 14 are usually called adolescence, 15 to 18 middle adolescence, and 18 and above late adolescence. The accomplishments realized during these three stages affect **physical appearance, social interaction, and thinking processes**. The physical changes are known collectively as puberty. Students in this age group develop a more comprehensive understanding of social roles and relationships. Furthermore, thinking processes evolve from concrete to formal, resulting in an increased ability to think abstractly. Counselors working with this age group need to be mindful of both the stage at which a student is operating and the next phase of development, so that they can provide opportunities for that development.

THERAPEUTIC STRATEGIES FOR WORKING WITH ADOLESCENTS

Adolescent students are increasingly able to apply **abstract thinking** to possible solutions and scenarios of situations. Counselors working with this age group can take advantage of this abstract thinking by soliciting the student's collaboration in generating and implementing solutions to problems. The beginning of this process could be asking a student to view a situation differently, allowing for a larger spectrum of possible solutions. Adolescent students are also able to think reflectively, allowing for a better sense of responsibility for actions. Students in this age group are also increasingly egocentric and **less dependent on external feedback**, sometimes resulting in reckless behavior. They are more **self-conscious**, particularly with students of their age group. Counselors are best served by facilitating the student's ability to balance these feelings with increased social awareness and abstract thinking skills. Counselors can also provide students in this age group with opportunities for the development and implementation of alternate approaches to problem solving.

EFFECTS OF PUBERTY ON ADOLESCENT STUDENTS

The onset and progress of **puberty** complements and often perpetuates role confusion for the adolescent student. Adolescence is a pivotal time, in which students refine self-concepts of worth, value in the larger society, and life goals. This self-definition is often validated by peer interaction. The counselor should work with students in this age group by encouraging them to develop goals and values of their own, not necessarily those of their peer group. Counselors can assist students in developing their own senses of identity and worth, separate from social cliques or idolized hero symbols. Students in this age group begin to understand that their actions and beliefs form an integral part of their role and their value system. Counselors can positively facilitate this connection when working with adolescents. It is important that counselors endorse the idea of the worth and significance of every individual.

PEER RELATIONSHIPS FOR ADOLESCENT STUDENTS

Adolescent students are simultaneously developing a sense of self-worth and self-identity and developing close ties with their peer groups. It is important for the counselor to assist the student in balancing the significance of **peer relationships** with the evolution of his or her own self-definition. Students in the adolescent age group often develop a sense of ethnic identity before they develop a sense of self-identity. While the role of a peer group can bolster and validate a student's ethnic or cultural identity, it is also important for the student to develop personal and individual goals. Counselors can work with adolescent students to help them identify personal goals as well as ideas and perceptions that diverge from the group identity. The influence of community beliefs and behaviors can hinder the development of individuality. Nonetheless, because peer relationships are very important to adolescents, counselors should also encourage and endorse healthy relationships.

Student Diversity

NEED FOR SENSITIVITY TO DIVERSITY OF CULTURE

As America becomes more **culturally diverse**, schools will be increasingly comprised of a mix of different races, religions, and socioeconomic levels. Counselors need to be aware of the significance of these factors in the learning environments of students. Certain ethnic groups may be victims of social and economic hierarchies, which can affect the availability of technology and other education-related amenities. Counselors can act as non-judgmental liaisons for students if they are sensitive to some of the situational differences defined by race. They can also work with groups of students on such issues as assertiveness and empowerment. A counselor should also consider the problems faced by second-language learners, as well as the religious and cultural factors that may affect academic and social success.

BECOMING MORE CULTURALLY AWARE

The first step in becoming more **culturally aware** is to recognize the need to do so. Counselors who work with a diversity of races and socioeconomic groups should invest the time and attention to understand the roots and ramifications of the differences. There are cultural sensitivity training sessions available, often through the school district. Although cultural sensitivity training is becoming more commonplace and is even required in some districts, counselors and their programs will be best served by a proactive approach. Some counselors reach beyond the school district to surrounding cultural enclaves, to further their understanding of a particular culture. Some counselors take further action by becoming involved in addressing policy and practices that better the overall academic achievement of a particularly underserved group, although the effectiveness of this has not been clearly demonstrated.

PROMOTING CULTURAL SENSITIVITY IN THE SCHOOL ENVIRONMENT

Cultural sensitivity helps counselors recognize culturally based differences within the school environment. Counselors observe interactions affected by cultural differences, and then address any problems while maintaining sensitivity to both the minority and the majority cultures. Counselors can involve school staff and counselors in discussions regarding the methods and policies for addressing cultural differences and conflicts among students, as well as between teachers and students. Certain school practices can lead to an appreciation and celebration of these differences. These practices can include talking with students and parents and actively learning about different cultures. Increasing cultural awareness within a school environment can lead to a rich, dynamic community, and can improve the value of a well-designed counseling program.

PROFESSIONAL SKILLS AND COMPETENCIES RELATED TO CULTURAL AWARENESS

Counselors striving to attain an **environment of cultural sensitivity** can begin the process by first presenting a professional demeanor toward all students and other members of the school community. It is important to recognize that cultural and socioeconomic differences can affect behavior and appearance, and to avoid responding negatively or differently to these manifestations. It is also important to remember that every person, including the counselor, lives with certain presuppositions, and to be cognizant of these presuppositions while developing an increased understanding of cultural differences and misunderstandings. Some of the bases for these misunderstandings include racism, stereotyping, socioeconomic oppression, and discrimination. Additionally, cultural differences could be gender-based, belief-based, or based on other distinguishing characteristics. Being aware of these cultural layers and learning to respond with dignity and respect can provide a healthy example for the school community.

LIMITATIONS OF LANGUAGE WHEN ADDRESSING ISSUES OF CULTURAL DIVERSITY

Counselors who have been sensitized to cultural differences, and trained in strategies for addressing these differences in the school environment, may still experience difficulty finding the right words when communicating with school staff, counselors, students and the rest of the school community. There is no one way to solve this problem; however, counselors should recognize that cultural differences can stem from historical traditions, racial or ethnic classifications, economic status, or cosmology. These differences can affect how people view and respond to life experiences, and can often divide populations into groups of similar experience and perception. Awareness of some of the roots of cultural diversity and cultural bias can help the counselor develop terminology for addressing issues of diversity and integrating cultural sensitivity into various aspects of the counseling program.

COMPONENTS OF CULTURE

Before broaching the subject of culture, counselors should first define culture and describe its influence. Listed below are some of the **key components of culture**:

- Beliefs or belief systems that define one's place in society, the world, and the cosmos. These beliefs can become assumptions and practices regarding social status, personal empowerment, and relation to material wealth.
- Perception of life experiences and how those experiences can affect life choices.
- Value systems including family, career, and education
- Religious beliefs and practices
- Definitions and circumstances relating to belief in life's purpose
- Accepted behaviors for self-validation

It is also important to remember that cultural distinctions are often rooted in historical tradition, supported by generations of practice and affirmation. Working with a culturally diverse population is best approached by recognizing and respecting the roots of culture.

RACE AND SEGREGATION IN THE SCHOOL ENVIRONMENT

Race can also be defined by biogenetic factors, socioeconomic grouping, distinctive traits and behaviors, language, traditions, and rituals. Individually or as an aggregate, these factors often play a part in racial discrimination and segregation. **Segregation** also may be based on economic status, academic achievement, level of fluency in English, or disability. In this sense, race can be viewed as a political and psychological concept. Counselors working in the school community to dissipate cultural biases and misunderstandings will be well served to recognize that race is a concept defined primarily by these behavioral and economic factors.

PARAMETERS OF ETHNICITY

In contrast to race, **ethnicity** is rooted in **national origin and/or distinctive cultural patterns**. In other words, ethnicity is based on more easily identifiable factors. Groups of students with the same ethnicity share the same general ancestral background. A group that shares ethnicity will often share religious beliefs; attitudes toward family, school and career; and customs, traditions and rituals. These beliefs and traditions are often reinforced by the fact that individuals who share an ethnicity tend to socialize together, providing a continuum of culture. However, counselors should be sensitive to the fact that individuals can present degrees of assimilation, developing practices and beliefs that differ from their ethnic origins. Ethnicity is generally associated with family, although it can also be defined by religion, race, and cultural history.

OPPRESSION

Although **oppression** may be rooted in cultural or racist biases, and is usually expressed through inequities of power or benefits. The general psychological basis for oppression is a fallacious assumption by one group that another group is intrinsically inferior or incapable of a particular quality of life. Unfortunately, these misperceptions often are perpetuated by the conditions that result from them. Individuals or groups who possess the power or benefits (e.g. better paying jobs, better access to technology, and better access to transportation) inherently define oppressed individuals as inferior by their lack of these quality of life indicators. **Oppressed groups** may internalize this definition, further perpetuating the oppression and exploitation. Oppressed individuals or groups will often accept their subservient position in the school or work environment because they do not feel empowered to challenge the dominant group. **Oppressive tactics** include exploitation, intimidation, and violence.

TYPES

The **forms of oppression** can be placed into five general categories. The first category is **individualized oppression**, which encompasses oppression stemming from assumptions of inferiority in another person based on race or culture. This process extrapolated to the group level becomes **cultural oppression**, which is comprised of actions or attitudes toward a cultural group that result in the targeted group changing its behavior. **Systemic or institutional oppression** is hierarchical practices that inherently discriminate against certain groups in the distribution of resources. Oppression that is internalized by the targeted group is insidious because the oppressed group believes and perpetuates its own perceived inferiority. Conversely, **external oppression** describes actions or beliefs targeting a particular group because they are perceived by others as inferior. Instances of oppression may fall into more than one category.

MULTICULTURAL COUNSELING

While developing a counseling relationship with a student or students, it is important to recognize whether multicultural factors obtain. **Multicultural counseling** occurs when the race or ethnicity of the students is different from that of the counselor. The multicultural counseling relationship will necessarily involve two sets of expectations, perceptions, social environments, beliefs and backgrounds, often beyond the usual disparities between two people. Sensitivity to culturally-based differences can be helpful in communication and setting expectations. The five major cultural groups identified by the Association of Multicultural Counseling and Development (AMCD) are African/Black, Asian, Caucasian/European, Hispanic/Latino/a, and Native American. Other cultural groups can pertain to gender, sexual orientation, religious beliefs, etc. A counselor should try to remain aware of multicultural counseling without falling into a biased taxonomy.

FORMS OF OPPRESSION THAT CAN AFFECT DISTRIBUTION OF RESOURCES

The terms below identify **oppressive belief systems** targeting specific groups. Often, public schools and other societal entities distribute resources unfairly based on these perceptions:

- Ableism – targeting persons identified by different abilities/disabilities
- Ageism – targeting persons younger than 18 or older than 50
- Beautyism – targeting persons who are obese or otherwise fall outside of expected appearance norms
- Classism – targeting persons based on income level or socioeconomic class
- Familyism – targeting persons whose family falls outside of expected norms, such as single parents, same gender parents, or foster families
- Heterosexism and Transgenderism – targeting persons who are homosexual, lesbian, bisexual, two-spirit, intersex, or transgender
- Linguicism – targeting persons because they do not speak the dominant language, or do so with a marked accent
- Racism – targeting persons of another color or of mixed race
- Religionism – targeting persons who do not practice the dominant religion
- Sexism – targeting persons of a different sex

ENSURING THAT COUNSELORS ARE COMPETENT IN MULTICULTURAL ENVIRONMENTS

Counselors who will be working with different cultural or ethnic groups are best served by not only receiving initial training in multicultural counseling, but also by attending workshops and other instruction in the field on an ongoing basis. Many schools and districts with a diverse student body require this of school counselors. Counselors who receive ongoing training in multicultural counseling will be less likely to impose their own belief systems and cultural insensitivity on the counseling relationship, and more likely to consider cultural differences when communicating and setting goals with students. School counselors and counselors can usually recognize when they are incorporating cultural sensitivity in their counseling methods by assessing the success of the sessions. If a counselor or counseling program is operating with multicultural competence, there should be no significant differentiation between success rates with students of different cultural backgrounds.

LEVELS OF MULTICULTURAL COUNSELING

Multicultural counseling incorporates three distinct levels of competence. The initial, foundational level is that of **awareness**. Counselors can begin to build multicultural competence by first becoming aware of the effects of culture on worldview, behaviors, etc. It is also a good first step for counselors to be aware of their own preconceived notions about cultures, as well as aspects of

28

their value system that are culturally based. Building on this, counselors can come to knowledge, respect, and understanding of other cultures, realizing that cultural assimilation is not always the recommended course of action for students. **Cultural sensitivity** includes refraining from imposing dominant beliefs and attitudes, unless appropriate. Balancing social protocol with cultural expression is a valuable skill that counselors can teach to students. Lastly, counselors can develop **skills** that enable them to implement effective and appropriate strategies when working with students from diverse cultures.

Types of Knowledge About Different Cultures That Will Enrich Multicultural Sensitivity

Counselors working with diverse cultures can increase and enrich their sensitivity by understanding the concepts and terminology of a particular culture, as well as by learning developmental theories related to that culture. In order to understand a culture, a counselor needs a working knowledge of the history, traditions, strengths, needs, and resources of it. Counselors can act as consultants and liaisons by assisting students who are misunderstood and misrepresented by school staff, students, public media, etc. Understanding the semantics and terminology of specific cultures can be particularly helpful in mediating between cultural groups, as well as in encouraging communication and sensitivity between groups. Counselors who approach diversity with a fundamental knowledge of specific cultures and the impact of culture can provide role models for dynamic multicultural understanding and communication in the school environment. Understanding the impact of culture in particular can lay a strong foundation for multicultural sensitivity, as counselors, students, and school personnel begin to recognize the cultural basis of many misunderstandings.

Counseling Skills That Indicate Multicultural Sensitivity

Counselors who are sensitive to cultural differences will more likely develop strategies and hypotheses that are free of **cultural biases**. Developing hypotheses that are not culturally slanted will allow counselors to more objectively plan and implement intervention strategies. **Multicultural sensitivity** enables counselors to design and deliver lesson plans that are free from stereotypical icons or remarks; it also helps them decide when and how to generalize instructions for diverse groups of students. With increased sensitivity, counselors can design activities and strategies that are inclusive of diverse cultures or that are individualized for different cultures. An example of an inclusive activity is eliciting student responses about a recent event on campus. An individualized activity could be asking students to write about holiday traditions in their home, which would allow students to respond from a cultural perspective.

Areas of the School System Positively Impacted By Multiculturally Competent Counselors

Cultural and ethnic diversity in the school environment often results in disparities in peripheral areas, particularly if issues of **oppression** and **bias** are not addressed. Some of the peripheral areas that can be impacted by culturally-based hierarchies include academic achievement, literacy competence, AP course participation, career planning, and, most significantly, disparities in standardized test results, which can negatively affect college opportunities and eventual income level. Counselors who operate with multicultural sensitivity can significantly mitigate these disparities by acting as a liaison between the student body and school officials. In this capacity, counselors can act on students' behalf when there is a culturally-based misunderstanding, as well help students develop strategies for bridging cultural gaps. Counselors can also help school staff and officials pinpoint practices that may inherently pose a disadvantage for certain cultural groups.

NEED FOR MULTICULTURAL AND ANTI-OPPRESSION TRAINING IN COUNSELING PROGRAMS

Traditional school counseling programs reflect long-practiced curricular parameters based on Western European culture and history. Consequently, practice and discussions tend to be non-inclusive of other cultures, particularly in regard to diversity and multicultural counseling issues. Counselors who have been trained in a traditional Western European program are usually inadequately prepared to address issues associated with multicultural identities, especially the practices and environments of oppression. Without infusing additional multicultural training into a counseling program, counselors often unknowingly perpetuate the Western paradigm. Counselors and the programs they create will then lack an understanding of oppression, cultural history, cultural identity, and the acquisition of multicultural competency. This is why the onus is usually on the counselor to obtain ongoing multicultural training, and to invest in research about multiculturalism and oppression, in order to bring a more comprehensive perspective into the school environment.

SOCIAL JUSTICE

Social justice incorporates awareness of inequalities based on cultural, race or ethnicity, and the ability to redistribute resources. Counselors who work with diverse student groups should know when and if those groups have been historically oppressed. This historical oppression usually reveals practices and attitudes that have been accepted and ingrained in the larger community as well as the school environment. Counselors can systematically and diplomatically address these practices and attitudes, in the interest of creating social environments that support social justice. Examples of these practices and attitudes include testing that does not allow for second language learners, and lesson plans that use examples that are only familiar to certain cultural groups. Counselors can work with students, school staff, and the surrounding community to establish an environment of social justice.

HELPING STUDENTS BECOME EMPOWERED

The idea of **empowerment** includes the distribution of resources, but is rooted in a larger context of social relationships and dynamics. **Culturally-based oppression** often depends on acceptance from both the dominant culture and the oppressed culture. Historically oppressed cultures sometimes adopt ways of thinking and behaving that originally were enforced by violence or other extreme means, but have continued because of cultural identity. Likewise, historically dominant cultures adopt ways of thinking and behaving that perpetuate a false sense of superiority. Counselors can help students develop personal empowerment by encouraging them to recognize that individuals, and groups of individuals, often share many similarities and are connected at a fundamental level. This kind of thinking transcends historical relationships and forges new interpersonal connections, giving empowerment to previously disenfranchised groups.

DEVELOPMENT OF CONSCIOUSNESS AND SELF-IMAGE THROUGH EMPOWERMENT

There are several key areas of personal dynamics and self-image that are impacted by empowerment:

- Individuals begin to relate to others based on commonalities of experience and belonging, rather than on preconceived notions of difference.
- Individuals begin to recognize social dynamics objectively, rather than internalizing them and view them in a subjective sense.

- A sense of empowerment and recognition of social dynamics can reverse students' thinking, from that of victim to that of change agent for social justice.
- Once individuals understand that social dynamics, and not any inherent inferiority, determine their social status, the implications for personal growth can be exponential.

Counselors who work with students toward empowerment are giving them back the power that taken by culturally-based beliefs, attitudes and practices. Empowerment should be understood as being not hierarchical, such that the oppressed group is now the dominant group, but rather as egalitarian, ensuring fair distribution of resources and opportunity.

STRATEGIES FOR HELPING STUDENTS FEEL EMPOWERED

Counselors can **help students feel empowered** by pointing out their membership in the larger community and helping them to develop ownership and responsibility for their actions. Counselors can begin by discussing the parameters of group membership, noting that each of us belongs to several groups. Students must recognize that they belong to groups based on their occupation, community, culture, gender, etc. This recognition enables students to transcend limits of identity. Counselors can then point out that social dynamics involve the whole community, affecting individuals in myriad ways. This allows students to broaden their understanding of social processes. Students should also be encouraged to take personal responsibility for their academic progress, as well as for other actions and behaviors. Counselors can help students develop new behaviors that reflect a stronger self-confidence, a perception of membership in the larger community, and a realization that they can positively contribute to that community.

SKILL-BUILDING AND DEVELOPING AN INCREASED KNOWLEDGE BASE WHILE PROMOTING EMPOWERMENT

Counselors working with students toward empowerment can first provide them with the knowledge and perspective that will allow them to approach their goals and circumstances differently. Even though students can understand their community membership in theory, often particular events or circumstances become a discouraging validation of the status quo. Counselors can partner with students to confront these circumstances, addressing them on a problem-specific basis, from an enlightened and empowered perspective. A good problem-solving strategy includes the following key steps:

- Identify the problem.
- Work together to set a goal that will mitigate or solve the problem.
- Develop incremental actions toward the goal.
- Identify available resources for achieving the goals.

Counselors can also provide support and encouragement, reminding students of their strengths, their desire to change their circumstances, and the support and resources available.

NEED FOR ADDITIONAL MULTICULTURAL TRAINING IN INDIVIDUAL COUNSELING SESSIONS

As with developing counseling programs, counselors who conduct **individual counseling sessions** can sometimes suffer from a dearth of multicultural knowledge, at least in part because of the limited scope of their training. This can affect counselors' interactions with students, as well as the strategies used to address problems. Many graduate programs fail to address cultures other than those with a Western European perspective. This can be a handicap for counselors working with a diverse student body, since they would lack an understanding of different cultural beliefs, terminology, historical oppression, and other factors. Understandably, their approach in counseling might be irrelevant or even offensive. Counselors working with a diverse student body should obtain multicultural training, develop relevant strategies for individual counseling, and collaborate with other counselors or school staff as appropriate.

EFFECTS OF CULTURE ON STUDENTS' PERCEPTION AND PARTICIPATION IN COUNSELING PROCESS

There are numerous **cultural factors that can affect the counseling relationship**. One of the primary factors is the difference between group-oriented cultures and individual-oriented cultures. Students who come from a culture that values the group above the individual will approach communication, goal-setting, and decision-making from a completely different perspective than those who comes from a culture that values the individual above the group (such as traditional Western culture). Culture can determine whether the student perceives the counselor as a helper or an intruder. Students from some cultural backgrounds may communicate more with body language than words, and could perceive the counselor's communication similarly. Culture can affect students' time orientation, sense of self, and ability to make decisions. This is particularly significant when counselors are working with students from a historically oppressed culture. Counselors can develop appropriate strategies for developing a student's sense of empowerment in harmony with his or her cultural values.

COMPOSING GROUP SESSIONS WITH MULTICULTURAL STUDENTS

The dynamics of **group sessions** can be particularly influenced by cultural factors. Understanding how different cultural groups respond to stereotypes, oppression, discrimination, and prejudice can assist the counselor in forming groups. Likewise, **student perceptions of the counselor** as facilitator or authority can affect the group dynamics. Although the recommendation is not necessarily to limit groups to similar cultures, and in fact in some cases it might be valuable to blend cultures, it is up to the counselor to be sensitive to the ramifications of multicultural dynamics. It is worth noting that culture can include gender, religion, and other criteria. Counselors should refer to literature, research, and other resources regarding considerations and practices related to cultural diversity.

FACILITATING MULTICULTURAL UNDERSTANDING IN GROUP SESSIONS

Although multicultural groups can benefit from the richness of blended cultures, these groups may be more susceptible to misunderstandings and conflicts as a result of the differences in perspectives. The counselor can provide valuable leadership by encouraging the interchange of ideas about such topics as self-identity, self-worth, oppression, and responsibility to society. Likewise, if there is conflict in the group, the counselor who has been trained in multicultural sensitivity can better recognize if the conflict is culturally based, and can take the opportunity to intervene and work with the students to develop strategies for resolution. It may be possible for the group to work as a whole on culturally-based conflict resolution, allowing other members to contribute newly learned skills or perspectives. Multicultural counseling groups can provide fertile ground for teaching multicultural sensitivity.

IMPORTANCE OF MULTICULTURAL SENSITIVITY WHEN CONSULTING WITH PARENTS AND TEACHERS

Sensitivity to cultural differences can be especially important when consulting with parents and teachers on a student matter, particularly when the student's family is from a different culture than the teacher or counselor. Often, the consulting/discussion group will be comprised of the student, his or her parents, the counselor, the teacher, and a school counselor. Counselors need to be especially sensitive to the following key factors:

- A parent who lives in a culturally isolated household or neighborhood
- A student who is bi-cultural
- The culture of the teacher/counselor
- The culture of the counselor

Counselors should create an environment that allows comfortable communication and input from all parties. Counselors should be sensitive to the cultural significance and perception of the issue at hand, as well as to the best ways to address the problem within the cultural contexts represented.

ADDRESSING CULTURAL BIASES OR STEREOTYPES IN CONSULTING ARRANGEMENTS

In the process of facilitating a discussion among parents, student, teachers, and other parties in a consulting discussion, counselors may find that one or more individuals may be communicating or acting from a paradigm of **bias** or **stereotyping**. This may develop into a resistance to resolution, particularly if the problem is culturally based. Counselors may need to challenge the individuals by pointing out the specific words or behaviors that perpetuate stereotypes and the negative effect that these actions have on the intervention process. Counselors can remind the group of the shared desire for resolution, and how stereotyping can detract from the purpose of the gathering. They can remind participants that the well-being of the student will be best served by collaboration and by refraining from expressions of cultural bias and stereotyping.

ASSESSING STUDENTS FROM DIVERSE CULTURAL BACKGROUNDS

In most school environments, there are a number of standardized tests that are administered to assess academic achievement and aptitude. Counselors can provide a valuable service to the school and its students by determining if tests are inherently culturally biased, and by suggesting **alternate assessment methods** as appropriate. Some of the aspects of testing that should be reviewed are references to events or individuals that are specific to particular cultures and language-based assessment that does not allow for second language learners. It may be appropriate for the counselor to help school counselors develop alternative testing methods, or to work one-on-one with students from disadvantaged cultures. Counselors should obtain training and use outside resources to identify **culturally biased testing** and to choose alternative methods. It is also important to understand how to communicate testing results to families of students from diverse cultures.

AVOIDING CULTURAL BIAS WHEN CONDUCTING ASSESSMENT

Counselors should be particularly vigilant about any personal biases that could obscure the assessment process. In other words, if a test is designed to assess student readiness for academic promotion, and half of the students perform at the readiness level, while the other half perform below the readiness level, the initial reaction might be that the test was successful, and that half of the class is ready for promotion. However, if a counselor finds that lines of success or failure fall in a quasi-line progression toward eliminating or isolating a particular cultural group, he or she should avoid the assumption that the test validates cultural differences, and instead should review the test and the testing process for cultural biases. Not only can these cultural biases negatively affect individual students, but the continued use of a **culturally skewed test** can be used to fallaciously document poor achievement by particular cultures, and further perpetuate academic oppression.

MAKING TESTS AVAILABLE IN LANGUAGES OTHER THAN THE DOMINANT LANGUAGE

Assessment vehicles that are language based, such as math word problems or reading comprehension tests, may intrinsically put second-language learners at a disadvantage. Counselors should be sensitive to this disadvantage, and should offer students alternate testing methods. These methods may include written tests in the student's native language or the presence of an interpreter. Translators may also be on hand to present the questions in both the **dominant language** and the **student's native language**, in order to assist the student in making associations between the two. It is important that the test be presented in a way that is comfortable, allows ample time for translation, and does not contain any implications of inferiority about second-language learners. Assessment of second-language learners should fairly and accurately test students' aptitudes, skills, and abilities.

USING CURRICULUM LESSONS TO ADDRESS MULTICULTURAL SENSITIVITY

Often, counselors are required to deliver **lesson plans regarding multicultural awareness and sensitivity** to diverse groups of students. Counselors can improve the cultural climate in a school setting by promoting multicultural sensitivity and educating students about best practices for positive diversity. They can begin by defining and identifying cultural differences, as well as appropriate language and behaviors for addressing these differences. A lesson plan about multicultural sensitivity can first identify that culture may include or refer to race, ethnicity, gender, sexual orientation, different levels of ability, etc. Counselors can illustrate how culturally-biased behaviors and attitudes can lead to oppression and conflict, whereas avoidance of these behaviors can contribute to the richness of a diverse student body. Counselors should also remind students of the negativity engendered by practicing and promoting oppressive behaviors among their families and other members of their own culture.

LESSON PLAN TOPICS ON POSITIVE DIVERSITY AND MULTICULTURAL SENSITIVITY

Counselors wishing to educate students on **positive diversity and multicultural sensitivity** can include both informational and reflective elements in their lesson plans. Informational elements can encompass the correct usage of multicultural terminology, identification of oppression and oppressive practices, and identification of cultural differences and how they can affect interaction. Counselors can explain culturally-based differences of world view and value systems. Reflective exercises can include group discussions, testimonies of personal experience, or journal exercises exploring personal biases and assumptions. Counselors can also include examples of racism, ageism, ableism, etc., to identify cultural bias and illustrate its negative impact. Students could be asked to identify cultural bias in historical texts. The class can also discuss ideas for addressing oppressive beliefs and practices throughout the world. Lesson plans can alternate between informational lecture and reflective discussion to best engage the students in the topic.

INCLUDING THE SURROUNDING COMMUNITY IN BUILDING MULTICULTURAL SENSITIVITY

Counselors can offer their expertise and act as **liaisons to the surrounding community** by including parents and neighbors in discussions and events promoting multicultural sensitivity. It is usually the responsibility of the counselor to coordinate this community outreach, which can take many forms. Counselors can develop peer mediation services, family counseling services, or hold workshops in the community to discuss cultural diversity. One of the common goals of a community outreach program is to increase multicultural sensitivity and communication, not only within the community, but also in the area surrounding the school campus. Since school campuses are often diverse, and the neighborhoods often culturally isolated, school counselors can be the vehicle for transcending cultural differences and encouraging multicultural understanding. Another method for involving the surrounding community is to hold programs, such as talent shows, on campus and invite the parents and neighbors.

Developing Relationships with the Surrounding Multicultural Community

Because students are in many ways required to **assimilate** the dominant culture, counselors may be only vaguely aware of the unique expectations, belief systems, and practices of a **student's native culture**. By developing and maintaining relationships with members of the surrounding community, counselors can be exposed to cultural practices and assumptions that are more pronounced because neighborhoods tend to be culturally isolated. In this way, counselors may gain insight about cultural identity from adults in the neighborhood. Students may be less likely to reveal some information, partly because of inherent role dynamics between the adult counselor and the adolescent student. Counselors can also find out about cultural holidays, traditions, and events in the neighborhood.

Significance of Data Collection and Sharing

Counselors can make a significant contribution to both the efficacy and the equity of a school's curriculum by **collecting and sharing data** related to the academic performance of the student body. This data can be invaluable in identifying chronic achievement inequities among racial, ethnic, and/or socioeconomic groups. Counselors should work with school staff and counselors to identify these inequities and to implement strategies to rectify the disparities. This may result in changes to course offerings or changes to the counseling program itself. Data collection may also identify strategies or courses of study that are successful. Since decisions related to curriculum are often made by committee, including school boards, clear and accurate presentation of the information is vital. Therefore, interpretation of the data is particularly important and should be conducted in collaboration with school counselors and staff.

Areas for Student Data Collection

The first area to focus on when **collecting data** is that of academic achievement. Sources include standardized test scores, grade point averages, other academic-based scores or results, and retention and graduation rates. Secondly, academic participation can be quantitatively assessed by looking at data related to course enrollment, discipline referrals, suspension rates, incidents involving illegal substances, parent participation, homework completion, and extracurricular participation. It should be noted that retention/drop-out rates can form part of both the achievement and the participation data bases. The third major area of focus for student data collection is the set of graduation-readiness competencies. These competencies include the number of students with four-year plans on file and the number of students who have participated in workshops related to career-planning, job-shadowing, and conflict resolution. Students who have completed their academic goals also form part of the graduation-readiness competency data.

Collecting Data on Multicultural Students

It is important to have appropriate variables when using data collection to determine inequities based on race, culture, ethnicity, and socioeconomic status. While there may be significant conclusions to be drawn by comparing results divided by gender, race, socioeconomic status, second-language learners, and other major categories, more useful information may be gained by comparing results in different areas within cultural groups. For instance, the results of second-language learners who perform well on aptitude tests that are number based, but poorly on those that are language based, should be assessed to determine if the testing and/or the curriculum inherently results in a cultural inequity. This kind of data gathering can identify which programs, courses, and strategies are most and least effective for diverse students, and adjustments can be made accordingly. In addition, if students do well on standardized tests, and poorly in the classroom assignments and tests, this may be an indication of poor participation in the classroom.

IMPORTANCE OF PERSONAL RESEARCH AND REFLECTION IN MULTICULTURAL COUNSELING

For counselors to be competent in multicultural counseling, it is important for them to develop a sensitivity to the significance of the distinguishing characteristics of culture. A good foundation for this sensitivity is **self-investigation and self-reflection** on the counselor's own cultural background. Counselors can develop an understanding of how their cultural and ethnic background has contributed to their value system, their traditions and rituals, their view of the individual's place in the larger society, and many other personal traits. Likewise, cultural history can reveal how particular cultures or cultural traits have played a part in social hierarchy. Counselors who are aware of their own ties to culture will be better able to understand the significance of culture for students who come from a different cultural background. A counselor with this valuable foundation can be an important liaison for students who need to balance tradition with assimilation.

ONGOING WORKSHOPS AND SEMINARS FOR MAINTAINING MULTICULTURAL COMPETENCE

The issues of diversity in the counseling and school environment are complex and multidimensional. As a society, our collective knowledge of diverse cultures and multiculturalism is continually evolving. Therefore, it is advisable for counselors to periodically attend **workshops and seminars** on the subject. Each workshop or seminar will help to **expand a counselor's sensitivity to diverse cultures**. From these events, counselors will learn how to work better with students and their families in the school counseling environment. They will learn strategies and terminology that reflect sensitivity and understanding of the scope of culture in general, as well as of the specifics of particular cultures. Fortunately, many professional organizations are aware of the need for ongoing training in multiculturalism and will usually offer numerous opportunities for the school counselor.

VALUE OF ORGANIZATIONS THAT WORK ON MULTICULTURAL COMPETENCE

The knowledge base formed from attending workshops and seminars can be greatly added to by meeting with other counselors on a regular basis or by joining organizations dedicated to increasing cultural sensitivity. The knowledge gained during periodic attendance at workshops can sometimes dissipate in an environment where it is not necessarily reinforced. Meeting with peers can repeat and validate this knowledge and can also provide the opportunity to implement and revise strategies. The combined expertise of the group can allow for **shared ideas and strategies** toward multicultural competency. Also, as a group, an organization of peers can collaborate on methods and strategies for combating oppression in the school and surrounding community through school counseling curricula and programs. These professional organizations include Counselors for Social Justice and the Association for Multicultural Counseling and Development.

READING LITERATURE ABOUT MULTICULTURALISM TO INCREASE KNOWLEDGE AND SENSITIVITY

The ability to read, analyze, and critically explore issues of cultural diversity through a written medium offers benefits not necessarily present in a seminar, workshop, or organizational meeting. Literature about cultural diversity can explore **historical and current events** through the eyes and **perspectives of several cultural groups**, especially when the written text is the culmination of research and interviews. Reading these texts, counselors can gain a comprehensive understanding of the historical factors and impact of events in relation to race, socioeconomic class, culture, gender, and the histories of other groups who have been oppressed or victimized because of culture. A good book dealing with these issues is Howard Zinn's *A People's History of the United States*, which contains personal testimonies and anecdotes about the subject. These personal stories

36

allow for a first-person perspective on issues of social justice, giving the counselor a sense of empathy to bring to the multicultural counseling environment.

BENEFITS OF CONTINUED READING OF LITERATURE ON MULTICULTURALISM

The benefits of reading **literature that addresses issues of multiculturalism** are generally two-fold: for one thing, literature on the subject of multiculturalism is always evolving, reflecting current research and other input. As with organizational meetings, literature dealing with cultural diversity is a compilation of the experiences and expertise of a number of people from a variety of perspectives. Counselors should become cognizant of this evolving expertise, in multiculturalism as well as other aspects of counseling. Secondly, teaching or counseling in isolation from the continued input of others increases the risk of personal biases and perspectives coloring the curriculum. Any one individual inherently has a limited worldview, and no individual or group of individuals could possibly know all there is to know about other cultures. Consequently, continued exposure to viewpoints and perspectives beyond their own horizon allows counselors to respond appropriately to a diverse student body.

IMPORTANCE OF A CHECKLIST IN DETERMINING OWN MULTICULTURAL COMPETENCE

A **checklist** can provide a rubric for counselors to assess their own level of multicultural awareness, sensitivity, and competence. For counselors commencing their own edification in multicultural sensitivity, or those who are relatively new and beginning the process of multicultural training, checklists can provide a set of goals to attain in the process of becoming more aware of multicultural issues. Counselors can see which issues or concerns are in need of further work, and can take advantage of the available resources for development in these areas. Once these goals are attained, counselors can periodically review the checklist to ascertain that they are continuing to incorporate the guidelines and strategies represented by the checklist, and can again refer to outside resources if indicated. The Association for Multicultural Counseling and Development, as well as other agencies, publishes appropriate checklists that address such issues as behavior, knowledge, sensitivity, and awareness.

IDEIA

The **Individuals with Disabilities Education and Improvement Act (IDEIA)** was enacted to ensure that eligible school-aged students receive the opportunity for a reasonable education. Eligible students are defined as those students who exhibit any single or combination of 13 identified disabilities. Reasonable education is distinguished as allowing students to make reasonable educational progress, not necessarily to achieve their highest possible performance. Eligible students can receive a **free appropriate public education (FAPE)** under IDEIA. The Act stipulates that these eligible students receive an education that is designed around their intellectual and physical levels. It is also mandated that the delivery of the curriculum be specially designed to meet the particular requirements of students. If the disability presented by the child has a minimal or non-negative effect on learning, then the student may not be eligible for IDEIA resources, but may be eligible for reasonable accommodations under Section 504.

AUTISM, DEAF-BLINDNESS, DEAFNESS, AND HEARING IMPAIRMENT PER IDEIA CRITERIA

Autism is a disability that affects social interactions as well as verbal and nonverbal communications. It can manifest in repetitive activities, stereotyped movements, resistance to changes in routine or environment, and unusual responses to stimuli. Most autism is evident in children before the age of 3. Academic performance may be mildly or severely impacted by autism, depending on the range and intensity of the symptoms.

Deaf-blindness refers to significant impairment in both hearing and vision. The combined impairments can result in severe suppression of development, learning, and communication, well beyond that which would result from deafness or blindness alone.

Deafness refers to a hearing impairment that is sufficient to affect the processing of linguistic information through hearing, with or without amplification. Academic participation and performance are affected accordingly.

Hearing impairment refers to a permanent or fluctuating condition that adversely affects the educational performance but does not qualify as deafness.

DEVELOPMENTAL DELAY, EMOTIONAL DISTURBANCE, AND INTELLECTUAL DISABILITIES PER IDEIA CRITERIA

Developmental delay refers to a significant cognitive lapse between ages 3 and 9 that cannot be accounted for by any other identified disability.

Emotional disturbance refers to a spectrum of symptoms that encompass a general inability to cope or learn which presents over a long period of time and to a marked degree. Symptoms include an unexplainable inability to learn, inappropriate behaviors or feelings under normal circumstances, a tendency to develop physical symptoms or fears that correlate with personal or academic problems, the inability to foster satisfactory interpersonal relationships with peers or teachers, and a general mood of unhappiness or depression. This condition adversely affects educational performance accordingly. IDEIA includes schizophrenia in this category.

"Intellectual disabilities" refers to a significantly sub-average intellectual functioning that may exist alongside deficits in adaptive behavior and may manifest during the developmental period.

IMPLEMENTING SPECIAL EDUCATION APPROPRIATION FOR STUDENTS

Generally, the steps involved in **appropriating special education accommodations** for a student include:

- Student will be recommended as needing special accommodations or additional instruction by parents/guardians, the school system, school personnel, or a state agency.
- History of student learning problems will be reviewed with parents/guardians, school counselors, school educators/special educators.
- Counselor should request written consent from parents/guardians to conduct further formal assessment.
- Students is formally assessed through tests administered by psychologists, special educators, specialists such as audiologists, etc., to determine the specific special needs and the extent of the special needs.
- Student eligibility for special accommodations is determined from results of assessment.
- If student is eligible, counselor will develop an individualized education plan (IEP) that will address student needs.
- Counselor will implement an FAPE in the least restrictive environment (LRE), as determined by the parents/guardians and educators.

> **Review Video: 504 Plans and IEPs**
> Visit mometrix.com/academy and enter code: 881103

Ethics and Legal Issues

LEGAL AND ETHICAL OBLIGATIONS OF SCHOOL COUNSELORS

Counselors are obligated both explicitly and implicitly to treat each of their clients **ethically and within legal boundaries**. Counselors need to be aware of all federal, state, district and other institutional laws and mandates regarding school counseling. Counselors also should recognize the ethical obligation to be cognizant of current research and resources pertaining to issues that students will be dealing with in the counseling sessions. Although it is understandable that no one can know resources for all the possible situations facing students, it is nonetheless ethically required of counselors to endeavor to add to their knowledge as is reasonable, to best serve the students. Counselors who are beginning their careers may spend more time researching specific issues, but will become more knowledgeable about issues affecting students. Professional associations provide guidelines and sources for counselors regarding this aspect.

> **Review Video: Ethical and Professional Standards**
> Visit mometrix.com/academy and enter code: 391843

STATE AND FEDERAL CONFIDENTIALITY REGULATIONS

Federal statutes generally address the right of a parent to access records of a minor student. Both state and federal mandates dictate that parents have the right of access to privileged information, although some state laws mitigate that right in the case of abuse or neglect. It is important for counselors to be cognizant of both federal and state statutes regarding the protection of information relating to minor students. Since federal law generally protects the right of parents to view their minor child's school records, counselors should probably keep counseling records separate from school records, in accordance with school and/or district rules. Awareness of both federal and state laws regarding confidentiality can impact not only a counselor's treatment of information, but also his or her approach to the counseling relationship, including informing both students and parents of these rulings.

OVERARCHING RULE AND IMPORTANCE OF CONFIDENTIALITY IN COUNSELING

The general **rule of confidentiality**, as denoted by the American School Counseling Association, specifies that counselors be mandated to protect the confidentiality of the student unless there is indication of intent to harm self or others. It is important to both the student and the integrity of the counseling relationship that this confidentiality principal be explained in a manner that is aligned with the student's age group and ability to perceive the explanation. This confidentiality ethic needs to be explained to parents also. The benefits of clearly explaining issues of confidentiality include the student's trust to divulge sensitive information, as well as the parents' understanding of the ethical obligation of the counselor to protect the student's confidentiality. It is also important that the student understands the counselor's obligation to breach confidentiality if he or she fears the student will harm him/herself or others.

> **Review Video: Ethics and Confidentiality in Counseling**
> Visit mometrix.com/academy and enter code: 250384

APPROACHING THE ISSUE OF CONFIDENTIALITY WITH STUDENTS

It is important that the student not only understands the tenets of **confidentiality**, but also feels comfortable with the counselor's obligations and respect of confidentiality issues. Younger students may participate in a counseling situation with their parents present, but it should be clearly explained to both parents and students that information divulged in a session without the parents will be protected. Although young students need to understand that this confidentiality can be breached in the presence of threat to self or others, it is more an assurance to parents to indicate that this aspect of confidentiality is in place. On the other hand, adolescent students are particularly sensitive to protection of their confidentiality, and it is important that they be aware of the criteria for breaching that confidentiality. To best respect the rapport established with an adolescent, a counselor could approach these criteria using humor or exaggerated examples.

ACA

The **American Counseling Association (ACA)** is a professional organization that promotes the development of counselors, advances the counseling profession, and promotes social justice within the profession. Their scope is all professional counselors. The ACA seeks to apply the profession and practice of counseling to the purpose of promoting and respecting cultural diversity, while enhancing the overall quality of life in society. The ACA includes 18 divisions, which focus on particular areas or work settings within the counseling profession, four geographic regions and 56 affiliate branches. It actually is comprised of a partnership of associations. The ACA influences many aspects of professional counseling, including credentialing of counselors, accreditation of counselor education programs, public policy and legislation, and professional resources and services. The ACA, operating in part through committees, holds functions and develops specific programs for the advancement of the profession.

STANDING COMMITTEES, TASK FORCES, AND OUTREACH

The following are the 15 standing committees of the ACA:

- Audit
- Awards
- Branch Development
- Bylaws
- Compensation
- Conference Program Selection
- Ethics
- Financial Affairs
- Graduate Student
- Human Rights
- International
- Nominations and Election
- Professional Standards
- Public Policy and Legislation
- Publications
- Research and Knowledge

Ad hoc task forces are created annually to address current concerns and business issues. Most task forces are brought together 1 year, but can stay together longer if needed. In that case, members must be re-appointed. The ACA offers training workshops, professional development conferences, and learning institutes. ACA publications address current research and are often used as textbooks in counseling courses.

ASCA, NBCC, AND CACREP

A subgroup of the ACA, the **American School Counselor Association (ASCA)**, addresses those issues in professional counseling that pertain to students, with a focus on academic, personal-social, and career development issues. School counselors are particularly pivotal in the lives of students, in that long-term life success patterns are often closely tied to academic success and a positive school experience. The ASCA provides additional information to school counselors through professional development, research and advocacy.

The **NBCC, the National Board for Certified Counselors**, is the only national credentialing organization for counselors. The Board also has established several specialty-area certifications requiring passage of the **National Counselor Exam (NCE)**.

A corporate partner of the ACA, the **CACREP, the Council for Accreditation of Counseling and Related Educational Programs**, establishes state-of-the-art standards for counselor education programs that address curriculum, program objectives, program evaluation, faculty and staff criteria and other requirements.

ETHICAL STANDARDS IN SCHOOL COUNSELING

Ethical standards are developed by most professional organizations, and are designed to direct the behavior of its members. The ethical standards for school counselors are frequently updated to reflect changes in the school system, usually at the federal level. These updated standards are revised in order to be relevant and appropriate for the school counseling profession. Ethical standards generally address the following three purposes:

- To educate members about sound ethical conduct
- To provide a mechanism for accountability
- To provide a mechanism for improvement of professional practices

The ACA's Code of Ethics is based on the following five moral principles:

- Autonomy: the ability to make independent decisions
- Justice: treatment that is fair and appropriate
- Beneficence: services and actions that are in the students' best interests
- Fidelity: commitment to the student regarding honor, loyalty and faithfulness
- Nonmaleficence: avoidance of actions or services that would cause harm to others

LAWS RELATED TO SCHOOL COUNSELING

Although **laws** are based on generally accepted norms, customs, values and beliefs, they are more binding and carry more severe penalties than ethical standards. Laws are codified into written governing documents. Laws are more prescriptive and require that counselors comply or be penalized. Both laws and ethical standards are designed to ensure that professionals follow appropriate behavior patterns and act in the best interests of the student(s). Laws and ethical standards should adhere to the same patterns and expectations, but if on occasion a law conflicts with an ethical standard, the counselor is encouraged to comply with the law. Counselors must advise the student if they encounter a situation where the laws and ethical standards are in conflict, and inform the student that they will follow the legal course of action, provided there is no harm to the student as a result.

DISCREPANCIES IN ETHICS CODES

There is some responsibility on the part of the school counselor to critically apply codes of ethics in his or her professional life. It is worth noting that there are minor differences in the codes of ethics published by different professional organizations, for instance between those published by the ACA for counselors in general, and by the ASCA for school counselors in particular. Counselors should be cognizant of the codes and any relevant disparities, and be prepared to apply the appropriate code based on both the counseling setting and capacity in which the counselor is operating. There are also, on occasion, ethical codes regarding a particular situation or relationship that seem to conflict with laws governing the same relationship or situation. Counselors are, within reason, obligated to adhere to the applicable law. However, counselors are encouraged to participate in the dynamics of setting ethical standards by initiating changes to mandates as appropriate.

ACA CODE OF ETHICS

Codes of ethics for the counseling profession generally apply to and are designed for actions and behavior that are best for the student, the situation, and the profession. These codes are reviewed and revised as appropriate. The most current revision in August 2005 addresses the following key areas:

- The Association asks for clarity regarding all ethical responsibilities for current members.
- The Association and its Codes support the mission of the membership.
- The Association endeavors to establish principles by which ethical behavior is identified, and the practices of its members are delineated.
- The Association assists its members in generating a course of action that will utilize counseling services and promote the overall values of the counseling profession.
- The Association establishes the manner in which ethical complaints should be processed, and inquiries against its members should be initiated.

ASCA CODE OF ETHICS FOR SCHOOL COUNSELORS

Since the **ASCA** falls under the organizational umbrella of the ACA, its **Code of Ethics** parallels that of the ACA in general scope of benefit to the student, the situation, and the profession. The ASCA Code is delineated more specifically through its eight major sections:

- Duties to Students
- Duties to Parents
- Duties to Colleagues and Professional Associates
- Duties to the School and Region
- Duties to Self
- Duties to the Profession
- Adherence to Standards
- Resource Materials

Counselors should treat each student with respect and consider the student's best interest. They should involve the parents when possible, and exhibit professional and ethical behavior. They should also maintain their expertise through continued learning and development. School counselors should be well versed in both the ACA Code of Ethics and the ASCA Code of Ethics. They should endeavor to incorporate the tenets of both in their professional lives, and carefully research both in the event of an ethical dilemma.

DETERMINING IF AN ETHICAL PROBLEM EXISTS

There are prescribed **steps to take in the process of identifying & addressing an ethical problem**. Both the ACA and the ASCA delineate these steps. The ACA model specifies:

- Recognize the issue.
- Consult direction from the ACA Code of Ethics.
- Identify the type of issue and its components.

42

- Consider possible courses of action.
- Compare the potential consequences of each course, and choose the most appropriate action.
- Assess the results of the course of action.
- Implement the course of action.

The ASCA model specifies:

- Identify the issue both realistically and philosophically.
- Consult direction from the law, the ACA Code of Ethics, and the ASCA Code of Ethics.
- Factor the developmental & chronological age of the student.
- Assess the student rights, parental rights, and circumstances.
- Adhere to ethical and moral principles.
- Compare the potential courses of action and consequences.
- Assess the results of the selected action.
- Consult.
- Implement the action.

LEGAL MANDATES FOR PROFESSIONAL COUNSELING BEHAVIOR

There are numerous **laws and levels of law governing the behaviors, expectations and limitations of school counselors**. Counselors are obligated to follow the laws of their state, and those of the federal government. However, these laws may be further tempered by statutory laws, common laws and/or appellate decisions. Although counselors are not expected to be legal experts, they should nonetheless be cognizant of the federal and state laws governing their scope of responsibility. As needed, they should critically analyze relevant interpretations of the law, such as in common law. They should also refer to peripheral mandates and appellate decisions if a particular situation warrants the time and clarification of researching it to this extent. If counselors are researching appellate decisions, they should have a working knowledge of the appeal process in their particular state, and any relevant appeal procedures in other states, should the situation call for reference to precedent.

STATUTORY LAW GOVERNING SCHOOL COUNSELING

Generally speaking, federal law serves to enact the Constitution. Under this umbrella, state laws generally address education, health, and other comparable programs through mandates. These state mandates, the body of which is referred to as **statutory law**, are created through legislation passed by state legislatures and the US Congress. State mandates generally are more specific and more prescribed than federal laws, although they cannot be more restrictive than federal law. State legislatures create state laws that implement federal legislation, as well as laws specific to the state. The federal government has also passed several laws, within the parameters of the Constitution, that affect professional school counselors and others in comparable fields. Because statutory law generally addresses issues related to health and education, school counselors should be well versed in relevant state law, but should also be aware of federal laws that can affect their profession.

TITLE IX

Title IX was put in place in 1972. Its intent is to prevent the **sexual discrimination** that for most of the history of this country, blocked girls from educational opportunities open to boys. Title IX made it a law that any educational institution receiving federal funding is required to provide equal opportunities in education. One effect on school counseling would be the expectation that counselors encourage girls to participate in clubs and courses—areas that have been either openly (by school policy) or covertly (by harassment and intimidation) denied to them, such as advanced

43

math, science, wood or metal shop, or chess clubs. Title IX also affected athletics, which had traditionally been a nearly all-male domain, with very few resources and little support accorded to female athletes. Title IX also supports male students who may want to enter fields considered nontraditional for males in this society, such as nursing, child care, or early education. Title IX also protects individuals from sex-based harassment or discrimination in federally funded public institutions such as museums, vocational rehabilitation organizations, and libraries.

TITLE IX OF THE EDUCATION AMENDMENTS OF 1972

Scheduling required girls' physical education at the same time as Advanced Placement (AP) Physics would prevent girls from being able to attend the AP class, effectively excluding them based on their sex. **Title IX of the Education Amendments of 1972** is the law that prevents schools receiving federal funding from denying students access to educational activities based on their sex. Schools that receive federal funding have to make sure that educational opportunities such as classes and academic clubs are not blocked to students because of their sex, and in a case where scheduling a single-sex class interferes with the potential for taking an advanced science class, even if the scheduling conflict is accidental, adhering to it violates Title IX.

TITLE II

Title II (also called the **Every Student Succeeds Act [ESSA]**) is the federal funding program, signed in 2015 by President Barack Obama, that provides for increased professional development of teachers and administrators or school leaders (including counselors). It improved on the earlier **No Child Left Behind Act**, by changing the requirement that funds be used only for teachers of core academic subjects. ESSA funding covers a wider range of professionals and provides ongoing professional development in the form of grants.

Title II recognizes that there is more to school than teachers and students: support staff and other professionals are also responsible for the well-being and education of students. Making sure that teachers and other school staff receive up-to-date training ultimately benefits students and the greater community by strengthening the school as a whole organism.

INCORPORATION OF STATE LAWS IN RULINGS AND GUIDELINES OF EDUCATION GOVERNANCE AGENCIES

In the broadest sense, governance is the interpretation and implementation of **codified laws**. Tailored to the school counseling profession, the state legislatures as a rule create legislation that addresses the field of education, from which **state and local agencies interpret and implement rules and guidelines**. The state boards of education generally enact regulations at the school district level that either address areas not specifically addressed in state legislation, or interpret it more specifically to that arena. These regulations or guidelines are not legally binding like legislation, but are representative of how agencies view certain circumstances. This interpretation is subject to the oversight of the state attorney general, particularly if a regulation is challenged. Local school systems may also develop guidelines and policies, tailoring state regulations to the local environment. Individual schools may further refine these policies, addressing the professional behavior of school counselors.

INCORPORATING KNOWLEDGE OF LAW IN PROFESSIONAL DECISIONS

For school counselors to act **professionally and ethically**, a basic **knowledge of the laws** governing their profession is expected. Beyond that, counselors should avail themselves of information regarding updates or interpretations of relevant law, and other pertinent data. Sources for this information can include on-site supervisors, ACA newsletters, professional journals, commercially available newsletters, the internet, etc. Counselors should recognize that the law and its interpretation are not static, and knowledge of the law needs to be maintained on an ongoing basis. Counselors also have the responsibility to implement and interpret the law reasonably. If state mandates appear to be in conflict with other regulations or ethical standards, counselors should apply common sense and critical thinking to the interpretation or application of the ruling. If this should occur, any decisions or actions should be documented carefully, and counselors should bring the conflict to the attention of appropriate parties as soon as possible.

PROVIDING CURRENT, OPTIMUM COMPETENCE TO CLIENTS

In addition to keeping abreast of laws and guidelines, counselors should include the following practices in order to **provide current, optimum competence** to their clients:

- Pursue opportunities for professional development. Most national and state credentials even require counselors to complete continuing education training in order to stay current on theories, trends, and new data in the field.
- Remain current within the counselor's area of responsibility by reading, consulting, networking, and otherwise bringing new research, trends, and information as added resources for serving the clients.
- Represent credentials accurately. Only earned and applicable credentials should be listed.
- Provide only those services for which the counselor is trained and qualified. Counselors should have training in a particular technique before they practice it and should not try to work with students who have conditions beyond the counselor's realm of knowledge.

RESPONSE TO SUBPOENAS

Counselors may be served with subpoenas, relating to **allegations of child abuse, neglect, custody disputes**, etc. Counselors should recognize that subpoenas are legal documents, but should respond within the context of his or her obligation to the student and the school guidelines. Counselors should not violate a student's confidentiality beyond that mandated in the school guidelines. The subpoena should always be discussed with the student or the student's attorney, and in some cases the school attorney, before any information is provided to a legal entity. Once the appropriate council approves compliance with the subpoena, school counselors should then discuss how the release of information will affect all parties, and should obtain a signed informed-consent form in order to release necessary records. If, on the other hand, the attorneys do not approve the release of information, they should file a motion to quash, which will release the counselor from the obligation to respond. All actions should be clear and documented.

LEGAL AND ETHICAL PARAMETERS OF CONFIDENTIALITY

Counselors are both **legally and professionally** committed to respect and protect students' confidentiality. The primary professional consideration relates to the establishment of trust with the student. Confidentiality essentially belongs to the student. It is his or her right and choice to disclose information. Counselors who respect this contribute to the cultivation of trust that is vital to the counselor-client relationship. However, if students are under 18, this legal right extends to the students' parents. In the case of counselors working with students under the age of 18, they can request that parents respect the student's confidentiality, but parents of minors are allowed to be present during the session(s). Nonetheless, whether a student is a minor or over 18, counselors can communicate with the students regarding their rights and responsibilities relating to confidentiality, such as whether it is optional that parents be informed.

INCLUDING PARENTS IN COUNSELING SESSIONS WITH MINORS

The ideal situation regarding a minor student is if a student readily accepts and invites his or her parents to participate in the session(s). However, if this is not the case, there are steps counselors can take to ease the disclosure. Counselors should discuss confidentiality with students at the initial session, and let them know the **legal parameters**. Students may be hesitant to let parents know about their problems, for fear of the parents' reactions. Also, when broaching the subject of disclosure, counselors should be sensitive to the possibility of family secrets, sensitive information, cultural issues and other factors that could be problematic when including parents in counseling session. Counselors can work students to get them comfortable with the idea of including their parents, and can discuss reasonable boundaries before the parents are invited to participate. However, if minor students refuse to include their parents or to give permission to disclose information, counselors may be obligated to inform the parents without the student's permission.

CIRCUMSTANCES FOR WHICH CONFIDENTIALITY MAY BE BREACHED

There are certain circumstances, as outlined in the **ACA Code of Ethics**, whereby a counselor may break, and in some cases is obligated to break, student confidentiality. Generally, counselors may **break confidentiality** if a student is in danger of harming himself or herself or others, if there is indication of abuse, or if there is any other life-threatening situation. There are other circumstances for which confidentiality may be breached:

- Counselors may disclose confidential documents with subordinates in the regular course of business.
- Members of treatment teams, consultation groups, families, and third-party players may break confidentiality through regular verbal interaction.
- Parents may be legally informed of the counseling discussions held with their minor children.
- Parents or family members may be justifiably informed if they could contract a life-threatening disease through association with the student.
- Court-ordered disclosure by way of a subpoena may require the counselor to share information, although that information can be restricted to what is necessary.

ASCA ETHICAL STANDARDS FOR SCHOOL COUNSELORS

The following statements are taken from standards comprising the first section of the American School Counselor Association (**ASCA) Ethical Standards for School Counselors**, Section A, Responsibility to Students. As each profession creates and standardizes ethical standards, the standards reflect the unique aspects of that profession. Although there are ethical standards for counselors, counseling psychologists, and teachers, the ethical standards for school counselors are constructed to account for counselors' particular responsibilities, their place in the school system and community, and their positions in regard to being trusted with the young to confidentiality and to acting on behalf of students while considering the impact of their roles and actions on parents, teachers, administrators, and other stakeholders.

In supporting student development, the school counselor has the following obligations:

- Acknowledge the vital role of parents and family.
- Provide brief therapy to students in need and obtain referrals to outside therapists when longer-term therapy is needed.
- Not provide DSM diagnoses, but keep students' diagnoses in mind when working with them.
- Understand laws regarding students, and keep parents and students informed of their legal rights.

Mometrix

MINOR CONSENT LAWS

Minor consent laws are mandated at the state level and define the circumstances under which counselors may protect the confidentiality of a minor student. These laws fall under the federal regulation that prohibits the breaking of confidentiality for patient recovery, regardless of the patient's minor status. Generally, minor consent laws allow confidentiality regarding issues such as substance abuse, mental health, and reproductive health areas, without releasing information to parents or guardians. There is some controversy regarding the interpretation of these laws, but a common implementation is a school-based student assistant program (SAP) comprised of teams that include a counselor, a counselor or a nurse, a teacher and possibly substance abuse assessors from local agencies. School staff can refer students to the SAP team who will collaboratively determine the best action for the student. Counselors should be well informed about the state mandates and local interpretations of the minor consent law.

PRIORITIZING REQUESTS WITHOUT ENGAGING IN TASKS OUTSIDE THE ROLE OF SCHOOL COUNSELOR

School counselors may have to educate others about the limits of the role and hold fast to professional tasks when administrators ask them to work outside their areas of responsibility. Being assigned other responsibilities may create dual relationships, which complicate the counselor role and are warned against in the **American School Counselors Association (ASCA) Ethical Standards for School Counselors**. School counselors may help by locating resources in the greater community, such as peer groups or mental health facilities for students whose needs exceed school-based, time-limited therapeutic interventions. The school counselor's ongoing challenge is to balance the students' needs with the ethical standards that delimit the range of school counselors' responsibilities.

Occasionally, as when a student is in danger or potentially endangering others, a school counselor will be faced with "betraying" a student's confidence to save lives. School counselors need to know and to consider the ethical standards in regard to their decisions, even relatively small decisions, at work. Being liked by all students is far less important than acting with integrity, even when the right decision is unpleasant.

PROFESSIONAL DEVELOPMENT OF SCHOOL GUIDANCE COUNSELORS

School counselors should be members of professional organizations and attend lectures, seminars, and state and national conferences sponsored by those and related organizations. School counselors should read journal articles and stay abreast of current research, which may inform their own school programming efforts. School counselors should also stay current with their legal and ethical responsibilities by attending trainings. Seeking consultation and supervision from more experienced school counselors helps build skills as well as providing much-needed emotional support for a career that balances so many activities—counseling and teaching, evaluating and reporting, working with individuals and groups, facilitating, mentoring, leading, consulting, and collaborating. Self-care is a vital part of a school counselor's mandate: if the counselor is suffering, trying to work without addressing personal problems is too difficult to sustain for long without negative effects showing up in one's work life.

MAINTAINING OWN MENTAL HEALTH

Research shows that our mental and physical health are inextricably linked. Counselors need to care for their bodies as well as their minds. Regular exercise and an intelligent diet are basic to good health. Using mindfulness and other stress reduction techniques helps bring a fresh attitude to work as well as increasing harmony in personal relationships. Creating healthy boundaries at work may mean finding a substitute at times, taking adequate time off and limiting communications with

47

parents, students, and administrators outside of school hours. Engaging a supervisor or participating in a group with other counselors can provide support and generate new ideas.

When a counselor experiences problems in his/her personal life (such as divorce, illness, or death in the family), self-care such as seeking help and support in crises is especially important.

BURNOUT

Burnout is characterized by lack of interest in the job, ironically, often while spending too much time on the job. When people burn out at work, their effectiveness drops: they make mistakes, get sloppy, or even lose the desire to do the right thing. In school counseling, students can too easily become the victims of counselor burnout. Counselors have a great deal of responsibility—as those who guide students in taking tests that will affect their college placements and future careers; as mentors, role models, and protectors; and as emotional supports and educators of academic and life skills. There's too much riding on a school counselor to have that person melt down over stress and overwork. And because the work is emotionally demanding, time-consuming, and often seriously underfunded, school counselors are at tremendous risk of burnout. To work ethically on behalf of students, the counselor has a responsibility of self-care that can't be avoided or put off.

Chapter Quiz

Ready to see how well you retained what you just read? Scan the QR code to go directly to the chapter quiz interface for this study guide. If you're using a computer, simply visit the bonus page at **mometrix.com/bonus948/praxsccoun5422** and click the Chapter Quizzes link.

Deliver

Transform passive reading into active learning! After immersing yourself in this chapter, put your comprehension to the test by taking a quiz. The insights you gained will stay with you longer this way. Scan the QR code to go directly to the chapter quiz interface for this study guide. If you're using a computer, simply visit the bonus page at **mometrix.com/bonus948/praxsccoun5422** and click the Chapter Quizzes link.

Guidance and Counseling

RESPONSIBILITIES OF COUNSELORS TO SCHOOL COMMUNITIES AND INDIVIDUAL STUDENTS

It is important to remember that the primary responsibility of the counselor is to the student body and the school community as a whole. This community includes parents, teachers, the student body and even other counselors. Within this context, counselors can and should strive to address the needs of individual students who will most benefit from individual counseling, particularly as it relates to their academic development and success. The counselor's role is to assess individual students to determine if one-on-one counseling would be beneficial, and then to implement it when appropriate. If a counselor feels a student is in need of additional therapy or therapy outside of the academic context, it is recommended that the student be referred to external agencies or other appropriate services.

CRITERIA TO BE ADDRESSED IN INDIVIDUAL SESSIONS

The school counselor should try to schedule sessions at times that are **least intrusive** to the academic day. The counselor should also be sensitive to student nuances: for instance, some students may be **more receptive** after school hours than during the middle of the day. Within each session, the counselor needs to honor the **particular needs of the student** while developing and implementing therapeutic goals. It is important to consider a student's developmental or situational hindrances. Furthermore, the counselor should develop a rubric for assessing the success of the therapy.

COUNSELING ADOLESCENTS

Counseling approaches and intervention strategies need to be determined and assessed within the context of developmental theory. In other words, counselors should be familiar with the different stages of development in adolescents, including the **appropriate behaviors for this particular age group**. Counselors may dismiss behaviors that would be unacceptable for an adult, but **perfectly normal for an adolescent**. Conversely, if a child is exhibiting behavior that is not typical of his or her age group, this may need to be addressed in the counseling session. Furthermore, counselors developing intervention strategies should be mindful of the range of reasonable expectations within an age group. It is important that counselors enter each session with an understanding of the age group of the student, referring to outside resources for that information if necessary.

ESTABLISHING A RAPPORT BETWEEN COUNSELOR AND STUDENT

Because of the importance students place on peer relationships, they are often less receptive to recommendations or inquiries from adults. It is important for the counselor to **develop a relationship of trust** with the student. One strategy is for the counselor to listen carefully to the

49

student's perception of a situation in order to develop and convey an attitude of empathy. Likewise, once a counselor has researched a student's background and situation or precipitating event, it is important to refrain from developing biases or expectations based on this research alone. Listening to the student's experiences and perceptions will allow the counselor to form a more realistic and comprehensive approach to resolution. As the counselor and student develop a history of tackling a situation in tandem, the counselor will not only encounter less resistance from the student, but also will benefit from the student's collaboration.

GENERAL AND AGE-SPECIFIC STRATEGIES

With all age groups, it is important for the counselor to listen attentively, and to refrain from judgmental or negative behaviors or comments. With specific age groups, there are particular activities that can facilitate the **establishment of a trust relationship** between counselor and student. For younger children, playing and creative activities can provide a rich medium for developing rapport. Students in middle childhood and adolescence also can develop a solid relationship with a counselor by playing sports or other games. Counselors should be versed in an array of **rapport-building strategies** in order to apply the best strategies for each student. Other strategies include drawing, collage-making, and writing on a board. Counselors can facilitate the therapeutic benefit of these activities by isolating and discussing particular pictures or words, always remembering to be attentive and respectful to the student.

RESPONDING TO STUDENT RESISTANCE

It is important to remember that the student has been referred to the counselor in most cases. Not only is the student not motivated to work with the counselor, but often is confused and suspicious of the purpose of the session. Counselors need to be sensitive to this apprehension by not immediately tackling the situation for which the student has been referred. One approach is to allow the student to begin talking to the counselor about an innocuous subject, such as objects in the room. This will sometimes help the student to feel more comfortable in the counseling environment, as well as to alleviate the feeling that he or she is the subject of a therapeutic spotlight.

COUNSELING A SELF-REFERRAL

In some cases, students will **refer themselves for counseling**. In this scenario, the counselor should experience less resistance from the student. However, there are nonetheless **legal and ethical issues to be considered**. It is first important to refer to government and school regulations regarding self-referral. One of the issues to be addressed is when and how to obtain parental consent. Limits of confidentiality in counseling a minor student need to be thoroughly researched and clarified before the counseling sessions, whether it is an individual or a group session. A counselor should be cognizant of all of the considerations and ramifications of working with a student who self-refers before meeting with the student, and in fact may decline the session based on findings.

EXPLAINING COUNSELOR'S ROLE TO STUDENTS

Counselors are responsible for **explaining their role in the session**. This explanation can and should serve to establish a relationship of trust and collaboration with the student. It is important for counselors to be sensitive to a student's age when explaining their role. In other words, for a younger student, the counselor might begin the discussion with by explaining that he or she wants to help the student feel better, whereas for an adolescent this type of explanation could easily be deemed condescending. For adolescent students, it might be advisable to first begin by asking the student of his perception of the goals and purposes of counseling, and then proceeding by clarifying the student's response. Counselors will often also be responsible for explaining the role of counseling to parents.

Topics Appropriate for Various Age Groups

As a part of a comprehensive counseling program that addresses specified needs, counselors should include topics that are generally **relevant to particular age groups**. Some of these age-specific topics are:

- For elementary students - Students in this age group are dealing with issues related to friendships, family roles, problem solving, social behaviors, success in school, expressing emotions, and self-esteem.
- For middle school students - Middle school students are particularly embroiled in issues relating to body image, interpersonal relationships, social skills, conflict management, social roles, diversity issues, self-esteem, transitioning to a new school, and academic development.
- For high school students - As students are preparing to become adults, topics that are most relevant are career exploration and planning, dating protocol, intimate relationships, self-identity, assertiveness training, stress management, and time management.

Although many of these topics overlap age groups, counselors need to be cognizant of the level of development present in the particular student group or population.

Determining Group Size and Length of Sessions

Both **group size** and **session length** are primarily determined by the age and developmental level of the participants. One of the key deciding factors is the ability of certain age groups to focus on a topic for a specific period of time. Since younger elementary children have shorter attention spans, a rule of thumb for them is to have group sessions last about 20 minutes, with about 5 members in the group. Older elementary students (roughly grades 4 through 6) can meet for periods ranging from 30 to 45 minutes, in groups of 7 or so. High school students will benefit from an expanded length of session, but still will fare better in smaller groups. The ideal group size for high school students is 6 to 8, meeting for 40 to 50 minutes. If a counselor feels that a particular group could extend the recommended time or group size, he or she should refer to research regarding both the topic and the group size.

Considerations Regarding Group Size

Group dynamics are very much influenced by the **size of the group**. There need to be enough participants to provide **feedback and support** as appropriate, but not such a large group that **individuals are ignored** or that **focus becomes dissipated**. In addition to consulting published standards regarding ideal group sizes for every age group, counselors can determine effective group sizes by considering the age or developmental level of the group. One important factor is the relative attention spans of the participants. The topic being addressed is also a factor. Sometimes the therapeutic strategy to be implemented will determine group size. Finally, counselors should consider the individual participants in the group, including their modes and likelihood of participation, when determining group size.

Scheduling Group Counseling Sessions

It is important to remember that the responsibility of the school counselor is simultaneously for the student as well as the school community. Because of that, the counselor should work with school personnel and school schedules when **developing counseling schedules**. This is particularly pivotal in high school and middle school because counseling sessions that are scheduled at the same time of day will interrupt the same class repeatedly. Collaboration with teachers and other school personnel is probably the best approach; the counselor should solicit their input about the best and worst times to schedule counseling sessions, for instance by avoiding sessions on days when standardized tests are administered. Beyond that, it is always a good idea to **stagger group counseling sessions**, especially in the middle school or high school setting, although this may be necessary in an elementary school also, if indicated by the teachers.

SELECTING GROUP MEMBERS

ROLE OF DEMOGRAPHICS

While it is not always indicated for counselors to specifically focus on **demographics when choosing group participants**, it is nonetheless a good idea to be aware of how the demographics relate to the topics being addressed. Sometimes the referral process might result in a default group of students that is primarily one gender or one ethnicity. Although there are no definitive rules about this, it is often a good idea to include a spectrum of cultures and mix of genders in a group setting. This is true when working with all age groups, but especially so when working with adolescent students. This often allows students to address personal and social skills in a mixed group, within the controlled environment of the counseling session. Younger children may be more comfortable in a group of their own gender. Of course, if the topic relates to culture- or gender-specific topics, then the group should be comprised of student falling within the specified category.

ROLE OF TOPICS

Selecting group members based on topic can be approached somewhat holistically, since topics may be interrelated. However, the group members will want to experience similarities and empathy among themselves. For instance, if the topic being addressed is dealing with authority, the group may include students who stay out after curfew as well as students who are perpetually late to class. Students whose parents are divorced may relate to students who recently moved from their home town, since all of them are dealing with separation issues and disenfranchisement. Nonetheless, if students are in fact dealing with the same issues, there may be enough diversity in personal coping skills to comprise a dynamic group. In terms of age similarities, it is a good idea to have students in a group who are within the same age group or developmental level, although a small spectrum of emotional maturity can provide the interactive component that is valuable in a group setting.

RECRUITING AND SCREENING STUDENTS

The primary considerations for **selecting** and **screening students** for group counseling are the willingness and capacity of the student to participate in a therapeutic group setting. Students may be self-referred, or they may be referred by parents, teachers, and other students. While self-referral indicates the student's willingness to participate, the other types of referrals indicate the need for counselors to screen students to see if they are amenable to group counseling. All students should be screened for capability to participate in a group setting, and to determine if a group counseling format would be beneficial for them. In general, the counselor should consider the parameters of the group setting, which include both speaking and listening, respecting confidentialities and differences among its members, as well as other components of the group format. Some counselors prefer to have individual meetings with potential members before the first group meeting; others devote the first meeting to information and screening.

SOLICITING PARTICIPATION IN GROUP COUNSELING

Finding appropriate members for a counseling group can be accomplished through a combination of advertising and referrals. Of course, counselors should have a profile of the groups that would be relevant and beneficial for a particular student body. This information can be obtained during

52

conversations and other interactions with students and school staff. Often, this input will include the referral of specific students and the request for group sessions focusing on particular topics. Once the need for a group has been indicated, counselors can **solicit additional members** with notices in newsletters, flyers, word of mouth, or by talking with students, groups of parents, or school personnel. The counselor should specify the topic to be addressed, the philosophy and general format of group counseling, and the proposed times for the sessions.

SCREENING PROCESS

A good way to begin the **screening process** is for the counselor to give the student an overview of the group counseling format. This overview should include the purpose of the group; the roles and expectations of the members; and the role and expectations of the counselor. The counselor should provide an opportunity for the student to ask questions, and to express any concerns or anxieties he or she has about the group format. In the context of this conversation, the counselor should look for indications that the student is either likely or unlikely to be able to participate in a group setting. Some of these indications relate to the student's ability to follow the rules of the group; his or her ability to attend, participate, and contribute in the group setting; his or her emotional capability to participate; and, lastly, his or her willingness to participate.

OPTIONS FOR STUDENTS INITIALLY DEEMED UNSUITABLE FOR GROUP COUNSELING

Students who are unsuited to the group counseling format may be referred to individual counseling. Although some students referred to individual counseling may never participate in group counseling, others may transition from individual to group counseling. For these students, the counselor will want to make a determination of readiness based on specific criteria. He or she then should communicate to parents the recommendation and the factors that indicate the student's readiness for group counseling. The intent, format, and expectations of the group setting should be distinguished from those of individual counseling. Counselors should refer to school policy regarding additional procedures to follow when transitioning a student in this manner. Also, students referred into group counseling from individual counseling should sign a consent form indicating their understanding of, readiness for, and commitment to the group setting.

GUIDELINES AND EXPECTATIONS OF GROUP COUNSELING

Once the members of a group are selected and brought together, at either the first meeting or a pre-meeting, the counselor should give an overview of the **guidelines and expectations of group counseling**. This first meeting or pre-meeting will define the individual members as a group brought together for a purpose. As a collaborative group, students can be given a presentation of the ground rules in group counseling, and can then individually sign forms of understanding and consent. These ground rules can include the importance of commitment, issues of conduct, and the importance of respect and confidentiality. It is significant that they agree to these ground rules as a group, since they will be implementing them as a group, with the counselor as facilitator. The counselor can also talk about group expectations, and allow members to voice their individual concerns and expectations.

GROUP GROUND RULES

Ground rules in a group counseling setting serve to bond the members in a unity of conduct and purpose. When reviewing ground rules, it is helpful to solicit input from the members, allowing them to participate in the establishment of the ground rules. **Rules also contribute to a healthy and productive dynamic** in a group setting. Lastly, rules can provide and ensure a sense of safety and trust in the counseling environment. Some typical rules which address these issues include, but are not limited to:

- Give respect to the counselor and other members by listening attentively and without interruption.
- Be willing to participate and contribute by sharing feelings and experiences.
- Respect the experiences, perspectives and backgrounds of the other members.
- Maintain confidentiality. (Although confidentiality cannot be legally mandated for group members as it is for counselors, it is nonetheless effective to have members include a commitment to confidentiality in their overall consent to the ground rules.)

MULTI-FACETED ROLE OF GROUP COUNSELOR

The counselor in a group setting must balance and maintain healthy and productive **group dynamics**. This includes attending to both the group as a whole and to the individual members. The counselor needs to be sensitive to the **levels of participation** within the group, ensuring **fairness** and eliciting **contributions** from all members. He or she should be available for consultation regarding any concerns, and should act as the overseer and reminder of the ground rules. Counselors should facilitate the interaction of the members toward the benefit of each of the members. This may involve working with a resistant student, or intervening when there is negative, unproductive behavior. The counselor in a group setting can encourage group dynamics, while honoring the individual needs of the members. He or she should also strive toward a more integrated and self-regulating group through encouragement and guidance.

MAINTAINING THE GROUP'S FOCUS

Counselors in a group setting need to be particularly sensitive to the possibility of the group becoming **distracted** and **losing focus on the topics and goals**. Although the counselor should be flexible in order to meet the individual needs of the participants, he or she also needs to maintain the focus and progress of the group as a whole. One of the early safeguards against distraction is clear communication to the members, parents, and school staff about the purpose and goals of the group; therapeutic format; and process of resolution in a group setting. **Defining and reviewing the goals** and parameters of the group with participants is also helpful. It is important for counselors to be well-versed in the basic tenets of group dynamics in a therapeutic setting.

COUNSELING THEORY AND DEVELOPMENTAL THEORY IN GROUP COUNSELING

Since school counselors are working with students of different ages and developmental levels, they need to be sensitive to any developmental issues that are relevant to counseling. When implementing group strategies, counselors may need to refine or revise their methodology in relation to the age group, or to the developmental level of the group members. Each age group has inherent developmental crises like separation anxiety, individuation, and self-worth, and counselors need to be sensitive to these crises in their topic-based strategies. A six-year-old will have different coping strategies than a fifteen-year-old, even though the problem for both may be divorce. These age-based sensitivities should not mitigate counseling strategies, but rather should make them more effective and readily received. Some therapeutic strategies that have been successful in the school setting are cognitive therapy, reality therapy, Adlerian therapy, and SFBC.

IMPORTANCE OF BEING KNOWLEDGEABLE ABOUT THE GROUP TOPIC

Although a counselor will not have personal experience with every crisis treated in group therapy, it is nonetheless important for him or her to feel a sense of **empathy and recognition**. This allows students to feel safe, understood, and not isolated in their situation. Therefore, it is important for counselors to have a basic knowledge of the topics that will be addressed in group counseling. They should be able to discuss the processes and effects of such situations as divorce, teen parenting, stress management, poor academic performance, and peer pressure. It is also valuable to develop a cache of information and resources about particular topics that can be shared with students. Counselors can also recommend activities or anecdotes that relate to the student's situation. Combined, these not only provide the empathy of knowledge, but also can serve to assist and empower students toward resolution.

Multisensory Stimulation in Group Counseling

Students exposed to **multisensory stimulation** are found to be more engaged, responsive, and attentive. This is particularly valuable in a group setting, since one of the inherent weaknesses is the ease with which members can become distracted. Multisensory stimuli involve the mind and senses of children and adolescents, targeting **multiple intelligences**. This is particularly valuable in a group, which will be comprised of unique individuals with unique coping and learning styles. These stimuli provide the group with a comprehensive, experiential mode for addressing issues. Through the use of such creative and multisensory stimuli as puppets, music, drama, and movies, counselors can generate response and participation when broaching difficult topics. An added benefit is that students will forge positive associations between the topic and the creative stimuli. Various media, such as film, or puppets for younger audiences, can present a problem in a manner that may be more palatable than a lecture.

Developing a Knowledge of and Sensitivity to Cultural Differences

It is particularly common for counselors in a school setting to work with students from **varied cultural and ethnic backgrounds**. Knowledge of the **belief systems, perspectives, and sensitivities** of an array of cultures and ethnicities is invaluable when working with students from varied backgrounds, especially in a group setting. The foundation of this knowledge lies in recognition of the far-reaching influence of culture, as well as recognition of the personal biases and perceptions that the counselor might have. Counselors should be aware of how misunderstandings and miscommunications within the group could be related to **cultural differences**, and should work with the group to resolve these misunderstandings. In this context, students in the group can also gain an appreciation for different cultures.

Planning Sessions in Advance and Flexibility Within Sessions

It is the counselor's job to **maintain focus** on the topic, goals, and strategies each group session. Therefore, it is important for the counselor to **prepare in detail for each session**. This preparation should include a list of discussion topics, planned activities, and an informal agenda. Within the grid of this agenda, counselors will often allow time and **flexibility** for longer group discussion, particular concerns that might arise in the session, or individual responses or behaviors that may require extra time and attention. However, because of the preplanning and the agenda, counselors can redirect the group toward activities, specific discussion topics, and the goals of that particular session, in order to maintain the focus and progress of the group. The activities and discussion topics in each session are understood as part of a larger agenda outlining the long-term goals of the group.

Beginning Sessions of Group Counseling

Before tackling the topics and goals of a counseling group, facilitators should first establish the tenor of the group. In the **first session** or sessions, participants can become acquainted and share a bit about themselves. The counselor's role is to assist in **establishing a safe environment**. It is important that participants feel a sense of camaraderie with the other group members. Throughout the remainder of the sessions, they will be sharing personal insights and experiences as well as addressing possibly difficult topics. Therefore, this initial introductory period is vital in developing a close and collaborative group. During these first sessions, the counselor can review the purpose of the group, ground rules for participation, and the importance of confidentiality, all of which will serve to establish a safe and controlled environment.

MIDDLE SESSIONS OF GROUP COUNSELING

Although particular activities will vary between groups, and especially between different age groups, there are similarities that all will share. Counselors should establish a relatively standard routine for the **middle sessions**, during which the group will be pursuing their goals most intensely. A good idea for each session is to include an initial greeting of the members, in order to **reinforce each member's importance** and contributions. Counselors can briefly review the ground rules and guidelines during the early part of the session. A **review of the previous session's events**, **activities, and accomplishments** is recommended. Counselors can then focus the group's attention on the current topic and a preplanned activity or discussion designed for that session. As the session draws to a close, counselors can briefly review the session's activities and insights, and establish a regular routine for ending the session.

ENDING SESSIONS OF GROUP COUNSELING

Developing a structure for the **closing sessions** of group counseling require a different focus than the beginning or middle sessions. The closing sessions **review accomplishments** as a group and anticipate individual futures. There will necessarily be a refocus and possibly some apprehension. Counselors should announce the upcoming final session at least three meetings in advance. An important component in the final session or sessions is a review of the initial goals, and the reminder of the achievement of those goals. Counselors should take this time to empower and encourage participants to remember their newly discovered skills and insights, and to apply them to future situations. Time should be allowed for participants to express feelings and for leaders or other group members to respond to those feelings.

COMPONENTS

Particularly in the closing sessions, counselors should refer to a defined **listing of topics and issues to be addressed**, in order to facilitate a healthy transition. Although the particular modes and media may differ between ages and topic groups, the following are key components to consider when structuring a closing session:

- Review of the initial goals from the first meetings.
- Review of the accomplishment of those goals in subsequent meetings.
- Review of strategies, resources, and activities experienced during the sessions.
- Validation of growth and new insights of the participants throughout the sessions.
- Direction for incorporating this growth and insight in future activities and behaviors.
- An opportunity to address any unfinished business or lingering concerns.
- An opportunity for the group to respond to unfinished business or lingering concerns.
- Allowance of substantial time for personal goodbyes.
- Counselors may also want to schedule a post-meeting for evaluation purposes.

COMPLETING GROUP MEETING EVALUATIONS

In order to assess the effectiveness of the group sessions, counselors should complete an **evaluation** at the end of each meeting. The format of these evaluations will in large part determine the kind of information that will be returned. If counselors are looking for the group response to particular components of the sessions, such as the scheduling or the structure, a multiple-choice or graded-response format can be used. The results of these surveys will be more quantitative and focused. Another model is that of questions or open-ended sentences that ask participants how they felt about a session, such as "my favorite part of the session was...".These types of survey instruments can provide more qualitative information, as well as provide an ongoing profile of participant satisfaction and involvement. Counselors may also provide pre- and post-surveys to parents and school staff, as well as post-surveys to participants several weeks after the last session.

SITUATIONS CALLING FOR INDIVIDUAL COUNSELING INSTEAD OF GROUP COUNSELING

Individual counseling would be chosen over group counseling when the **student's problems are severe** enough that paying attention to the student takes priority over investigating or changing how the student interacts with others. When a student is in a personal crisis, if he/she has been bullied at school, if the student is working with problems that are long-standing, group work will not be helpful and may even cause harm. Students struggling with issues related to trauma or current or past abuse should not be placed in groups.

When people are fragile, individual therapy is usually the best course of action as it removes the added complications of dealing with others.

In general, if a student is highly resistant to the idea of group work, it may be better to avoid it. Groups are usually short term, and working against resistance or outright sabotage from highly resistant members may take all the resources of the group and leader, with no appreciable results.

INDIVIDUAL COUNSELING FOR BULLIED CHILDREN

Counseling research has shown again and again that when counseling works, it is primarily due to the strength of the counseling relationship. **Establishing trust is crucial** in any counseling relationship, and with children who have experienced **bullying**, the adult world has already let them down—trust is greatly diminished, and children are traumatized. Children who have experienced bullying need the support and encouragement of an adult who cares for them while teaching them about how to set and defend their own boundaries. In group counseling, the counselor's attention and support are distributed among all the members of the group, and a child whose self-esteem has been damaged will be less likely to connect and thrive as a group member.

Bullying is part of a loop, and bullied children often need training in emotional and verbal self-defense on a **one-on-one-basis** to develop the skills and confidence to participate in a group.

GROUP WORK WITH CHILDREN IN CRISIS

When children have experienced the same type of crisis, group work can facilitate healing—and in some cases, the need for **responsive service** to a recent disaster requires group work when there aren't enough counselors to provide individual services. Children who have experienced a natural disaster, or who have all suffered a similar loss or family situation such as divorce, can be formed into a group based on their similar experience. The fact that others have been through the same experience provides validation of feelings and the opportunity to learn how to empathize with and support each other. Group leadership must be strong enough to act as a container and prevent members from becoming overwhelmed by their own feelings and the stress of the current situation.

There are **limitations to group work** with children who have experienced trauma. Those whose boundaries have been violated in various ways may not have the ego strength or the capacity for trust to benefit from group work. Anyone who is seriously decompensating is not capable of group work. Counselors must vet potential members carefully and prepare placements in individual therapy for those too fragile for group.

APPROPRIATE SITUATIONS FOR GROUP WORK WITH STUDENTS

Psychoeducational groups are helpful when students need to combine practical learning with more subjective experiences in the emotional realm. Groups are helpful in teaching study skills, stress or anger management techniques, and life skills such as organization and time management. Putting a group together based around a goal more concrete than "feeling" work can do two things at once: achieve the concrete goal (such as learning a set of study skills for college entrance examinations) and give students an experience of working in a group—a skill set that can serve them in various situations all their lives.

Groups helping students address **cognitive-behavioral challenges** like test anxiety and social skills building can maximize resources and help many students at one time. Groups are appropriate for teaching skills, and students can help each other learn. Students can bond, form friendships, and practice emotionally intelligent skills, like empathy, active listening and providing support and encouragement. Students also practice mature skills such as maintaining confidentiality, resolving conflicts in the group, and being peer mentors to each other.

ACADEMIC ADVISING USING A PYCHOEDUCATIONAL GROUP MODEL

Group advising is most effective with students of a similar age or grade who have similar interests. After taking a career inventory, for example, a group of students with a particular common interest could be identified and formed around the concept of career exploration in their common areas of interest. Students might pair up to investigate and report to the group on particular careers, even going so far as to determine the best course to take after high school to enter the career. Colleges, trade schools, and universities might be identified based on their study programs, financial aid opportunities, and postgraduate employment statistics.

Students who are particularly interested in a certain occupational path could be encouraged to come together to study for placement exams, participate in field trips, create projects, or build portfolios for later applications. Using the energy of the group and its interests, the school counselor can take a role as facilitator and advocate, allowing students to work as a group and only stepping in to assist in conflict or "stuckness."

SCHOOLWIDE ASSEMBLIES

Schoolwide assemblies may be a necessary response to a variety of circumstances that affect a large number of students within the student body. These kinds of circumstances can take the form of behavioral issues, tragedy, urgent new policies, or any other reason that the school as a whole is affected. When the target subject of an assembly is a sensitive topic, such as the death of a student, drugs, violence, or some other responsive matter, the counselor should speak gently and broadly, without bringing up the impacts on a specific student. School counselors should remain ethical and produce an air of safety when discussing a topic in front of the student body. Student assemblies should also be held as a gateway or informational setting in which students are reminded about paths they can use to get help when needed. Because schoolwide assemblies are generally used to open the doors for further services, clear presentation of contact information is particularly important so that students can know how to follow up.

PEER MEDIATION

In **peer mediation**, students help each other resolve interpersonal problems using peaceful interventions. **Peer helping programs** teach students the skills that build **character education**; empathy, integrity, respect, and honesty are pieces of the constellation that make up good character. In peer mediation, students learn how to listen empathically, communicate respectfully, handle difficult emotions, and solve problems. Peer mediation is a group process requiring more

58

than two people. **Conflict resolution** is the primary purpose of peer mediation, and peer mediation programs have been shown to reduce school violence. Those who participate in peer helping programs are developing deep areas of emotional learning that too often go ignored in education—making them better citizens, more responsible family members and friends, and stronger, more caring human beings. Aside from the great good of building a peaceful, accepting school community and keeping each other safe, they are learning skills that will serve them anywhere they go in life.

Addressing Specific Concerns

CONCERNS ADDRESSED IN COUNSELING

For concerns such as relationship issues, anger or stress management, family dynamics, sexual topics, and academic goals, the counselor acts as a **guide and mentor** for students in their academic, personal, and professional lives. Since students may be referred by school officials, family members, or other students, the counselor should anticipate varying levels of openness by the student and/or the family. It is vitally important for counselors to be trained in the strategies for recognizing and addressing issues in a manner that will capitalize on the counseling session to the maximum benefit of the student. The first step in this process is recognition of the key issue or issues, which may take more than one session to identify. Beyond that, counselors can use various strategies focusing on the particular situation as well as the idiosyncrasies of the student.

AT-RISK STUDENTS
FACTORS AND BEHAVIORS

It is important for counselors to be aware of the **events and influences that place students at risk**, as well as the potential ramifications of unstable behavior and mental state. Counselors should be aware of **changes in student behavior** that may signal depression or other mental or emotional fragility. It is worth mentioning that the leading cause of death for young people is suicide, and therefore that counselors are in a pivotal position to notice and respond to these symptoms. Some students may need more intensive treatment than school counseling. Some of the factors that can contribute to emotional vulnerability for at-risk students are rising levels of poverty, substance abuse of the student or parents, domestic violence, and community violence. Other kinds of behavior problems may be a result of ADHD or other behavior disorders, and may indicate the need for the student to be referred to special education resources in the school.

INCLUDING NEEDS OF AT-RISK STUDENTS WHEN DELIVERING CURRICULUM

Counselors are generally responsible for addressing the **academic** as well as the **career** and **social development** needs of students. To that end, they should be well versed in the areas of leadership, advocacy, systemic change, and collaboration. Also, they should develop and continually refine the skills to teach these subjects to diverse groups of students, including at-risk students. Within the category of at-risk students are included those students whose behavior and performance are a result of family or socioeconomic factors, as well as students who come from a more stable background but suffer from physiological disabilities.

AT-RISK

Although the behaviors of at-risk students fall within a rather large spectrum, there is an umbrella definition that can be used to identify at-risk students. Generally speaking, if a student shows **decline in any or all of the areas of physical, mental, social, spiritual or economic health, then the student is considered at risk**. In addition, community and social circumstances may contribute to a student's sense of isolation, increasing the possibility of deterioration in one or more of these areas. Students who are at risk in any or all of these areas have a diminished likelihood of becoming productive members of society. Counselors are encouraged to refer to guidelines from professional organizations or literature to identify and appropriately respond to at-risk students. Counselors can provide the support, resources, and encouragement that can significantly mitigate deteriorating factors.

CAUTIONS WHEN IDENTIFYING A STUDENT AS AT-RISK

There are **five key areas of caution** to consider when identifying a student as at-risk:

- Students who fall within the definition of at-risk may nonetheless be very resilient, with strong coping skills, and therefore at-risk may be a temporary status for that student.
- If a student is overtly and obviously treated differently than other students because of the at-risk designation, this may discourage creativity or confidence.
- The term *at-risk* can easily become a label rather than a status, in which case there is no mechanism to identify when the student is no longer at risk.
- The term *at-risk* by itself encompasses so many situations and behaviors that the response may be also very generalized and not address the issues specific to a particular student.
- Cultural factors should always be considered, as they may be contributing to or masking an underlying issue.

DIFFICULTY OF ASSESSING AT-RISK YOUTH FROM CULTURALLY DIVERSE BACKGROUNDS

When a student is identified as at-risk, the identification is usually based on overt behaviors or shortcomings. These may include poor academic performance or inappropriate behavior. An initial assessment may point to the need for more native language materials or conflict resolution workshops. However, for some **first- or second-generation immigrants**, these outward circumstances may be noticeable, but **not the underlying or most problematic issue**. Often, the underlying issue can be masked by overt behaviors, until the need for treatment is long past due. Students from diverse cultures may be contending with issues related to isolation, sadness for loved ones left behind, bridging the gap between cultures, and other issues directly related to poor cultural assimilation. Although there are no clear guidelines for identifying such cultural factors, counselors should be aware of the possibility of precipitating circumstances when dealing with at-risk students from other cultures.

PEER ASSOCIATION

Adolescent students between the ages of 14 and 17 are particularly **susceptible to peer association and influence**. Youth in this age group generally gravitate to peer groups besides their family. Often, young people join groups that are formed around a common ethnicity. Unfortunately, if some of the members of the group engage in violent or illegal activities, those who join the group often mimic this activity in order to be accepted. Consequently, students who participate in violent behavior or drug use engage in a lifestyle that leads to the decline of their physical, mental, social, spiritual, and/or economic health, which places them clearly in the at-risk category. Although counselors need to refrain from making assumptions based on associations, they nonetheless should be aware of a student's associations, particularly as they relate to at-risk behaviors and attitudes.

CURRENT AND DECLINING TRENDS

Within a large student body, there will be a small percentage of students engaging in at-risk behaviors. Counselors should be on alert for this type of behavior. At-risk youth commit various **crimes** after school, generally between the hours of 3 and 8, and especially right after school. Robberies are sometimes committed by youth, usually during the week and usually after 9 p.m. Today's students still face problems with **premarital sex and unwanted pregnancies**, which can put them at significant risk of **poor academic performance**. However, the incidence of student suicide is on the decline, as are the incidences of students riding with drunk drivers and carrying weapons to school. Although these activities and behaviors still occur, counselors should be aware of rising and declining trends in at-risk behavior in order to be aware of the signs and symptoms associated with them.

REJECTION OF AT-RISK STUDENTS BY THE SCHOOL SYSTEM

Students who are displaying at-risk behavior often pose a challenge to educators who are striving for academic success and good classroom management. The at-risk behavior can cause a disruption on both fronts. This can be exaggerated when there are multiple at-risk students in multiple class periods. Teachers and school counselors faced with this disruptive activity will first attempt to remedy the behavior using known strategies. However, if this proves unsuccessful and the disruptive, at-risk behavior continues, teachers may become discouraged and begin to **develop an attitude of complacency** about the behavior. This can grow into complacency about teaching in general. Consequently, faced with this possibility, counselors will sometimes make the decision to **remove a student or students from the school**. Unfortunately, this solves the short-term problem by creating a longer-term issue of underserved youth becoming unproductive adults. Counselors can provide a valuable service by preventing this downhill slide in at-risk youth.

DESIGNING PROGRAMS FOR ALL STUDENTS TO BENEFIT THE LARGER COMMUNITY

Since schools are the primary focal point for issues relating to adolescents, counselors and educators often work with other **community entities** in discussing and developing strategies for **addressing the needs of youth**. Some of these entities are libraries, police departments, private schools, recreation centers, and other organizations. One of the ways that counselors can work as **liaisons between students and these entities** is by dispelling the idea that the burden of at-risk behavior lies with the student. They can work with community representatives who feel that students are solely or primarily to blame for their behavior. Counselors can collaborate with educators to develop programs that are designed to address the needs of not only mainstream students, but also at-risk students. These programs can incorporate the needs and concerns of the larger community as well as the academic goals identified for the student population.

REASONS EDUCATORS HAVE NOT ADDRESSED NEEDS OF AT-RISK YOUTH

Many educators have not addressed the needs of at-risk youth for some or all of the following five reasons:

- Funding has not been allocated for programs focusing on at-risk youth. Counselors can assist appropriate entitles in reevaluating the need for programs to address the needs of these students.
- Existing systems and programs do not include strategies for at-risk students, and changing the systems can be very challenging. Counselors can work with educators to overcome this challenge.
- There is an assumption that at-risk youth will always be at risk. Counselors can implement goal-setting strategies that guide and encourage at-risk students to adopt productive behaviors.
- Social and community groups usually do not have programs that focus on at-risk students. Counselors can increase awareness for the need to do so.
- Graduate programs do not always include pedagogy focusing on at-risk youth. Counselors can collaborate with their peers by educating each other about at-risk youth.

GOVERNMENT FUNDING AND ALLOCATIONS FOR ASSISTING AT-RISK YOUTH

Federal and state departments of education and mental health have developed the 1967 **Elementary and Secondary Education Act (ESEA)**, which provides for continuing public education through grade 12. There is also funding allocation for disadvantaged children, focused on the goal of drug-free schools and available after-school care. The National Defense Education Act (NDEA) of 1958 authorized schools to hire counselors who encouraged students in the areas of math and science. Counselors and other educators who are committed to assisting at-risk youth can find government support that relates to a guaranteed education for all youth, safer schools, and improved academic performance.

COUNSELOR'S ROLE AFTER A SCHOOL OR COMMUNITY TRAUMA

Numerous kinds of **trauma** can affect a student population, from individual crises to those affecting the entire student body. Counselors need to be aware of the types and levels of trauma and how they impact students. It is prudent for them to be aware of the possible ramifications of trauma, how to identify these effects, and the strategies for intervention. Counselors need to be aware of the scope of trauma, and the scope of the needed intervention. **School-wide traumas** can include natural disasters, school shootings, and widespread gang activity. **Individual traumas** can include family illness, depression, domestic abuse, and even suicide. Sometimes an individual crisis can escalate into a school-wide trauma like a school shooting or suicide. Counselors should be well versed in the types of trauma and how to assess and treat victims.

CRISIS

A **crisis** is defined in part by the event, and in part by the response to the event. Generally speaking, a crisis is a situation that is perceived as **overwhelming and intolerable** by the individuals facing it. Crises can affect people cognitively, psychologically, behaviorally, and even physically. Although full-scale disasters necessarily affect entire populations and inherently pose overwhelming circumstances, counselors also need to be aware of how individual students are equipped to cope with a crisis. For most crises, which fall significantly short of full-scale disaster, counselors can employ intervention strategies that help students through the present crisis and help them develop coping skills for future challenges. Early intervention will minimize the possibility of traumatic response to a crisis.

> **Review Video: Crisis Management and Prevention**
> Visit mometrix.com/academy and enter code: 351872

CRISIS INTERVENTION

Since crisis by definition is a situation that is overwhelming and intolerable, **crisis intervention** serves to provide immediate support and help victims develop coping skills. It is good to remember that one of the factors that can contribute to a crisis is that the situation or event poses a new challenge to the individuals. Some of the components of crisis intervention include:

- Defusing of emotions to allow the exploration of possible solutions.
- Interpretation of the event or situation causing the crisis.
- Organizing of the situation in terms of information, resources, etc. Proper preparation to calm the student and help him or her handle the situation.
- Integration of the event into personal experience. Assistance to the students in recognizing the life lessons to be realized.
- Recognition of the positive impact gained from a crisis, e.g. the coping skills or new awareness gained.

CRISIS RESPONSE PLAN

Counselors can work with school staff and counselors, both at the school and district levels, to develop a **crisis response plan**. Counselors should facilitate regular meetings with school personnel, parents, and other professionals as appropriate, to educate them on crisis intervention both at the school and at the community levels. **Crisis response teams** should coordinate campus-wide and community-wide services as part of the critical response team. Counselors can educate and prepare the team on strategies and methods for handling the crisis. The team should be versed on methods for crisis prevention, strategies to employ during a crisis, and post-crisis needs. The team should work together, with the counselor acting as facilitator, to develop a well-organized, systemic response plan. The coordination of the team and the crisis response plan should be implemented as a matter of preparation, and not in response to an immediate crisis.

LOGISTICAL CONSIDERATIONS IN SCHOOL CRISIS INTERVENTION PLANS

Crisis response plans need to address the possibility that normal logistical operations may be suspended, particularly in the case of a school-wide or community-wide crisis. Therefore, a good crisis intervention plan will address the following needs:

- **Locations** should also be established for communications, first-aid treatment, emergency personnel, storage of supplies/food, and a break room or safe room.
- **Communication needs**: Crisis response teams will need to communicate with one another. They may also need to communicate with parents, as well as with the press. Part of the communication requirement will be the oversight and monitoring of team activities.
- **Other considerations**: An overall plan, including assigned assessment personnel and assigned intervention tasks.

IDENTIFYING AND ADDRESSING SUICIDAL BEHAVIORS

School counselors need to be educated on potentially **suicidal behaviors**, and need to be prepared to intervene if necessary. These behaviors can include ideation, or any other behavior that indicates a student is contemplating suicide. **All threats of suicide should be taken seriously**. Counselors should consult institutional directives and state laws regarding responsibility for notification. In some cases, parents should be notified immediately, and may even need to pick up their children from school as soon as possible. In any case, students who are at risk for suicide should be in the presence of an adult at all times during the school day. Since the possibility of suicide can be extreme and immediate, intervention may include referral to an outside agency or institution. Counselors can work with parents and consultants in order to transition to treatment facilities, and should be familiar with the community services available.

ADDRESSING THE POSSIBILITY OF SUICIDE

Suicide is all too prevalent among young people, and has been deemed the most common cause of death for adolescents. School counselors working with youth need to be well versed on the factors and behaviors contributing to suicides. There is no guaranteed strategy to prevent suicide and, in fact, suicide may occur despite the best efforts of the student's support network. However, counselors should still be informed and prepared in the event of suicidal behavior. It should be noted that suicidal ideation may be expressed differently in different cultures, and therefore counselors should respond to every potential ideation seriously. Some of the **common circumstances** precipitating suicide are alcoholism, depression, and a sense of hopelessness or helplessness. Counselors who observe suicidal tendencies should meet with the student regularly to discuss and work on the student's problems and state of mind.

HELPING STUDENTS RECOVER EMOTIONALLY FROM SUICIDE IDEATION

Working with students who are presenting **suicidal ideation** includes reconnecting the student to his or her network of support. In the process of working with a student, a counselor can determine which activities and people in his or her life provide meaning, and can contribute to an attitude of hope and resiliency. If a counselor deems that suicide is an imminent threat, the first consideration is the **student's safety**. This may include the involvement of the parents, within the parameters of relevant privacy mandates. Counselors can also encourage the student to reach out to his or her network of support for encouragement. This network could include parents, friends, church, and coworkers. As the student's ideation begins to subside, this network can also provide a grid upon which the student can reestablish positive connections. Counselors can remind students of their responsibility, purpose, and place in this network and in the larger community.

WARNING SIGNS OF SUICIDAL IDEATION

Although there are innumerable manifestations that **suicidal thoughts** can take, there are seven key identifiers that counselors should take note of:

- Communication, either spoken or implied, which incorporates suicidal thoughts and possibly includes themes of escape, punishment, or self-harm.
- Well-thought-out plans for dying. If the plans are feasible, concrete, detailed, and specific, this may be a good indicator that the student is seriously contemplating suicide.
- Well-thought-out plans for self-harm or for murder. Remember, suicide is self-murder.
- A rush of completed business, closure, or a potential suicide note.
- Extreme stress, such as a traumatic loss, illness, or failure. Counselors should also be wary of the anniversaries of significant losses in a student's life.
- Mental state indicators pointing to alcoholism, depression, or any recent changes in attitude.
- A sense of overwhelming hopelessness or helplessness.

INDICATORS FOR VIOLENT BEHAVIOR IN A SCHOOL ENVIRONMENT

Often, students who feel disenfranchised will act out by bullying or otherwise victimizing other students. This sense of separation can result from a **student feeling isolated** from peer groups, cultural groups, family, or other groups from which the student feels excluded. This sense of exclusion may precipitate the student attacking, bullying, ignoring, or otherwise harassing other students. This sense of isolation may also be a precipitator of suicide, or attacking the self. Students may intensify this attacking behavior by bringing weapons on campus, or by inciting physical violence. Recent years have seen more covert and violent victimization on school campuses. Counselors and other school personnel need to be attentive to any incidents of bullying, which can escalate into more intense behaviors. Bullying and other victimization may be more prevalent among certain groups of students, and should provide the counselor with the opportunity to address the prevailing attitudes and behaviors.

IMPLICATIONS OF BULLYING

Any act of **bullying** or other **victimization** implies a **power hierarchy**. The victim is perceived and treated as powerless against the perpetrator, and each act of victimization further endorses that hierarchy. Often, social injustices and inequalities in a community or school environment provide fertile ground for bullying and victimization, which perpetuates the inequalities. If a comprehensive program to balance inequalities is not implemented, the bullying and victimization will most likely continue. Counselors can begin to address **chronic victimization** problems by educating students and relevant adults about how to effectively break the cycle of victimization. Victimization can also take the form of gossiping or excluding certain individuals from group activities. Although some schools have rules specifically prohibiting victimization, counselors can provide a valuable service by working with the parties involved to recognize and stop the cycle of victimization.

IMPACT OF ABUSE OR NEGLECT ON AT-RISK STUDENTS

Students who have been **abused**, **neglected**, or who have been **witness to abuse** within their own family are **inherently at risk of decline** in any or all of the areas of physical, mental, social, spiritual, or economic health. Often students with a history of neglect or abuse display chronic behavior problems including anxiety, depression, substance abuse, and/or other emotional or mental disturbances. Furthermore, victims of childhood abuse or neglect often feel a deep-rooted sense of shame or embarrassment, which translates to chronic social and emotional isolation. They often exhibit poor academic performance and retreat from normal activities with friends and fellow students, particularly if they have been helpless bystanders to abuse perpetrated against a parent or siblings. Counselors find that there is often a clear correlation between at-risk behavior in school, and abuse or neglect in the home.

GROWING INCIDENCE AND IMPACT OF DATING VIOLENCE

The definition and parameters of **dating violence** vary between studies. However, the overall incidences of dating violence have been steadily increasing in recent years. The figures of violence occurring in a dating situation range from a few incidences to a significant portion of the student body. As indicated by the term *dating violence*, the general parameters define an individual victimizing another individual in a dating environment. This can occur with middle school, high school, or college students. Most of the victims are women. The impact of this dating violence is felt at the individual level, often throughout the students' school, family and community network. The victim often is left with feelings of helplessness, which can expand into depression, substance abuse, and risky sexual behavior. Counselors need to be aware of the possibility of dating violence in a student who is presenting at-risk behavior.

PREPARING FOR CAMPUS-WIDE STUDENT VIOLENCE

Counselors should first be assured that the frequency **of campus-wide student violence** has declined in recent years. Nonetheless, there is always some possibility of a student or students committing violent acts that harm the campus as a whole. Unfortunately, there are not always clearly identified indicators of potential campus-wide violence. Most experts agree that this type of wide impact violence is usually the culmination of several factors in at-risk students. The best preparation strategies for counselors include both individual interventions for at-risk students and an intervention plan for the school. On the individual level, counselors should always work with students to mitigate their violent tendencies or fantasies, regardless of whether or not they appear to pose a threat to others. On the campus-wide level, counselors can work with school officials to develop a rubric for threat assessment, as well as an intervention plan to minimize the casualties should a campus-wide event occur.

FACTORS ASSOCIATED WITH VIOLENT TENDENCIES IN STUDENTS

One of the factors that makes it difficult to **predict violent incidents** is that many students who display violent behavior do so on an **impulse**, meaning that most violent incidents are unplanned. Generally speaking, students who feel disenfranchised, helpless, or threatened may act out by perpetrating violent acts or behaviors. Often, violence will be motivated by feelings of desperation or an irrational fear that others may be threatening harm. Males are generally more likely to commit violence than females, and the highest incidence of violence falls between the ages of 15 and 24. Lower socioeconomic status is also a common factor in violent tendencies. In addition, if a student has a history of violence, he or she will be more likely to commit violence. Lastly, students who have disorders related to conduct, ADHD, hallucination, delusions, etc., will be more likely to commit violence.

FBI CLASSIFICATIONS FOR THREATS OF VIOLENCE

Most of the research on the violent tendencies of students has been completed by governmental and FBI profilers and analysts. This research is made available to counselors and other educators to mitigate the possibility of future occurrences. There are four basic classifications of threats of violence identified by the FBI:

- **Vague threats** that imply violence. The threat is implied in the terminology, but not specified. Time and place are not generally specified.
- **Veiled threats** of violence. The terminology is more specific, but time and place are still not specified.
- **Conditional threats** of violence. The terminology refers to violence if certain conditions are not met. A common example of this is extortion.
- **Direct threats** of violence. These threats are clearly stated and straightforward. The terminology is in the form of a warning which specifies a target, time, and place.

LEVELS OF THREAT SERIOUSNESS

According to government publications, the likelihood or seriousness of a threat can be classified according to three sets of criteria:

- Low-level threats are generally characterized by vagueness or a lack of specificity. Students may make a general, indirect statement of threat with little or no detail and little or no specific plan of action. Minimal risk is associated with low-level threats.
- Medium-level threats are more direct and plausible but do not appear to be realistic. They may contain details about time and place, but lack evidence of comprehensive planning. A medium-level threat may include phrasing that indicates seriousness, but lack the specificity to make it happen. The risk level for a medium-level threat is higher than for a low-level threat, but generally does not indicate imminent danger.
- High-level threats are distinguished by their high levels of specificity, and by the comprehensiveness and plausibility of the plan. High-level threats should be taken very seriously, and school officials should always contact the local authorities when they are discovered.

FBI'S FOUR-PRONGED ASSESSMENT MODEL FOR THREAT ASSESSMENT

The **FBI has developed a four-pronged model of threat assessment** that focuses on the specific characteristics of the student making the threats:

- Prong 1 assesses the behavior and emotional dynamics of the individual, including signs of alienation, poor anger management, poor coping skills in general, lack of trust, or marked changes in behavior.
- Prong 2 assesses the circumstances of the family and home of the student, including a lack of limits or lack of monitoring, access to weapons, lack of intimacy, and/or volatile relationships within the family, particularly between the student and parents.
- Prong 3 assesses the student's perceived marginal place in the school community, evidenced by bullying, a lack of attachment to the school, inflexibility about culture, and hierarchy among the students.
- Prong 4 assesses the student's other connections, including peers at school, use of drugs or alcohol, and other outside activities or interests.

INTERVENING WITH AT-RISK YOUTH AND MITIGATING THE POSSIBILITY OF VIOLENCE

Counselors can provide at-risk students with opportunities to develop **healthy dynamics** and **self-validating experiences** among their peers as well as with significant adults. Threat assessment teams can be formed and trained to focus on preventative strategies. Peer mentor groups should be established so that at-risk students and students not considered at risk can interact under the guise and facilitation of the counselor. These groups can provide an **insulated environment** for learning healthy strategies for coping with bullying, neglect, and other forms of abuse. Counselors can teach healthy interpersonal skills within these groups. Counselors can also collaborate with local authorities and community groups to provide opportunities for at-risk youth to have positive experiences with adults and outside groups. At-risk students can be encouraged to join community support groups such as Big Brother/Sisters. Counselors can also encourage family members to develop connections with available support groups and resources.

IDENTIFYING AT-RISK BEHAVIOR ASSOCIATED WITH SUBSTANCE ABUSE

Since the prevalence and diversity of substance abuse among youth is increasing, counselors should be at least generically educated on common legal and illegal substances and behaviors associated with substance abuse. Counselors should also be aware of the local resources available for students involved in substance abuse. Although school guidance counselors cannot be expected to be experts on substance abuse, it is nonetheless a good idea to be aware of the behaviors and other signs of possible substance abuse. However, many students will not admit or discuss substance abuse, so the counselor should be prepared for referral if necessary. In addition, counselors should be aware of how substance abuse affects academic performance and mental ability, in order to best address these issues with students for whom substance abuse appears to be a contributing factor.

ENCOURAGING STUDENTS TO SELF-REPORT SUBSTANCE ABUSE

Although students may be hesitant to self-report or even to recognize substance abuse, counselors can facilitate this recognition and self-reporting through a series of questions. The following questions target alcohol abuse and are identified by the acronym CAGE:

- C – Questions about **cutting down**. Ask the student if he has thought he should cut down on alcohol/substance use.
- A – The **annoyance factor**. Ask the student if he becomes annoyed when people criticize his drinking.
- G – The **guilt factor**. Ask the student if he ever feels guilty about the amount of alcohol/substance consumed.
- E – Alcohol as the **eye opener**. Ask the student if he ever needs alcohol to get going in the morning or to calm his nerves.

Counselors should also have regular access and referral to the Physician's Desk Reference to maintain current knowledge about drugs and alcohol, including possible side effects.

ALCOHOL AND PRESCRIPTION OR OTHER DRUGS

The following questions can be used as a guide for encouraging students to **recognize and self-report substance abuse**. Counselors can ask students that may have a substance abuse problem:

- If they are taking over-the counter or prescription medications.
- The reason they take the medications.
- Any other medications/drugs they take.
- How long they have been taking these medications.
- Side effects, including severity and when they noticed the effects.

- If they drink alcohol.
- How they are affected by alcohol.
- About their drinking and substance habits – alone, with friends, etc.
- If their alcohol/substance use has affected their personal, financial, professional, or legal circumstances.
- If anyone in their network of family/friends has asked them to stop using drugs/alcohol.
- If they attempted to quit alcohol/drug usage.
- If an attempt to quit caused withdrawal symptoms.

LOSS THAT STUDENTS MAY EXPERIENCE

One thing that counselors should remember is that a loss is still a loss, even though it may be as severe as the loss of a parent or as seemingly trivial as failing a class. Divorce of parents can be a particularly devastating but unfortunately a commonly experienced loss for young people. In addition, friendships are very important at this age, and the loss of a friendship can be very upsetting and can be experienced as a major loss. What is significant about these different types of losses is that young people feel loss just as intensely as adults, and that each loss needs to be grieved and processed. Students need to move through the grief, and on to acceptance. By understanding that a sense of loss can be experienced regardless of the precipitating event, and by knowing about the grief process, counselors can provide the support and the guidance to move students through the loss and on to acceptance.

STAGES OF GRIEF PROCESS

The **grief process** encompasses the following **five major stages**:

- Shock and denial usually define the first stage of the grief process. Counselors can help students identify their fears.
- The second stage is usually anger, which involves indignation and questioning of why this loss was perpetrated on them. The student may argue that he or she did not deserve this loss.
- Bargaining is generally the third stage. The student may attempt to negotiate with a higher power in an attempt to undo the loss. Bargaining is commonly accompanied by a sense of guilt that the student's actions or inaction may have caused the event leading to the loss, and that therefore they did deserve the loss.
- The fourth stage is hopelessness and depression. This tends to be the longest stage, and may include feelings of sadness. As this stage becomes less intense, this is usually a signal that the student is almost ready to move on to acceptance.
- Acceptance is the fifth stage, in which the student adjusts to his or her new life circumstances.

ASSISTING STUDENTS THROUGH THE GRIEF PROCESS

Throughout the **grief process**, counselors can assure and remind students that their feelings are normal, and that eventually life will improve for them. This is not intended as a denial of their feelings, but rather as an assurance that grief is a process, and not a permanent state. Counselors can work with students in the grief process, remembering that there are four major tasks to be accomplished during grief:

- **Accept** the reality of the loss, both emotionally and intellectually.
- **Experience** the pain, both internally and externally.

- **Acclimate** to life after the loss, accepting help from others as appropriate.
- **Assimilate** the loss and reinvest energies elsewhere.

Counselors should be watchful for the stages and tasks involved with the grief process and be prepared to refer to the student to outside or specialized resources if the situation becomes overwhelming or too complicated for the counselor to be of assistance.

DROPPING OUT OF HIGH SCHOOL
PRECIPITATING FACTORS AND PREVENTATIVE MEASURES

Counselors should be particularly alert and responsive to the possibility of **students dropping out**, especially if students present any or all of the following:

- High rate of absenteeism
- Low or dropping grades
- Low participation in extracurricular activities
- Limited parental support
- Evidence of alcohol or drug problems

The following are recommended **intervention strategies** for students at risk of dropping out:

- Tutoring services – either peer tutoring or other trained assistance
- Career and skill training for success after high school
- Expressing high but reasonable expectations for students
- Additional general/foundation classes for students with disabilities

Continued support and **resources** are recommended for at-risk students who stay in school, including:

- Relevant curriculum
- Significant support and assistance from teachers and others as appropriate
- Useful and accessible textbooks and other classroom materials

KEY AREAS TO BE ADDRESSED AND INTERVENTION STRATEGIES FOR AT-RISK STUDENTS

During all interventions with at-risk students, counselors should address interpersonal skill-building and self-reflection. It is important for counselors to encourage students to develop strong relationships with peers and school staff/counselors, in order to increase their sense of community and belonging. Throughout the intervention, counselors should always assure students that they can discuss personal issues in both individual and group sessions. Often, at-risk students are struggling with numerous issues in several areas of their lives. There are four key areas that are possibly involved when students are at risk of dropping out:

- **Personal/Affective** – counselors can offer retreats or other groups to encourage interpersonal participation
- **Academic** – counselors can arrange for tutoring and/or other individualized methods of instruction
- **Family Outreach** – encompassing increased feedback to parents
- **School Structure** – possibilities include class size reduction or alternative school options
- **Work/Career** – vocational training

COLLABORATING WITH COMMUNITY RESOURCES TO DEVELOP A NETWORK OF SUPPORT

Many schools will have ongoing relationships with **community groups** as a part of a general philosophy of community outreach. However, for at-risk students to receive any direct benefit from these groups or relationships, counselors may have to initiate and coordinate auxiliary relationships for addressing the specific needs of at-risk students. Understanding that at-risk students are often overwhelmed by a variety of life challenges, counselors can collaborate with a number of **community resources**, including:

- Businesses
- Families
- Recreational Centers
- Police Departments
- Universities

Counselors should cultivate these relationships, possibly in tandem with existing school relationships. With the counselor's facilitation and coordination, these resource groups can cooperatively address many of the needs posed by at-risk students. This comprehensive coordination of resources can provide a significant hedge against students dropping out.

FACILITATING CHANGE IN INTERVENTION POLICIES TO BETTER ACCOMMODATE CULTURAL DIVERSITY

Counselors who work with **at-risk youth from diverse cultures** are in a good position to reduce the gap between intervention strategies designed for the dominant culture and those that address the needs of minorities. Counselors need to communicate to school officials that under the umbrella of at-risk students may be ethnic groups whose problems are defined or exacerbated by their marginalized status. Counselors can consider the **cultural differences of at-risk students** and how they will interpret different activities when creating preventative and intervention programs. If necessary and when appropriate, counselors can act as liaisons on behalf of students from diverse cultures, making recommendations for program changes to better accommodate cultural diversity. Counselors can make significant and important changes in the school system, which will benefit present and future students.

MODELING AND ADVOCATING EMPOWERMENT FOR AT-RISK STUDENTS

Recognizing that at-risk youth are generally overwhelmed and under-supported, counselors can be particularly effective by providing students with numerous opportunities to develop empowerment and self-confidence. When setting goals, it is important to set **achievable, short-term goals** to best ensure success by the students. Each success should lead to further and **larger successes**, and counselors can provide **scaffolding goals and challenges**. Counselors can also encourage listening and cooperation among family members through their own willingness to take a back seat and emphasize the importance of collaboration and teamwork, facilitating when appropriate. In terms of advocacy, counselors may be aware of policies or procedures within the school system that inherently pose an obstacle or inequity for at-risk students, and may need to intervene on behalf of the students. This is another way that counselors can model empowerment.

AUTHENTICALLY DOCUMENTING INTERVENTION OUTCOMES

In the absence of available success/failure rates for many intervention strategies, the onus is often on the counselor to document the outcomes of the strategies used. In order to authentically and effectively produce this outcome assessment, it is at first important to document student responses during and/or after an intervention. In keeping with the assessment model, counselors should produce documentation that either quantifies or clearly identifies specific outcomes. Counselors should also be mindful of their role as advocates for the students by realistically reporting successes and failures, so that program improvements can be made if necessary. By doing so, they can also provide a model for reflection and willingness to change. Counselors who provide authentic documentation and are willing to revise strategies are excellent candidates for added funding or other resources, and can provide comprehensive parameters for the role of school guidance counselor.

VARIOUS ROLES WHEN WORKING WITH DISABLED STUDENTS

As defined by the ASCA, the school counselor should address the following **functions in his or her role as facilitator and advocate** for student needs:

- Lead and facilitate activities of the comprehensive school counseling program.
- Collaborate with other student support personnel to deliver appropriate services.
- Provide services to both disabled and other students.
- Provide individual and group counseling.
- Work with staff and parents to develop an understanding of students' special needs.
- Refer students as appropriate to auxiliary resources in the school system or in the community, to address needs not met in the context of the counseling program.
- Advocate for the rights of disabled students in the school and the community.
- Assist school staff with issues related to students transitioning between grade levels.
- Serve on interdisciplinary groups that assess students who may have undiagnosed special needs.

MULTIPLE DISABILITIES, SPECIFIC LEARNING DISABILITY, ORTHOPEDIC IMPAIRMENT, AND OTHER HEALTH IMPAIRMENT

The term "**multiple disabilities**" refers to a combination of impairments, such as intellectual disabilities with either blindness or orthopedic impairments, whereby the student's educational needs cannot be accommodated in the traditional classroom. Excluded from this group is deaf-blindness.

Specific learning disability refers to a disorder whereby a deficiency in one or more of the basic psychological processes inherent in using or understanding spoken or written language causes a person to have difficulty communicating linguistically or performing mathematical calculations.

Orthopedic impairment refers to physical impairments that adversely affect a student's academic performance. Included in this category are loss of a limb, clubfoot, cerebral palsy, and disease-related conditions like poliomyelitis and bone tuberculosis.

Other health impairment describes the presence of such chronic or acute health problems as diabetes, epilepsy, ADD, heart conditions, or sickle-cell anemia, that adversely affect the student's educational performance.

INTERVENTION STRATEGIES FOR EATING DISORDERS

Eating disorders in youth commonly manifest as either bulimia nervosa (BN) or anorexia nervosa (AN), or both. Because both of these disorders result in extremely poor nutrition, and bulimia nervosa can result in esophageal injury, students who are suffering eating disorders are at risk for poor health, poor intellectual and social development, and in some cases death. Counselors can implement intervention strategies through a complete medical assessment and multifaceted therapeutic assessment. In particular, the combination of behavioral therapy and cognitive therapy can be very effective in treating eating disorders. **Cognitive therapy** can address issues of control and self-esteem, while **behavioral therapy** can promote healthy eating habits and discourage destructive behaviors like purging. **Group therapy** may also be quite helpful and in some cases, family therapy may be indicated. **Medical assessment** may also be indicated, to ascertain if the student is in immediate physical danger from an eating disorder.

INTERVENTION STRATEGIES FOR TIC DISORDERS

Tic disorders are characaterized by recurrent, non-rhythmic sequences of movements and involuntary sounds from certain muscle groups. These disorders can include Tourette's tic, transient tic, and not-otherwise-specified (NOS) disorders. Counselors should initially garner enough information to recognize the condition and should direct the parents to a doctor who can diagnose the disorder and educate the family on the condition. Therapy can include identifying any underlying stressors as well as assessing family interaction and understanding regarding the disease. Various therapeutic strategies can be effectively implemented for tic disorders. Cognitive-behavioral therapies can address stress management. Self-monitoring, relaxation training, and habit-reversal training are effective strategies to consider, once initial data about the tic have been collected. Habit-reversal training is more commonly indicated, requiring the student to relax the affected muscles and introduce a competing response. If students present with frequent or explosive outbursts, counselors should collaborate with a physician to determine if medication is indicated.

INTERVENTION STRATEGIES FOR MOOD DISORDERS

Mood disorders are generally defined as those in which students externalize feelings of depression, sadness, guilt, or other negative emotion, possibly including thoughts of suicide. Students with mood disorders may present with somatic complaints. Counselors should be wary of misidentifying a mood disorder when a student may just be experiencing temporary sadness. On the other hand, counselors should be cognizant of the signs of mood disorder, especially symptoms that may signal the risk of suicide. Effective therapeutic strategies for mood disorder include cognitive and behavioral interventions, as well as psycho-educational programs that focus on improving social skills and promoting rewarding activities. Some students suffering from mood disorders have improved with antidepressants. However, studies regarding the efficacy of medicinal treatment for depression are inconclusive, and therefore the use of antidepressants should not be immediately considered, if at all.

INTERVENTION STRATEGIES FOR SUBSTANCE-RELATED DISORDERS

One of the **initial intervention steps for substance abuse** is to identify the pattern of abuse and the substances involved. Parents may conduct drug tests at home, although students may also self-report. An important factor to remember is that students with substance abuse problems may have family members with substance abuse problems, since the correlation is very strong. In addition to individual counseling and education, counselors can conduct school and community workshops that address the benefits of early detection, the risk factors involved, and the treatment options available. Based on the type of substance abuse, duration, and intensity, various treatment models are available, ranging from outpatient therapy to intensive inpatient treatment. The spectrum of treatment options encompasses very restrictive models as well as more participatory models. Treatments include detoxification, contracting, self-help groups, behavior therapy, family therapy, social skills training, as well as nutritional and recreational counseling.

INTERVENTION STRATEGIES FOR GENERALIZED ANXIETY DISORDER

Generalized anxiety disorder (GAD) is defined as a pervasive anxiety that is characterized by excessive, uncontrollable, and often irrational worry about everyday things, which is disproportionate to the actual source of worry. Physical, somatic symptoms may include shortness

72

of breath and/or muscle tension in other parts of the body, both of which can be difficult to control. Although GAD is not limited to adolescents, it does present problems particular to students, in that the physical symptoms and the irrational worry can overshadow attention to academics, and therefore negatively affect performance. Students who are chronically anxious are unable to focus on their lessons. Counselors can use cognitive-behavioral strategies to mitigate the intensity of the anxiety and the accompanying physical symptoms. Students can be taught coping strategies such as identification, modification of anxious self-talk, education about emotions, modeling, relaxation techniques, and related self-regulating models.

DRUG ADDICTION

In recent years, medical professionals have shifted from viewing **drug addiction** as a sign of immorality to seeing it as a legitimate physiological disorder, which can be treated by medicine and psychological therapy. Scientists believe that prolonged use of drugs can cause chemical changes in the brain that create addiction, and can endure for the entirety of the person's life. The most common traits of **chemical dependency** are loss of control over dosage and frequency of use, and continued use despite harmful consequences. Unfortunately, one of the other common characteristics of drug addiction is the refusal to admit that it exists. Many doctors believe that only by removing the stigma of drug addiction will it be possible to treat all those who need help.

Academic Advisement and Career Planning

ADVANTAGES OF EVIDENCE-BASED CURRICULA IN HELPING STUDENTS MEET SEQUENCED OUTCOME GOALS

Counselors can facilitate students in **meeting short-term and long-term goals** by using either curricula they have developed, commercially available curricula, or a combination of both. There are several advantages of using commercially available curricula, the first of which is that they are usually evidence-based, having been developed and revised in response to professional research and tracked success rates. Counselors using **evidence-based curricula** experience the added benefit of more widespread institutional support for an established, evidence-based curricular model. Counselors can collaborate with school staff and administration to select an appropriate commercial curriculum, and from there identify pedagogy that best addresses student outcomes. When a commercial curriculum is selected and adopted, outcomes can be matched with appropriate pedagogical methods. Often these evidenced-based curricula provide both students and school faculty with the confidence and efficacy that result from utilizing established pedagogy.

CONTRIBUTING TO ACADEMIC ACHIEVEMENT WHILE TARGETING PERSONAL AND SOCIAL DEVELOPMENT

Counselors can best serve their students and the school system as a whole by continually **integrating developmental goals with academic goals**. Since students mature and move through the graded school system simultaneously, counselors should maintain a conscientious awareness of achievement standards in the areas of academic development, personal-social development, and career development. These areas are inherently interdependent, and an effective counselor will consciously integrate them toward the holistic development of his or her students. The ASCA identifies three key strategies for this integration:

- Counselors should be aware of the academic content and schedule of classes, and should tailor counseling sessions to the academic needs of the students.
- Counselors should refer to the school documents and personnel for explicit and implicit goals and competency standards for the students.
- Counselors should be proactive in enriching certain academic areas for students.

ADDRESSING CAREER DEVELOPMENT WITH STUDENTS IN GRADES K TO 5

For young students, **career awareness** is the primary goal of career development. Children can be made aware of the different kinds of jobs, and it's to their long-term benefit if that learning also addresses the idea that they need not feel limited by gender, socioeconomic status, or ethnic background—or even the attitudes of their family members. In early school years, career awareness can be facilitated by field trips to places where people do interesting work, by having adults come to the classroom to talk about and demonstrate their work, by playing games and creating stories about different kinds of work, and by watching videos and reading books about occupations. Children can be encouraged to notice how their favorite activities might relate to work. Reporting on the work their parents and other family members do can be another way to engage the curiosity and awareness of the world of work. Craft fairs or farmers' markets, where children make (or grow) and sell their work are another way of showing children that they can work for themselves in ways that they might not otherwise consider if they've grown up in a corporate-focused work culture.

CAREER COUNSELING FOR MIDDLE SCHOOL STUDENTS

Middle school students should be encouraged to explore careers, investigating how their interests and strengths could lead to satisfying work. Students might go with their parents to work, might interview other adults about their occupations, and might read about unusual career choices. At this time of life, grades will begin to impact the options children have regarding college: it's also a time for career counselors to assist students whose life paths might lead them to the trades, to entrepreneurial activities, to the arts, or to other nontraditional vocations. Students whose families have traditionally been involved in particular professions might be discovering that they're well-suited to the tradition or that they will need support in pursuing other interests. Part-time jobs after school give students a little spending money, a feeling for what makes a strong work ethic, and a taste of what it's like to work in a particular occupation. Volunteering is another way that students can explore potential interests and gain skills.

CAREER COUNSELING FOR HIGH SCHOOL STUDENTS

Career counselors may administer **career inventorie**s to help students identify personal strengths and interests associated with particular occupations. Students will need guidance in choosing high school courses relevant to their future paths in college, trade school, or business. Preparing for college entrance exams and locating funding for training are parts of student career development work that may require the help of a school counselor, especially when students' families are not familiar with the course of the students' proposed occupational fields.

Students from disadvantaged background should be helped to take courses, prepare for exams, and locate scholarships that will help them overcome those disadvantages. Personal encouragement and locating mentors or guides are valuable strategies because building hope will increase the student's motivation to use the tools. Without hope and support from a trusted advisor, students whose social/familial environment does not support their career paths can be overwhelmed by the process and mired in pessimism.

HELPING STUDENTS WHEN CAREER INTERESTS DON'T MATCH CAREER ASSESSMENT

Career assessments measure interests, but many factors contribute to career choices. For example, a student with a **Holland code** of artistic-entrepreneurial-social (AES) may state the determination to become an engineer. The counselor can discuss with the student how the AES code doesn't seem to match up with the student's ambition and explore possible reasons for the incongruence without telling the student that "you're wrong." It's possible that the student's parents have raised their child to take up a "solid occupation," and the student is either trying to please the parents or has other personal goals. Perhaps the student isn't aware of potential careers available for the Holland codes and needs to explore.

Perhaps, the student is **multiskilled**, wants the security of a higher-paying job, and plans to keep art on the side while becoming a consulting engineer (satisfying the entrepreneurial tendencies.) The main purpose of the counselor in the situation is not to force the student to see "reality" but to support the student, using the discrepancy in the test to fully explore, actively choose, and fully prepare for the chosen career.

Promoting a Healthy School Environment

BENEFITS OF ESTABLISHING A RELATIONSHIP OVER A NUMBER OF COUNSELING SESSIONS

Foremost in the school counseling model is the **establishment of a trust relationship between counselor and student**. Trust and cooperation sometimes needs to be established over a period of several visits, and is augmented by a strict policy of confidentiality by the counselor, which further contributes to the perception of a safe environment. The process of identifying and addressing key or underlying issues can be much more productive when the relationship between the counselor and student is fully established over a number of sessions. An added benefit of numerous sessions can be the student's increased receptiveness to the counselor's recommendations.

CONTRIBUTING TO ACADEMIC DEVELOPMENT IN CLASSROOMS

Since school counselors are primarily concerned with personal issues that affect academic performance, they are often expected to devote a percentage of their time to developing programs that deliver guidance and instruction to all students. Incorporated in these programs are strategies that address such topics as academic performance, career planning, and social skills. Counselors may also be asked to contribute to curriculum implementation. **School counselors are expected to contribute significant resources to teaching**. Although the guidelines for counselor contributions to curriculum implementation may differ between schools, there are generally understood percentages, based on age groups. In elementary school settings, 35 to 45 percent of the counseling program should be devoted to curriculum implementation. In the middle school milieu, the percentage is 25 to 35 percent. High schools generally expect 15 to 25 percent of the counseling program to be devoted to curriculum implementation.

COUNSELORS AS TEACHERS

School counselors can have a positive influence on classroom instruction, specifically in the areas of personal and social growth related to academic performance. Although in the past guidance counseling was often an added role for teachers, students are now able to benefit from the expertise of trained guidance counselors, both in and out of the classroom environment. One of the benchmark criteria for **classroom instruction by school counselors** is empowering students to be productive members of society. Throughout their school years, counselors can assist students in such areas as study skills, time management, social skills, and career planning. The American School Counselor Association (ASCA) is a strong proponent of school counselors contributing their expertise to the classroom environment. Counselors can also assist students with preparation for standard-based testing and other academic goals set by the school.

CLASSROOM GUIDANCE

BENEFITS

The **benefits of classroom guidance** are found to be extraordinary and exponential. Results show that students who have experienced classroom guidance are significantly more successful academically and socially than those who have not had classroom guidance. This seems to be the case across the board, regardless of school district or even geographic area. In terms of academic success, these students fare noticeably better in attendance, test success, and overall grade-point average. Socially, their in-class behaviors improve markedly, and they are better able to cope with personal issues. Finally, students who have had the benefit of classroom guidance are more likely to attend college and to participate in career planning.

ASSESSING EFFECTIVENESS

As with any counseling strategy, it is important to both qualitatively and quantitatively **assess the success of classroom guidance**. It is important to establish a rubric that includes such criteria as grades, test scores, and graduation rates. Both pre- and post-intervention surveys are recommended. There can also be a qualitative appraisal of the effectiveness of intervention strategies in the classroom, delineating changes in behavior or classroom tenor. Note that demographic information can be valuable in assessing classroom strategies, but that it should not be included in pre- or post- intervention surveys. In other words, data gathering (grades, etc.) needs to be free of demographic categories, whereas ethnicity, gender, socioeconomic status and other demographics may be included on final evaluative reports. A significant added caution is that all data gathered should be confidential, with little or no reference to identifiable specifics.

STUDENT RESPONSE EVALUATION METHODOLOGY FOR MEASURING CONTENT

Counselors may want to assess student perceptions and **student responses** in order to qualitatively evaluate the effectiveness of classroom guidance content. The approach should be informal, gearing the evaluation in a way that is not readily perceived as an assessment. Younger children may respond well to a fill-in-the-blank cartoon; older students may be able to write or complete narratives that allow them to express their feelings about academic success, their role in the classroom or society, or other relevant perceptions. Other recommendations include scaled devices to self-report feelings, or another spectrum-like instrument, so long as they are user-friendly and informal. Counselors will generally want to assess the effect of classroom strategies on behavior, motivation, increased coping skills, and interest in planning. As with quantitative assessments, these more informal qualitative assessments should be administered both pre- and post-intervention, to more effectively assess the effect of the interventions.

STUDENT RESPONSE EVALUATION METHODOLOGY FOR MEASURING PROCESS

Process evaluation is necessarily more focused and formal, since it is administered to solicit feedback on specific components of the classroom guidance strategies. This type of evaluation is particularly valuable when developing or introducing a new strategy, since it provides a kind of rating system to assess the value of the strategy. The format for this type of evaluation should be more formal and quantitative than an evaluation of content acquisition. Surveys can be administered with rating systems, using terms like extremely helpful, helpful, not helpful, etc. It is also a good idea to include a comments section that will provide qualifiers for the rated responses. In other words, if a strategy was not particularly well received, what about it could be changed, if

76

anything? This type of evaluation is often administered during the first classroom sessions using a strategy, providing valuable feedback for refining and revising the strategy in subsequent class meetings.

ADHERING TO AN OVERALL THEORY OF COUNSELING

According to the tenets of an overarching theory of counseling. School counselors should be familiar with a number of theorists and models, in order to select one that is applicable to the school setting. Human development theories can serve as a viable foundation for many program designs, as can peripheral models of developmental phases within age groups. However, not all counseling sessions or students will necessarily be well served by same theoretical paradigm, so counselors should be watchful that a particular approach will address the situation or student group appropriately. Counselors should consider age levels and other defining factors in each counseling situation.

SEQUENTIAL NATURE OF STRATEGIES BASED ON DEVELOPMENTAL STAGES

Counselors need to be cognizant of developmental stages as they implement strategies for different age groups and developmental levels. A recommended approach is to dovetail a particular **developmental theory** with sequential task order as it is standardized in the K-12 curriculum. Certain learned life skills and levels of awareness may be negated if a student encounters significant life changes after the strategy is implemented, or if the strategy is implemented too early. By incorporating the K-12 model with the particular developmental theory, counselors can build a comprehensive model of guidance that introduces sequential skills in a meaningful order. It is important for counselors to be aware of students' developmental level before introducing a task or awareness that is beyond the student's capability or understanding. A good reference is the Adlerian-based framework of five key stages:

- Understanding self and others
- Development of empathy
- Ability to communicate
- Ability to cooperate
- Responsibility

DELIVERING CURRICULUM THROUGH CONSULTATION

School counselors are in the valuable position of liaison between students and school staff. They work with students on personal and academic issues, and collaborate with school personnel on appropriate strategies to facilitate student learning and development. Although counselors may directly design curriculum or deliver guidance in a classroom setting, often they will act as consultants to school staff in curriculum design, program development, or other related issues. **Collaboration** seems to work best when teachers follow a standardized curriculum and counselors solicit and assess student feedback. The counselors will advise the teachers, who will in turn implement the curricular changes. Counselors can infuse personal guidance and development into standardized curriculum to create a much richer program for students.

DELIVERING CURRICULUM THROUGH COLLABORATION

In some cases, the best model for curriculum delivery that incorporates counseling guidelines is a partnership between the counselor and teacher. The particular value of this model lies in the fact that each partner is able to contribute his or her expertise in curriculum delivery. An example of this is teaching social skills through role playing, which can be designed around a historical setting. In this particular model, the counselor would contribute a set of guidelines for social skills, based on the agea and developmental levels of the students. A history teacher would plan the lesson

77

around the historical period indicated by the grade level, and a drama teacher could contribute expertise regarding performance and role playing. This **collaboration** would culminate in a lesson addressing different modes of learning, while delivering curriculum and honoring counseling guidelines.

DELIVERING CURRICULUM THROUGH DIRECT TEACHING

Counselors who work according to the **direct-teaching** model function much like regular instructors, although they deliver a different type of information. While standard instruction focuses on information-based academic areas, direct teaching by school counselors focuses on life and social skills. Referring to appropriate topics for each age and grade level, counselors can plan and deliver the lessons that are most useful for specific developmental levels. Elementary students might benefit from a lesson on friendship or independence, while middle school students may need lessons on anger management, conflict resolution, or stress management. For high school students, these lessons could expand to incorporate planning for the future. Some topics under this umbrella could be college preparation skills, career planning, and goal setting. Other topics appropriate for high school students fall in the categories of relationships and responsibility.

DELIVERING CURRICULUM THAT ADDRESSES CAREER PLANNING AND CONFLICT RESOLUTION

One of the qualities that differentiates school counselors from teachers is their training and knowledge base, both in areas pertinent to school-age children and in appropriate expectations for each age and grade level. Although **conflict resolution** is a valuable skill to learn at any age, the delivery method and context will differ greatly between age levels. Counselors are particularly knowledgeable about this. One example of this is teaching young children how to get along with their friends through a puppet lesson; for high school students, an example is role-playing to address relationships with parents. It is important that high school students be given a wealth of information about career and college planning, which is an area of expertise for school counselors. Counselors can talk to high school students about setting goals, researching options, and planning for the future.

ROLE OF SEATING ARRANGEMENTS IN CLASSROOM GUIDANCE LESSONS

Seating arrangements can be very important in establishing tone and expectation, as well as in contributing to the efficacy of a guidance lesson in the classroom. Counselors can choose other seating arrangements that are most conducive to the planned activity or lesson. Just the process of rearranging the established seating in a classroom can signal a change in the group dynamic. If students are asked to break into small groups, the expectation is that group discussion will occur. Counselors can implement this seating arrangement to address interpersonal skills. An added benefit to this kind of seating arrangement is that student groups can address different topics. Conversely, if the activity is one that requires the group of students to listen to the counselor, the chairs and desks would all face the front of the classroom.

IMPLICATIONS OF VARIOUS TYPES OF SEATING ARRANGEMENTS

Two key **areas influenced by seating arrangements** are formality and communication, specifically whether communication is one-sided or open and interactive. At one end of this spectrum is an arrangement in which seats are all facing one direction, toward a speaker or screen. This arrangement inherently discourages interaction, and implies one-way communication by the person or event at the front of the room. At the other end of the spectrum is an arrangement of small groups, in which the participants face each other. This arrangement allows for a great deal of interpersonal dialogue, and relegates the counselor to the role of facilitator. The gradations in between include U-shaped seating, which encourages discussion with a speaker; seats in a circle,

Copyright © Mometrix Media. You have been licensed one copy of this document for personal use only. Any other reproduction or redistribution is strictly prohibited. All rights reserved. This content is provided for test preparation purposes only and does not imply an endorsement by Mometrix of any particular political, scientific, or religious point of view.

which encourages discussion without a speaker; and seating around a table. Counselors should consider how much participation, if any, is appropriate for a given session when looking at seating arrangements.

ENCOURAGING POSITIVE PERCEPTION OF ROLE AMONG SCHOOL TEACHERS

School counselors run the risk of being perceived as disruptive and counter-productive to the class. One of the ways to mitigate this negative perception, besides conversation and collaboration with teachers, is to understand and respect certain aspects of the classroom dynamic. Particularly when working with younger children, maintaining routine is important to the continuity of the class. The counselor should strive for a role that is complementary and not disruptive. It is also important for counselors to understand and respect the established rules and behavior standards in classrooms. By recognizing that classroom dynamics have been established and providing a continuum, counselors can fulfill the role of facilitator and gain the respect and trust of teachers and other school staff.

MITIGATING CLASSROOM DISTURBANCES

Managing classroom tone and behavior is best accomplished by developing appropriate lessons and incorporating dynamic content, vocal and body signals in lesson delivery. It is important to develop lesson plans that are challenging yet manageable for the age and developmental level of the students. In addition, counselors can incorporate words of encouragement and validation in lessons, giving students a sense of connection to the classroom discussion and activities. Counselors can add a bit of humor to maintain interest and to pique students' creativity. In addition, utilizing changes in voice pitch, moving around the room, and making eye contact with different students can add to a counselor's ability to manage the tenor of a classroom. Not only does this contribute to the credibility of counselors in the classroom, but also greatly improves the efficacy of the lesson.

ROLE OF SMOOTH LESSON DEVELOPMENT

Giving students not only interesting and informative classroom content is another pivotal factor in mitigating the occurrences and opportunity for **classroom disturbance**. It is important for counselors to provide a consistent flow of content and interaction with students in order to keep the class focused on the lesson at hand and away from any possible distractions. This consistent flow also provides a standard backdrop of activity, so that any distracting activities are easily noticed; whereas if a lesson includes lulls or unfocused time, distractions can not only occur more easily, but also can occur relatively unnoticed and pave the way for increased distractive activities. Practices for developing sufficient classroom content include good preparation as well as familiarity with the lesson content. During the lesson, no matter how well planned, the counselor should continue to be watchful for any classroom disturbance, and should bring students back into focus as appropriate.

ADDRESSING CLASSROOM DISTURBANCES WHEN THERE ARE EXTRANEOUS FACTORS

If a counselor feels that a **classroom disturbance** is rooted in a relationship outside of the classroom or the personal issues of one student, he or she may be able to restore the learning environment in the classroom and provide empathy at the same time. In the process of reminding a student or students to support the classroom learning environment, counselors may discover that there are underlying issues feeding the disturbance. It is important to approach each situation from a position of mutual respect and group consideration, so as to not be perceived as an unsympathetic, top-down authority. On the contrary, a counselor wants to be perceived as a knowledgeable person whose concern is the well-being of all students. A counselor can serve as a sounding board and resource expert for students who are experiencing problems that interfere with their learning experience.

ADDRESSING INDIVIDUAL DISCIPLINE ISSUES

In order to manage with empathy, a counselor should maintain his or her role as authority while conveying a message of accessibility and expertise. When first approaching students, counselors should try to establish a kind of partnership, allowing students to participate in addressing issues that are disruptive to their learning environment. Students who feel they can participate in this resolution are less likely to feel isolated and singled out. However, counselors need to maintain the students' respect for the counselor's role. Not only does this prevent disruptions from becoming more pronounced, it also serves to give students confidence in the counselor's expertise. In the process of **working with a disruptive student**, counselors can suggest to the student underlying problems that may be fueling the disruption, providing an effective, holistic response to a classroom disturbance.

ADDRESSING ATTENTION-SEEKING BEHAVIOR

Because of the When a student exhibits **attention-seeking behavior**, it is important that counselors do not reward the behavior with undue attention while disciplining the student. Counselors can develop consistent consequences for disruptive, attention-seeking behavior, and make these consequences known to students when first beginning work with them. Counselors may want to work with teachers and other staff to develop and communicate these consequences to students. Consequences should be directly related and proportional to the behavior. The effect of implementing these consequences should validate a perception that the counselors and teachers are interested in ensuring a calm and productive classroom environment for all students. Disciplinary actions should be free of anger or other emotional volatility. It is also important for counselors to remain objective, and to not infuse personal or moral assessments into their discipline. All of this will serve to downplay and neutralize attention-seeking behaviors in the classroom.

EXPECTATIONS FOR STUDENTS

A counselor should set high **expectations** regarding students. However, it is important for the counselor to remember that every student is different and that expectations should be set accordingly. One of the first considerations to take is the student's developmental level. A counselor needs to be aware if the student has any learning disabilities or is developmentally slow. Another factor to consider is the instructional level for the students. Expectations should not be set so high that they go beyond the instructional level. A kindergartener cannot be expected to perform on the same level as a sixth grader. The opposite is also true; expectations should not be set too low that the students will be performing below grade level and unmotivated to achieve anything higher than that.

AWARENESS OF NATIONAL PERSPECTIVE CONCERNING EDUCATION

It is vital that counselors are aware of the **national perspective concerning education**. They need to know what is expected of them, their staff, and their school. Counselors should know what the expectations are and make sure they are trying everything to meet those standards. The nation has certain goals that they expect schools to achieve, and counselors need to know what is expected of them and ensure their school is moving in that direction. When a counselor knows what the national expectation is, they can look at their school and ask whether they have the means to achieve those expectations. If they do not then they will know what their educational needs are and find the means to achieve those goals.

SELECTING A CONFLICT MANAGEMENT TECHNIQUE

In most cases, when a counselor is deciding which technique is the most appropriate to resolve conflict, they will choose a contingency approach, meaning that they choose the technique based on the nature of the situation. However, a counselor should also consider the individual personal needs of the staff when selecting a conflict management technique. Other important factors to consider are the people involved in the conflict, how serious the situation is to them, the type and intensity of the conflict, and the authority that the individuals possess. A counselor is likely to encounter several different types of conflicts and therefore there will be a number of alternative techniques from which to choose. One technique will not be suitable in all situations.

GAINING SUPPORT FOR CHANGE

There are certain groups that will be affected the most when there is change: the faculty, the students, the parents, the school board, the counselor's superiors, and the state department of public instruction. These groups can also provide the most support or the most resistance to change. Counselors must remember that every group will have their opinions, and the most professional thing to do is respect, listen, and accept those opinions, even if they are not agreed upon. One of the most important groups a counselor needs to consider during the change process is the faculty. It is crucial to get the faculty involved, because if the faculty does not understand why there needs to be a change, there will be less support, and in return, an implementation of a new program might not be successful.

ADOPTION OF AN INNOVATION

The first stage a counselor will go through is the awareness stage, which is becoming aware of a **new innovation**, but not having enough information about it. Many times, a counselor may not even have a strong enough interest to find out more information about the subject. During the interest stage, a counselor is beginning to show signs of wanting to gather more information, and may even begin to develop negative or positive feelings. At the mental stage, the counselor has decided this is something worth trying and is evaluating the innovation and deciding how it will be implemented. They may also ask respected members of the school community to assess it. During the trial stage, the innovation is implemented on a limited basis. Next is the adoption stage, the point when the innovation is implemented fully. The last stage is the integration stage, in which the innovation has become a routine.

USE OF REFERENT INFLUENCE TO CHANGE A PERSON'S BEHAVIOR

If a counselor possesses a **referent influence**, this means others are able to identify with the counselor as a person. Certain characteristics that others can identify with are a strong character, an outspoken personality, and a compelling leadership style. Characteristics like these may enable a counselor to gain cooperation from others even if teachers, parents and students question the decisions made by the counselor. However, there are no particular character traits that have a positive impact on everyone. While some groups respond positively to certain traits, others may view them as a sign of weak leadership. Another issue with referent influence is that if a counselor is in a position of leadership, their authenticity has already been established; if certain traits are not there, the probability of them developing is small.

USE OF REWARD INFLUENCE TO CHANGE A PERSON'S BEHAVIOR

A counselor is said to have **reward influence** when he or she provides incentives for individuals who act and obey the rules of the program. One issue with this type of influence it that a counselor may not have enough rewards to be able to distribute equally. There may occasionally be a time when rewards may be offered to an individual or group without the same reward being distributed to others. This may seem like preferential treatment, which is not viewed favorably in the education field. Another problem that may arise is that the counselor may receive very little reward to give from the school board and other bureaucratic agencies. Although these problems may occur, a counselor can develop their own unique rewards. These rewards can include a free period, an additional lunch break, or support for a new activity a teacher wants to implement.

Consultation, Collaboration, and Coordination

COLLABORATION WITH TEACHERS AND SCHOOL PERSONNEL

An effective counseling group relies on the support, endorsement, and **collaboration of parents, teachers, and school counselors**. It is important that these individuals and administrative groups understand and support the importance and goals of the counseling group. Counselors can help sensitize parents and school personnel to the importance of counseling groups. One of the common concerns is that counseling groups require students to spend time that could otherwise be spent in the classroom. It is important to stress to parents and school personnel that the time students spend in the classroom is generally more effective if students are allowed to address personal, time management, and other issues in counseling sessions. Once counselors have established this understanding with parents and school personnel, they can unite in a partnership for the students' benefit.

INTRODUCING SCHOOL PERSONNEL AND PARENT GROUPS TO NEED FOR COUNSELING GROUPS

It is important for individuals **advocating the creation of counseling groups** to emphasize first the comprehensive nature of a counseling program within the school setting, pointing out that an effective counseling program works collaboratively with parents and school groups. It should also be stressed that counseling groups address personal issues that can hinder academic performance. A counseling program should include vehicles for input from school personnel and parents. It might be advisable to hold meetings in tandem with PTA or other parent groups, providing a forum for open communication about the need for and implementation of a counseling program. It is recommended that these presentations be held early in the academic year, to allow for discussion and consensus. It is also important for these meetings to be facilitated by professional counselors who can appropriately address questions and concerns.

VEHICLES AND MEDIA FOR COMMUNICATING DEVELOPMENT OF COUNSELING PROGRAMS

Regular communication with parents and school personnel provides continued interface regarding future and existing counseling groups. Some of the channels for keeping this communication open include:
Regular, informative meetings with school counselors discussing current counseling groups, future plans, and any peripheral activities

- Distribution of surveys assessing specific needs for groups, or for topics to be addressed
- Sharing information about groups needed as well as groups being formed, as appropriate, with parents and school personnel
- Being available on a regular basis to hear from school personnel regarding student issues or concerns that may precipitate the need for a counseling group
- Speaking with students in their classrooms about the availability of counseling groups, and providing a clear and confidential process by which they can bring concerns forward
- Developing and communicating clear procedures for group formation, group participation, and parental and school permission

COMMUNICATIVE METHODS FOR DETERMINING TOPICS TO ADDRESS IN COUNSELING GROUPS

The **choice of topics for counseling groups** should be representative of the needs of the school community and/or student body. Many topics will arise out of regular meetings between counselors and the school staff, or from meetings with parents. Others may be revealed in the surveys that are distributed to parents, students, and school staff. Students can also be a source of potential topics, particularly if they are provided with a clear and confidential protocol for bringing these concerns forward. Counselors can be proactive in the process of choosing topics: they can ask groups to suggest topics, or they can choose from a series of topics that might be of interest. Once the counselor has established him/herself as a responsive conduit for topic suggestions, there should be a body of recommendations available from which to determine best topics to be addressed in counseling groups.

TOPIC DETERMINATION ARISING FROM SCHOOL RECORDS, RESEARCH, OR OTHER DOCUMENTATION

School records are another resource for assessing the need for counseling groups and for generating topics. These records contain profiles that may **reveal patterns** of low retention, poor attendance, low test scores, or other identifiable areas of need. Counselors can also research the commonalities of specific age groups to determine which topics would be appropriate and well received. These topics can range from healthy social behavior to career planning. Some of these general areas can be addressed through a specific focus on life experiences, such as beginning a college prep program in high school. It is important that development of groups and group topics be well researched not only to discover common topics for a particular age group, but to determine the applicability of these topics to the particular student body, as documented by school records and the input of school personnel.

FOLLOW-UP MEETINGS
IMPORTANCE

Even when counselors have met with students for a number of sessions and feel that learning objectives have been met, it is nonetheless a good idea to schedule **follow-up meetings** with the students. It is important to realize that students may have effectively mastered particular objectives within the insulated environment of the facilitated classroom sessions, but that they may be inclined to revert to prior behaviors once they are in their familiar milieu. Follow-up sessions can serve as reminders to students of their progress in the classroom, as well as of strategies that were successful for them. They can also give students an additional opportunity to assimilate the lessons and imprint them in their everyday lives. Counselors can use some discretion in determining the best timing for scheduling follow-up meetings, but they generally occur within days or weeks of the final session in the sequence.

BENEFITS

Follow-up meetings with students who have completed a sequence of counseling lessons are beneficial to the counselor, as well as to the students and the overall success of the program. Counselors who meet with students shortly after the final session in a sequence can continue to assess the effectiveness of the strategies employed. As with intra-lesson assessment, follow-up assessment may identify particular areas that need to be targeted more or in a different way in future sessions. Additionally, and more importantly, follow-up sessions can provide counselors with the opportunity to reinforce the lessons and strategies employed in the sequence of sessions. This benefits the students and the program exponentially, in that it decreases the chances of repeated negative behaviors, and mitigates the need for redundant sessions targeting objectives that had been previously met. All of this contributes to the overall effectiveness of the program.

COLLABORATING WITH PARENTS AND SCHOOL STAFF

Because the average student to counselor ratio can range from 100:1 to 300:1, the accessibility of counselors is sometimes well below optimum. The moderate needs of many students can be eclipsed by attention paid to the more severe needs of a few. Therefore, it is advisable for counselors to consult with parents and school personnel in the design of effective prevention and intervention programs. Parents and school personnel experience day-to-day contact with students, and are able to observe them in the classroom and home environments. The combined student contact that parents, teachers, and school counselors have can provide valuable feedback to counselors for designing programs and intervention strategies that will benefit the most students most effectively, augmented by individual sessions as indicated. Counselors who meet with the larger school community are able to maximize the efficacy of the school counseling program.

TRIADIC-DEPENDENT CONSULTATION MODEL

The **triadic-dependent consultation model** is essentially a partnership formed between the counselor, parents, and/or school staff to provide indirect services to a student. It is a problem-solving solution for some students and situations in which strategies implemented at home or in the classroom can augment strategies implemented in the counseling sessions. In this model, the counselor works directly with the student, but augments that work by consulting with parents, schoolteachers, and school counselors. Those third parties are identified as the consultees, and the counselor as consultant can provide information and advice toward the goal of improving relations with the student. The triadic-dependent consultation model does not exist for the benefit of the student, but rather so that the parents and/or school personnel can develop strategies to improve the student's academic or personal situation.

CONDUCTING A CONSULTATION

In the **triadic-dependent consultation model**, counselors initially meet with family and/or school personnel to discuss the student's problems and goals, within confidentiality guidelines. In these meetings, counselors can obtain additional information about the student that will help in the individual sessions. Since many student problems can affect and/or be exacerbated by their social and family network, this model can address the interrelations of various dynamics in the student's life. Counselors may also want to include other members of the student's network, such as peers or other family members, as appropriate, in the process of developing a more comprehensive profile of the student. After assessing the student more comprehensively, counselors can then recommend particular prevention or intervention strategies to the family and/or school personnel. Counselors may recommend interventions focusing on changes for the student, consultee, and/or the school system.

BEHAVIORAL CONSULTATION

Counselors can apply the principles of behaviorism to a triadic-dependent consultation format very successfully. Using these principles, counselors can meet with parents and school personnel to identify and define the student's problems as well as any peripheral circumstances that could be contributing. Once the counselor has developed a comprehensive profile of the student's problems in the context of surrounding circumstances, he or she can the create strategies for changing the student's behavior, and possibly the consultee's behavior or actions. Counselors can also work to modify the social context of the interrelationship between the student and the consultee. Possible therapeutic strategies include behavioral contracting, positive reinforcement, and response cost. The behavioral consultation model can be represented by the following four areas of focus:

- Initial assessment: Identify problems and contributing circumstances.
- Analysis: Develop a comprehensive profile of student needs.
- Implementation: Develop and implement behavior modification strategies.
- Evaluation: Evaluate the efficacy of strategies and revise as appropriate.

PARAMETERS FOR COUNSELORS MEETING WITH CONSULTEES

Counselors meeting with parents and school personnel should strive to make the environment and the dynamics comfortable yet professional. This is particularly important when meeting with parents. Initially, counselors can restate the purpose of the consultation, identify the student, and define the issues of concern. Initial interaction can serve to ease any anxieties and to establish a professional, comfortable dynamic. The student's behavior should be the focus of the meeting, and counselors should redirect the conversation within those boundaries if needed. Nonetheless, consultees should be given the opportunity to give input, as with any therapeutic group. Counselors should probe for any relevant conditions that would affect the treatment planning, and should glean any additional information about the student from classroom observations. Counselors may also want to provide reference materials to the consultees to offer a better understanding of the issues and behaviors involved. All consultant/consultee interactions should be in writing, and follow-up actions should be scheduled during the initial consultation.

COLLABORATIVE-DEPENDENT CONSULTATION MODEL

The **collaborative-dependent consultation model** is also a partnership, but one in which the counselor/consultant may play more of a role as participant rather than as facilitator. The counselor is expected to contribute to problem-solving expertise, but is not the sole expert. The consultee in this model may have a more in-depth knowledge of the student or the system on which the consultation is focused. In this model, the consultant and the consultee can be educated on both the problem-solving process for the student and the response of the student. Both consultant and consultee may have working knowledge of normal and abnormal student development. The consultee may be able to contribute knowledge about the efficacy of previous interventions, and/or the impact of peripheral factors. In the collaborative/dependent consultation model, the partners collaborate to develop an intervention plan, with the counselor defining the problem and completing any evaluation and follow-up services while the consultee is implementing the intervention plan.

APPLICATION FOR ORGANIZATIONAL SYSTEMS

When the **collaborative-dependent model is applied to an organizational system**, the focus can be on the student, the consultee, or the initiation of change within the system. Family dynamics, or a family system, can also be included in this paradigm. In the system application of the collaborative-dependent model, the counselor participates as process consultant to address problem-solving within the context of the system. He or she can contribute his or her expertise on the assessment and interventions that are related to system change. This application should address the following six variables:

- Communication patterns within the group
- Roles and functions of the various group members
- Processes and procedures involved in group decision-making or problem-solving
- Normal group performance and expected growth

- Leadership and authority within the group
- Intra-group cooperation and competition

COLLABORATIVE-INTERDEPENDENT CONSULTATION MODEL

The **collaborative-interdependent consultation model** is one that is more complex and comprehensive, and is most appropriate for addressing the multiplicity of issues related to at-risk youth. In this model, the partnership may be comprised of family, counselor, students, school personnel, and community members, and all may act as equal partners. This model is a collaborative, dynamic one in which the combined input and efforts of the members enable the group as a whole to develop and implement a comprehensive plan. The counselor is not expected to be the sole expert or the central source of information. The onus does not lie on the counselor to develop and implement a plan. The collaboratively developed plan may include change for an individual student, additional knowledge and skills for the team, and/or a change to the system.

POSSIBLE DIFFICULTIES

There can be inherent difficulties in the **collaborative-interdependent model**, relating to the fact that its members are included in the partnership because of their knowledge or perspective of the issue at hand, and not necessarily because they are good collaborators. The collaborative-interdependent partnership can be comprised of parents, school counselors, community members, and others, each of whom may have a different strategy to address the student issues. This can be particularly problematic if the members are each implementing a portion of the solution strategy, and not working together to do so. The ability to work effectively presupposes the ability to work collaboratively. Collaboration should be present at all levels of interaction: identifying the problem, determining the necessary goals, creating strategies, implementing procedures, and evaluating outcomes.

DISTINGUISHING FEATURES OF COLLABORATIVE STYLE OF CONSULTATION

The **collaborative style of consultation** is distinguished by five key features:

- Voluntary participation of members toward resolution of a problem, as opposed to hierarchical direction from a counselor.
- Shared input for decision-making: This is opposed to a model in which the outcome is decided before the group convenes, or in which presuppositions color the outcome.
- Shared responsibility for decision-making: This implies both the expectation and the privilege of addressing the issue at hand. All parties participate in identifying the problem, developing objectives, implementing strategies, and evaluating outcomes.
- Shared investment and ownership of the problem and solution for all parties, potentially including family, school, and community: All parties recognize what needs to be accomplished and contribute their particular expertise.
- Shared resources: This implies less ownership, so that the group decides how the resources will be utilized.

COUNSELOR'S ROLE IN FACILITATING COLLABORATIVE CONSULTATION

The role of the counselor in the **collaborative consultation** format is that of both **facilitator** and **role model** for the consultation. The distinguishing advantage of the collaborative format is that of shared and interactive input regarding the student. Each person's perspective, expertise, and knowledge of the student and the situation is valuable and contributes to a whole that is often greater than its parts. Counselors can model this format by encouraging input from all the members, and can facilitate the group by maintaining the guidelines that allow for interactive sharing. The counselor's role in the collaborative model is not that of leader, but more of guide and facilitator. Some of the key points to address in collaborative consultation include:

- Open consideration of other perspectives
- Willingness to revise one's perspective
- Integration of others' ideas in intervention
- Flexibility of counselor to de-emphasize his or her role as leader
- Guiding the group in a manner that encourages collaboration

IMPORTANCE OF DEVELOPING STRATEGIES WITHIN THE CONTEXT OF THE LARGER SCHOOL SYSTEM

Particularly in a school counseling environment, any kind of intervention or therapy must be conceived and delivered within the context of the larger school system and community. The primary purpose behind this is **efficacy of treatment**. Counselors who are working with at-risk students or students who are facing personal problems will benefit the student and the counseling program by collaborating with school personnel. This may include a collaborative consultation, or may just be a matter of using the available resources. Counselors may also want to serve as liaisons in suggesting student-oriented changes to the school system. Counselors can also adopt a holistic approach to therapy, within the context of the school community. It is important to remember that students have classmates, take course work within a prescribed curriculum, and operate within the mandates of the school system. Therefore, when working with students, counselors should be cognizant of a student's daily routines and environment.

COUNSELOR'S ROLE WITHIN THE CONTEXT OF THE LARGER SCHOOL SYSTEM

It is important for school counselors to remember that they are just one member of the school personnel community. Their role is to provide individual or group therapy to student members of the community who are at risk for self-destructive behaviors, which usually include academic failure. It is the intervention focusing on the dangers of academic failure that serves as the linchpin of the collective goals of the entire school community, including the school counselor. For school counselors to be most valuable to their student clients, it is important for them to remember that serving their students is also serving the greater good of the school community. This greater good includes the safety of the student body, and the academic goals of the school and the district. Those academic goals can be reflected in test scores, retention, and other quantifiable data.

BECOMING AN INTEGRAL PART OF THE SCHOOL COMMUNITY

When becoming a part of a school community, a school counselor can take proactive steps toward **developing a collaborative relationship** with other members of the community. These steps include:

- Recognize that the school staff is in a fiduciary role, implementing the academic goals of the school and the district.
- Be open to the evolution of your role within the school community, as opposed to imposing preconceived ideas about your role on the school staff.
- Become familiar with the rules and expectations of the school community.
- Recognize that any operational entity will have both explicit and implicit hierarchies, and become aware of those levels of authority and power.
- Cultivate alliances and friendships through shared agendas and recognition of individual strengths.
- Develop effective and collaborative vehicles of communication with members of the school and the larger community.

- Maintain objectivity when working with any educator or family member.
- Refrain from provocatively challenging the authority of an educator or community member.

AREAS IN WHICH UNDERSTANDING OF POLICIES AND PROCEDURES OF THE SCHOOL SYSTEM IS IMPORTANT

Each school system will have particular nuances and interpretations with respect to **issues of confidentiality and parental rights**. Counselors should be aware of these policies/procedures when working with students in order to know:

- When and how to notify parents of student participation in counseling.
- How to respond to a suspicion of child abuse.
- Issues of confidentiality in the therapeutic environment, e.g., when and how to report severely at-risk behavior, and when and how to recognize and report students who may be at risk of harming others.
- When and how to open up the counseling strategies to include collaborative consultation.
- When to involve teachers and other school staff in intervention strategies.

Understanding the policies and procedures includes not only reading them but also understanding how these policies are implemented in a particular school environment. Maintaining open communication and cultivating relationships with school staff will be beneficial to the counselor in developing an understanding of school policies and procedures.

SPECTRUM OF POLICY INTERPRETATION AMONG DIFFERENT SCHOOL PERSONNEL

Although most **school policies and procedures** are clearly delineated in written form, their interpretation can be less clear-cut, and can even vary between teachers and classrooms. One policy area that can easily vary between educators is that of allowing students to participate in counseling during time normally set aside for classroom instruction. Some teachers may support student counseling, and may be willing to let students leave their classrooms to do so. Others may also be in support of students receiving counseling, but may feel that it should not be done at the expense of classroom time, but rather before or after school. Teachers may also have differing opinions about collaboration with school counselors, particularly about the implementation of behavior modification strategies in the classroom. Counselors should be sensitive to these differences in opinion, and the spectrum of teachers' responses to the need for and implementation of a counseling program.

DEFERRING TO THE EXPLICIT AUTHORITY OF THE PRINCIPAL

The principal of a school administrates the allocation of both monetary and personnel resources. For a school counselor to successfully plan and implement a counseling program at a school, the **support and endorsement of the principal** is pivotal. In deference to the principal's responsibilities, counselors should keep him or her apprised of the scope of the current counseling program, as well as revisions or plans for future revisions to the program. Not only is this respectful of the principal's agenda; it is also a good way to retain the support and endorsement of the administration. It is also recommended that counselors meet with principals on a regular basis, at the principal's convenience. Counselors should allow sufficient time to apprise the principal of updates and for discussion as appropriate. Principals may also make suggestions and recommendations for the counseling program, which should be taken into account by the counselor.

RECOGNIZING INDIVIDUALS WITH EITHER EXPLICIT OR IMPLICIT INFLUENCE IN THE SCHOOL SYSTEM

When a counselor recognizes that he or she is just one member of a school community, he or she should also recognize that a community contains both **formal and informal power structures**. Although it is necessary for a counselor to keep open communication with the principal, that line of communication may depend on the counselor's interactions with the principal's secretary or other assistant counselor. School counselors should also be cognizant of the network of communication and influence that exists within the school system, as it does within most communities. Counselors can cultivate relationships with teachers, parents, other counselors, etc., in order to gain an understanding of underlying concerns and agendas within the larger school agenda. These relationships can also provide a vehicle for counselors to inform the school community of their concerns and plans for an appropriate counseling program to address those concerns. A healthy environment for a school counseling program includes shared agendas and collaboration.

CULTIVATING RELATIONSHIPS WITH INFLUENTIAL INDIVIDUALS IN THE SCHOOL COMMUNITY
IMPACT

When counselors are able to communicate and collaborate with influential and interested members of the school community regarding the counseling program, there are positive far-reaching effects. By recognizing and incorporating the interplay of agendas and concerns in a school community, counselors are able to **gain the respect, endorsement, and contributions** of those individuals. When counselors can recognize and utilize the strengths and contributions of individuals working in the school community, the counseling program is able to thrive and grow within the context of the school system. The added benefit is that when the program is working within this context, peripheral individuals and programs will associate the counseling program with the larger agendas of the school community and will more readily accept and endorse the program. As these working relationships evolve, the counselor can develop rich alliances and friendships within the school community to the benefit of all the members.

CONCERNS

As with any group dynamic, the interplay of agendas and concerns within a school community may be organic and healthy, may be dysfunctional and conflicting, or may be somewhere in between. Although it is not necessarily the counselor's role to analyze the dynamics at play in the school setting, he or she nonetheless needs to be aware of conflicts between individuals and agendas, particularly if individuals or groups are in opposition to the principal's goals and overall agenda. Counselors should exercise some caution when forming alliances to the benefit of the counseling program that may be in opposition to other groups or the overall agenda of the school principal. It would be better to cultivate relationships with a measure of caution, until a counselor understands the overall interplay of agendas within the school community. Counselors can also strive to facilitate cooperation and collaboration between the parties involved.

WORKING WITH MEMBERS OF SUBSYSTEMS IN THE SCHOOL COMMUNITY

The larger school community is comprised of many **subsystems**, including but not limited to parents, service staff, librarians, and community groups. Even within the teaching staff, there are subsystems comprised of education specialists, resource teachers, etc. Although not necessarily in conflict with each other, these groups may operate quasi-autonomously and be unaware of their effects on the larger school community. This is best illustrated within the experiences of the students, who interact with and depend on many of these subsystems. Counselors working with students with complex needs may have to involve several subsystems in order to provide effective treatment. It might be beneficial for counselors to form acquaintances with members of the larger school community, in order to better understand the complexities of subsystems in the school and facilitate communication between these entities.

EMOTIONAL OBJECTIVITY WHEN INTRODUCING OR IMPLEMENTING COUNSELING PROGRAMS

When counselors join a school community, they may **encounter resistance to their contributions** from certain members of that community. Although the school community as a whole may endorse and support the counseling program and its inclusion in the larger efforts of the school, the resistance of a few may manifest in covert or overt actions that undermine or impede the counseling program. Counselors need to maintain objectivity when facing these kinds of challenges, which should be recognized as symptoms of systemic change. Recognizing this objectively, the counselor can then approach the challenges professionally. Relying on their knowledge of systems change analysis, counselors can isolate and identify the resistance, and openly approach the individuals or entities involved to find a mutual resolution. It is important to remember that, without this objectivity, counselors can become mired in conflict and programs can be rendered ineffectual.

INITIAL STAGES OF PROBLEM SOLVING ON A SCHOOL CAMPUS

Once a consultant is in the school system, he or she is in a position to **initiate problem solving**. Regardless of the problem, or the complexity of the problem, the initial stage of problem solving is generally that of identifying the problem to be addressed. This involves collecting the information necessary to comprehensively assess the issue at hand. If the difficulty relates to a student, the information collecting may involve parents, teachers, and/or the student. The problem-solving process can also require other educators or family members to form a collaborative problem-solving team. Problems to be addressed might also be more macrocosmic, involving several students with violent behavior, or possibly system-wide issues affecting the entire school. Once the problem has been comprehensively isolated, counselors should determine the most appropriate consultation model for working toward resolution.

IMPORTANCE OF PROCESS IN PROBLEM-SOLVING GROUPS

School teams brought together to resolve an issue are often task-oriented, and generally are not focused on process. Without some attention paid to process, the collaborative effect of the team can be diffused and the efficacy of the group diminished. The counselor as consultant can contribute to the group discussion with not only knowledge about a particular issue, but also specific expertise in group dynamics. As **facilitator**, he or she can encourage the group process necessary to complete the problem-solving task. As with any professional interaction, counselors should remember they are a part of a larger whole and maintain an openness to the strengths of the group and the individual members. If approached well, a successful collaborative process will significantly contribute to the overall success of the task team, as well as establish the counselor as a valuable member of the school community.

FACILITATING A COLLABORATIVE GROUP DYNAMIC

After the counselor as consultant has been assigned a role in the group, he or she may have the opportunity to **facilitate collaboration**. When working with a problem-solving team, counselors can initiate specific practices and procedures toward a collaborative group dynamic. These practices include:

- Noting and encouraging behaviors among the group that contribute to collaboration and cooperation.
- Noting and discouraging competitive remarks and behaviors.
- Working with the group to establish a collaborative group norm.

- Creating an open communication policy that allows the input of all participants to the problem-solving process.
- Recognizing and respecting the expertise and contributions of all members of the group.
- These practices can lay the foundation for a collaborative group process. Facilitating a collaborative group dynamic may also occasionally include soliciting the support and endorsement of a school counselor by explaining the value of the collaborative process in a problem-solving group.

FRAMING THE OBJECTIVES OF PROBLEM RESOLUTION IN GROUP SETTING

The counselor as facilitator can work with members of the group to set goals and create a viable action plan. It is important that the parameters of this action plan fall within the capabilities and contributions of the group members. Individuals in the group should be able to recognize and embrace their role in facilitating change in the students. Specific steps in the **process of developing an action plan** include:

- Identifying the goal and the action plan for achieving it.
- Determining an appropriate and reasonable measurement of outcome.
- Empowering group members to act as change agents.
- Identifying the individual and group strengths appropriate to the action plan.
- Encouraging flexibility of roles and expanded boundaries as appropriate.
- Encouraging collaboration within the group and with other entities as appropriate.
- Developing a plan to implement and retain the changes.

IDENTIFICATION OF GOALS AND OUTCOMES

It is important to remember the initial process of problem solving is comprehensive problem identification. This identification should define the scope of the problem, specifically whether it is isolated to a particular student and/or the student's family dynamic, more generalized within a group of students, or dispersed throughout the school system as a whole. Once the problem is identified, the problem-solving team should clearly **identify goals** for the student or the particular group, as well as **anticipated outcomes**. Academic goals for students should fall within the academic parameters and mission of the school. Inherent in the process is the need to develop viable outcome assessment measures, which will be made easier by clearly-stated objectives. When the group can articulate the objectives, as well as the measurements of outcome, they can formulate goals that are reasonable and achievable.

FRAMING ISSUES IN AN INCLUSIVE MANNER

When a student's behavior or problem becomes such that intervention is necessary, blame is often laid at the feet of various parties. Parents may blame the school for their child's problems, and schools may hold parents accountable for student behavior. As consultants, counselors can stress that the student's situation should be viewed as a **catalyst for change** that will involve the student, the school, and the family. Viewed in this way, intervention becomes a **collaborative goal** rather than an exercise in finding evidence to support blame. Counselors can encourage participants to feel committed to resolution, and to each embrace his or her respective role in its achievement. The strengths of the teachers and family members should be affirmed and used to bring about the desired objectives. Counselors should remind participants that change is a process that will take time and the commitment of those involved in the student's life.

APPROACHING AN IDENTIFIED NEED FOR SYSTEMIC CHANGE

When student intervention necessitates a group effort, it usually correlates with a multiplicity and complexity of issues. Consequently, resolution is usually complex, and may involve many entities. Sometimes, any change anticipated in the student relies at least in part on changes in family dynamics and/or school systems. Counselors should remember that student behaviors indicate a need for change, and should refrain from blatantly identifying any system or individual as a cause for the problems. Rather, counselors should use diplomacy in suggesting changes in family or school dynamics, particularly if the respective parties are operating under the assumption that the student's behavioral problems are not connected to other influences in his or her life. This is a situation in which the trust and alliances gained from members of the school community are particularly valuable. Counselors can work separately with teachers or family members to encourage change as applicable.

ENCOURAGING MORE FLEXIBLE ROLES AND BROADENED BOUNDARIES IN PROBLEM-SOLVING TEAMS

The **optimal consulting group** is one in which the whole is greater than the sum of its parts. Practically speaking, each of the participants comes to the task with particular expertise, a specific set of skills, and a paradigm or perspective regarding the problem and the anticipated resolution. Each member sees himself or herself in a predetermined role. Educators generally approach student problems from an academic perspective; psychologists will tend to be most concerned about the student's mental health. However, in a group setting, with good facilitation, the participants can be encouraged to step beyond their prescribed roles and expectations toward a comprehensive intervention strategy that will bring their collective expertise to a cohesive front. In this setting, counselors may ask a teacher to co-lead the group, or a psychologist to facilitate a discussion about academic goals. This shared crossing over can be most beneficial in a consulting group.

HOW CONSULTANTS CAN PLAN AND STRATEGIZE FOR PROTECTING CHANGE

Counselors understand that any kind of **behavioral change is an ongoing process and will often include backsliding or digression**. When facilitating a consulting group, counselors can first remind the group that any intervention strategy needs to include plans for protecting the anticipated change. Knowing this initially will enhance the long-term success of an intervention strategy. Consultants can assist the group in developing a post-plan for this purpose. This post-plan should include a delineation of the responsibilities and benchmarks to be used in evaluating progress. It may also include mechanisms that will allow for ongoing communication among the members, as well as support resources. In a school setting, student progress is generally associated with academic achievement, which can provide a clear marker for determining strategy success. Behavioral changes can also be monitored by noting clearly identifiable actions.

EVALUATING SUCCESS OF IMPLEMENTATION

When an action plan has been developed and implemented, the **evaluation process** should begin. The action plan should include strategies for evaluation and outcome measurement. It may be appropriate for each member of the consultant group to participate in the evaluation process by monitoring such successes as academic progress and changed behaviors. The evaluation should focus on **whether any change has occurred**, and to what degree that change can be **measured**. Participants can develop vehicles for collecting as well as presenting the relevant data. Counselors should provide oversight for this phase of the action plan. They should be attentive to the degree of change, and should determine if it is sufficient to be considered successful. They should also be attentive to any changes that constitute digression or negative change. If this is the case, they might want to assess possible factors, and meet with the group to develop alternate strategies.

BRINGING THE AD HOC CONSULTATION GROUP TO CLOSURE

If the consultant is not a regular member of the school community, **closure** may be more definitive than if the counselor as consultant is a part of the school staff. In that situation, counselors can maintain communication with the participants and provide confirmation of successful completion. The counselor can also conduct **debriefings** with the participants to **reflect on the process, the degree of success, and the value of collaboration**. Counselors can also maintain communication with school counselors and peripheral professionals as a follow-up to a successful intervention. If, on the other hand, the counselor as consultant is a regular member of the school staff, it is important to be attentive to sensitivities that the student might have regarding regular proximity to the participants of the consulting group, including the counselor. In that event, formal follow-up might be less appropriate than if the consultant is regularly away from campus.

CROSS-CULTURAL CONSULTATION

When working with consultees from diverse cultural backgrounds, counselors should refer to their knowledge of **cross-cultural counseling** in order to facilitate the group with confidence and skill. Multicultural participants in a consulting group will inherently present special considerations regarding diversity of culture:

- Impact of culture: how diverse cultural paradigms affect the consultation process
- Recognition of culture: understanding the richness of contributions from diversity of culture

A counselor should also strive to do the following:

- Be sensitive to cultural differences when developing rapport within the group.
- Be aware of cultural factors within the group as well as between the group and the student.
- Develop appropriate interventions with these cultural considerations in mind, if indicated.
- Respond objectively to diverse circumstances.
- Identify and emphasize similarities between the represented cultures, as appropriate.
- Address balance of power issues.
- Endorse the success of the student and consultees.

APPLYING COLLABORATIVE CONSULTATION TO A BROADER COMMUNITY

It may be the case that a student is already interacting with other professionals or professional groups outside of the school community. Often this is the case when students present a complexity of issues. In order to approach the student holistically, counselors may want to include these individuals in a consulting group, or as part of the school-based consulting group. Through **collaborative consultation**, the individual members should endeavor to adopt an integrated approach that will result in **shared input and shared responsibility**. It is generally recommended that each member's interaction with the student should be suspended or altered in deference to the participant's involvement in the collaborative consultation model. Counselors as consultants should become familiar with the expertise and scope of each professional/group, and should try to involve the parents in the consultation. Overall, the collaborative consultation model can prove much more effective than if counselors were to meet individually with respective professionals or professional groups.

INCLUDING PARENTS IN A COLLABORATIVE CONSULTATION MODEL

Counselors as consultants are in a position to recognize when a student issue could be best addressed by generating dialogue between parents and members of the school community. The initial process should involve bringing the parents together with educators or other school members as appropriate, to discuss and come to an agreed understanding regarding the needs of the student. Through collaboration, parents and school members can recognize that each of their efforts as individual entities would likely not be as effective as the collaborative efforts of the group members, including the parents. Counselors can facilitate the process by helping members to understand each other's roles and prospective contributions. Counselors can guide the group discussions by allowing each of the participants, which may just be a teacher and a parent, to understand their mutual goal of academic success for the student, and to encourage trust in the collaborative process.

INCREASING PARENTAL INVOLVEMENT IN STUDENT ACADEMIC ACHIEVEMENT

Increased **parental involvement and awareness** strongly correlates with **increased academic success** in students. There is also a significant benefit to students who are able to dovetail their school experience with their home experience, such that their parents become more involved in their academic requirements. When parents are able to supplement classroom instruction with additional teaching at home, their children generally perform better and are more engaged at school. Counselors and other members of the school staff can cultivate parental involvement through a number of vehicles. Open-house events and parent-teacher conferences are common modes for increasing parental involvement. Other recommendations are parent resource centers, phone calls, or even visits to the home when appropriate. If the school community as a whole recognizes the value of parental involvement and endeavors to forge a partnership with parents on a regular basis, overall student achievement can be expected to improve.

There are numerous arenas in which counselors can **encourage parental involvement** in students' academic achievement. Augmenting those events in which parents are invited to visit the campus, counselors can build on this involvement by including parents in planning and decision-making programs as appropriate. Another suggestion is to research the talents and skills of parents, and develop a volunteer pool. Educators and counselors will need to give specific directions for participation, and can diversify the selection of areas in which parents can contribute their time and expertise. Counselors can also acknowledge parental involvement through written newsletters or at school events. Counselors should emphasize the goal they share with parents: namely, the academic success of their students. Counselors can **distribute additional academic resources to parents**. The school should be portrayed as welcoming to families. Counselors may want to coordinate transportation and baby-sitting for parent visits.

EFFECTIVE COMMUNICATION WITH PARENTS

Counselors can set a welcoming tone each year, by proactively welcoming parents and encouraging their participation in the academic lives of their children. The following are some effective ways to set this tone:

- Send a welcome letter at the beginning of the year that includes a calendar of events and invites parents to participate.
- Provide a resource brochure or informational handout with general school policies and the an explanation of the counselor's role in the students' lives.
- Distribute informational resources describing the counseling programs, community resources, and pertinent contact information.

- Regularly send event and meeting calendars, which should include contact information for support resources and counselors.
- Generate a school newsletter that will give parents and the surrounding community information about school resources and any other material of interest.
- Schedule new-family meetings right before school starts.

Chapter Quiz

Ready to see how well you retained what you just read? Scan the QR code to go directly to the chapter quiz interface for this study guide. If you're using a computer, simply visit the bonus page at **mometrix.com/bonus948/praxsccoun5422** and click the Chapter Quizzes link.

Manage

Transform passive reading into active learning! After immersing yourself in this chapter, put your comprehension to the test by taking a quiz. The insights you gained will stay with you longer this way. Scan the QR code to go directly to the chapter quiz interface for this study guide. If you're using a computer, simply visit the bonus page at **mometrix.com/bonus948/praxsccoun5422** and click the Chapter Quizzes link.

Counseling and School Guidance Program Design

DESIGNING AND IMPLEMENTING INTERVENTIONS

The procedure for **intervention** entails **setting goals**, **designing intervention strategies** toward achieving those goals, and **evaluating the success of the intervention**. One of the first considerations in the intervention process is the counselor's consideration of a student's developmental stage, as well as the social and environmental settings and context. A counselor will want to make the decision to apply either formal or informal assessment methods, which in turn will affect evaluation procedures. Other factors to consider are informally assessing the level of parent and teacher support available for an intervention, as well as gauging the time constraints. Counselors should carefully consider all aspects of a student situation when determining intervention strategies. Another thing to be considered is whether resolving a situation may be beyond the scope of the school counseling setting, at which point the student should be referred to an outside resource.

INCORPORATING COLLABORATION AND FLEXIBILITY IN SETTING GOALS

Although it is important for each session, with each student, to be guided by clearly defined therapeutic goals, it is also important to recognize that reaching those goals is often a result of **collaboration** with the student, and may require some **flexibility** on the part of the counselor. The counseling relationship is inherently a dynamic one, which is most successful when there is a partnership between the counselor and the student. Setting and realizing goals in counseling should include the following considerations:

- What is particular about this student or this situation that needs to be incorporated into the strategy for intervention?
- What are the student's goals for this situation?

Answering these questions will enable the counselor to develop and refine goals, timelines, best approaches to each phase of the goals, and possibly even adjustments to the physical counseling environment. All of these and other interactive, collaborative considerations will contribute to the success and efficacy of the counseling session and relationship.

CRITERIA FOR DETERMINING APPROPRIATE INTERVENTION

Initiating an intervention for a student or situation is a complex strategic decision that should take account of a number of factors. It is important to remember that a number of strategies are applicable in most situations, so counselors are wise to isolate those strategies that are most effective in an academic setting. It is also important to remember that a particular strategy that is appropriate and effective for one student and one situation might not be suitable for another student with the same situation. Counselors should **implement interventions** that will serve to develop and maintain a dynamic counseling relationship; that will work in tandem with a student's evolving development; that have reasonable goals for the allotted time frame; that are flexible in relation to individual student circumstances;to the student's overt behavior; and that are respectful of diversity and culture.

Choosing Interventions in an Academic Setting

The general considerations for an **intervention in an academic setting** are the age, development, cultural background, and social skills of the student. Cultural and social considerations are particularly pivotal because they can provide the parameters for establishing recognition and context for some interventions. It might be useful to consult the families of students when determining the cultural and social relevance of a particular therapeutic method. Categories of therapy generally fall into broad areas of multimodal counseling, family counseling, direct and indirect play therapy, and expressive art therapy. Common therapy strategies for school-age children include drama, storytelling, music, art, puppetry, use of tactile materials like clay and sand, and an array of play therapies. Other formal methods include reality therapy, Gestalt techniques, cognitive-behavioral counseling, and Adlerian counseling. Knowledge of the spectrum of available therapies is particularly valuable for counselors seeking appropriate interventions for students in an academic setting.

Determining Appropriate Interventions According to Behavior and Symptoms

Once a counselor has narrowed down the **choice of appropriate therapies for a particular situation**, it is then a good idea to further narrow the options to those that would be appropriate for a particular student, with **particular overt behaviors** or **symptoms**. For instance, a student with ADHD might benefit most from a therapy that focuses on impulse control and self-monitoring, while a student who displays difficulty completing assignments might be better served by a kind of reality therapy that allows him or her to apply abstract thinking to consideration of the impact of their actions and to develop alternative behaviors. Another significant example is working with a student suffering from depression, who may need to first work on thought patterns through cognitive therapy, before or in tandem with other therapies targeting the situation. It is always appropriate to consider the cultural background, age, and developmental level of the student when choosing therapies.

Intervention Implementation

A **successful intervention** is best preceded by the establishment of a strong relationship between counselor and student. From there, the counselor can recommend an intervention to the student, who in turn will feel empowered by the effect of collaboration. This approach also provides students with validation, encouragement, and the endorsement of their own desires for resolution. Once the intervention is in place, it may be appropriate for counselors to discuss the progress and goals of the therapy with parents, teachers and others included in the student's support network. Likewise, if the intervention therapy is not progressing as anticipated, it may be appropriate to work with teachers to develop behavioral strategies in the classroom to complement the therapy. This communication and collaboration with teachers and/or parents should be within the context of the counseling sessions, and should honor the counselor's responsibilities to the school and the community.

Including the Student in Evaluation Procedures

Communicating with the student about the success of interventions, and the progress toward therapeutic goals, should take account of the counseling relationship. Indeed, the **student's response to evaluation practices** helps decide the success of the intervention. Without student response, counselors run the risk of losing the student's trust. A counselor can determine if a particular student, in a particular environment, would be best served by an informal or a formal evaluation of progress. In a collaborative informal evaluation, both student and counselor are present and the counselor can observe and monitor student response. Formal evaluations take into account reports from parents and teachers, as well as the student's documentation of his or her success in a particular area. With either formal or informal evaluation of progress, the counselor should make it a practice to take into consideration the relationship that has been established with the student.

CAUTIONS AND SAFEGUARDS REGARDING EVALUATION PROCEDURES

While counselor-generated evaluations are to some extent inherently subjective, there are several recommended safeguards to ensure a **reasonable level of objectivity**. In terms of the relationship to the student, the counselor should maintain a professional emotional distance, while still demonstrating sensitivity to student needs and feelings. The counselor should guard against becoming too emotionally attached to a student, since this could obscure the counselor's ability to evaluate empirically the level of success of the therapy or intervention. It is also important that the counselor and/or counseling team develop evaluation techniques and a rubric that will appropriately assess the achievement of therapeutic goals. A single-case study experimental design may be advisable. Another common suggestion is for the counselor to implement both formal and informal evaluation techniques to allow for more objective assessment.

SENSITIVITIES INVOLVED IN ENDING THE COUNSELING RELATIONSHIP

The academic counseling relationship is perhaps more susceptible to difficulties in closure than the professional relationship, for the mere fact that the student and counselor may have met several days a week, or even several times a day. For this reason, the **termination of the relationship** needs to be approached carefully and methodically. Although there is no definitive research regarding this process, there are some generally agreed-upon practices. Termination can be an abrupt or a gradual process, but it is nonetheless recommended that the counselor use his or her discretion in choosing a time to prepare the student for the last session. It is a good idea for the counselor to take this time to reinforce with the student the success of the counseling relationship, including the progress and improvements made by the student. Counselors should be attentive to student feelings and responses, and should recommend outside resources as appropriate.

BRIEF-COUNSELING METHOD
PARAMETERS AND PURPOSE

The brief-counseling method, sometimes referred to as **solution-focused brief counseling (SFBC)**, is often indicated in schools that have regimented time constraints for counseling. The parameters of these brief-counseling sessions are designed to mimic the parameters of longer individual sessions, but modeled for the indicated time period. The SFBC model also incorporates the unique aspects of the school counseling session. The model includes an opportunity for the student to concretely describe his or her particular situation, present any previous attempted resolutions, and then develop and implement an intervention. The SFBC model is most effective when the counselors utilize the time to endorse student strengths, successes, and resources. This model is often found to be effective for students of diverse backgrounds and cultures.

BASIC PREMISES AND STRATEGIES

Some of the key premises that underlie the SFBC model are:

- Focus should be directed toward solutions, and not toward the problems.
- Within each problem is an identifiable exception that should be isolated and addressed when formulating a solution.

- Large changes often begin with small changes.
- Within each student are the resources needed to solve his or her problem.
- The basic strategies of SFBC are:
- If the counselor determines that no problematic issue exists, he or she should be cautious not to create one.
- Counselors should develop tasks similar to those with which the student has found success.
- Counselors should be open to the necessity of changing strategies, if it is found that a particular strategy is unsuccessful with a particular student or situation.

These premises and strategies have been carefully researched and formulated by a consortium of counselors well versed in the SFBC model.

CORE CONCEPTS

The strategies indicated for SFBC are based on the following set of core concepts:

- If the counselor develops and presents the goals in a positive context, then cooperation, collaboration, and positive response from the student are more likely.
- In the SFBC model, a pragmatic approach is much more indicated than a theoretical one; in other words, this model focuses on what works rather than what the problem is.
- Counselors should be careful to formulate intervention strategies that can be reasonably attained within the allotted time frame.
- Because of the nature and parameters of the SFBC model, counselors should encourage students to focus on present and future circumstances, and to avoid past experiences as much as possible.
- Counselors should focus intervention strategies on students' behaviors and actions, rather than on reflective insights.

All of these strategies contribute to the efficacy and success of the SFBC model of counseling session.

INTERACTIVE FORMAT IN THE FIRST SESSION

One of the goals of the **first session** of the SFBC model is for the counselor to present the student with a series of questions designed to **elicit a response**. These responses will form the foundation for developing an intervention. A recommended format for introducing these questions is for the counselor to first present the basic goals and premises of SFBC. Second, he or she will inform the student that questions will be asked, and that the questions could prove to be difficult or challenging. This precursor strategy often sets the stage for the student to be poised with a response to a challenge. The student's response will often provide the counselor with a starting point for intervention. This posturing will contribute to the efficacy of questioning in the first session of the SFBC.

EMPOWERING AND ENCOURAGING STUDENTS TO CREATE POSITIVE GOALS

Creating positive goals requires the capacity to envision oneself realizing those goals. Some of the strategies that counselors can use to facilitate this process include:

- Asking the student how he or she would feel and react if his or her situation were suddenly resolved.
- Asking the student to identify instances where the current situation was not problematic, or when there were exceptions to the situation. This can be a very powerful step, in that it may recall a recent instance of resolution that the student can recognize and respond to.

- Asking the student what actions or behaviors led to some resolution, or mitigation, of the situation. The counselor should encourage positive actions and results.
- Asking the student to rate their feelings about their behavior or the situation on a scale of 1 to 10.
- Anticipating possible obstacles, and working to guide the students around and/or past those obstacles.

BENEFITS OF GROUP COUNSELING IN ADDITION TO INDIVIDUAL COUNSELING

As a rule, adolescents tend to learn better and respond more when interacting with peers. Therefore, **group counseling that augments individual counseling** can be beneficial. In group counseling, students have the opportunity to both give and receive support for positive behaviors. Likewise, group counseling provides immediate feedback for negative behaviors and thought patterns, allowing the student to reflect on his or her choices. The format of a group counseling session can also serve as a microcosm of larger society, providing a venue for students to experiment with behaviors in a controlled environment, and to experience the feedback of peers with whom they have developed a trust relationship. Group counseling, in tandem with the more remedial individual counseling, provides a comprehensive therapeutic environment for the student. Counselors who utilize both formats reap the benefits of opportunities for preventative therapy, as well as a richer school counseling program.

TYPES OF GROUP COUNSELING

There are many **models of group therapy**, including **psycho-educational groups, crisis-centered groups, problem-centered groups**, and **growth-centered groups**. Each of these groups carries its own considerations as a model for various situations. The psycho-educational group is generally helpful in promoting a student's awareness of common issues in life. Crisis-centered groups are often short-term and responsive to a major trauma on a community-scale. Problem-centered groups and growth-centered groups are preventative in nature. Growth-centered groups are designed to help students grow in areas of deficiency, such as self-esteem, whereas problem-centered groups are designed to reduce risk of major problems occurring in the future or developing over time. The problems in question include substance abuse or stress-related issues in students' lives.

PSYCHO-EDUCATIONAL GROUPS

DIFFERENCES BETWEEN PSYCHO-EDUCATIONAL AND COUNSELING GROUPS

To appreciate the distinctions between **psycho-educational** and **counseling groups**, it is a good idea to first identify the similarities. Either group can address life management issues such as loss, stress issues, academic success, etc. Either group can be categorized into developmental, remedial, or school environments. Where they differ is in the focus within the groups and group sessions. Counseling groups tend to address matters of managing crisis, targeting issues of process more than specific content issues. Psycho-educational groups, on the other hand, apply a more concentrated focus on particular content. Counseling groups tend to be less structured than psycho-educational groups. The effect and impact on students in the two groups is often perceived as distinctively different, although counselors tend to view them as similar in format and purpose.

PARAMETERS AND BENEFITS

Psycho-educational groups serve to address and develop **personal growth factors within an academic or educational setting**. The academic setting provides a framework for targeting common adolescent issues like emotional development, self-image, identity definition, and interpersonal skills. The student in the psycho-educational group develops socially and emotionally while addressing academic skills. The counselor in the psycho-educational setting can provide students with increasingly difficult developmental tasks, resulting in optimum benefit for the student. An important added benefit of this model is that it provides students with an array of resources, contributing to an increased feeling of self-worth and self-confidence. An effective psycho-educational counseling group can contribute positively to the futures of the students involved, by both mitigating future problem occurrences, as well as by providing a cache of resources that will be useful in career planning.

CHOOSING TOPICS OR THEMES

The initial consideration for **choosing topics for psycho-educational groups** should be the age and developmental level of the students involved. While adolescent and pre-adolescent groups will respond better to a focus on social and interpersonal skills, groups of younger students thrive in a friendship or playgroup, or a group focused on problem solving. These topics or themes can provide a framework for students to address peripheral issues. It might be advantageous to refer to the school's agenda for academic and social skill development, in order to compile topics for psycho-educational groups. Some typical topics, particularly for adolescents, are stress management, romantic relationships, time management, and career planning. It is also a good idea to ask the school if there are any survey instruments they have used to identify topics of interest among their students.

COMPONENTS IN CREATING A GROUP

The first step in creating a psycho-educational group is to define the following:

- Purpose of the group
- Anticipated membership
- Focus of the group
- Interventions and expected outcomes

Then, the counselor should clearly identify both long-term objectives and measured short-term steps toward those objectives, applicable to each session. The counselor should develop content and exercises that use an experiential framework which will incorporate and address the following:

- The demographics and targeted needs of the group
- Educational content that fits within the students' academic agendas
  * Opportunities for students to learn from experience
- A format that allows students to make connections between tasks and skills
- Exercises that generate group discussion and response

Finally, evaluation of the success of the group should include evaluation of each session and the process involved in achieving the long-term objectives.

COUNSELING GROUPS
FOCUS AND STUDENT POPULATION

Counseling groups are generally formed to address **personal issues that hinder or prohibit academic success**. The groups can target behavioral problems such as outbursts of temper, class disruption, social maladjustment, etc.; or they can target specific life-altering events such as the death of a loved one or a pregnancy. The groups are formed to work solely on the personal issues, aside from any resulting academic problems. Students referred to counseling groups have demonstrated an inability or diminished ability, particularly in the case of a personal crisis, to manage and positively respond to their academic responsibilities. Within the counseling groups, facilitators can provide an environment for students to benefit from peer support, particualrly by removing the sense of isolation. Benefits include a stronger sense of self-worth and the adoption of healthy strategies to handle emotions.

PARAMETERS AND FORMAT

The counseling group provides a **safe venue** for students to express and process overwhelming emotions. The **overall tone of the group** should be one of caring, compassion, and empathy. Many of its members will have experienced, or will be experiencing, similar events and emotions. The **format of the group** should be one of support, trust, and understanding. Members of the group should feel a sense of camaraderie with the other members. Acting as facilitator, group counselors can encourage peers within the group to provide support and suggestions for emotional healing to the other members, contributing to the general benefit of the entire group. Counselors should also be cognizant of each student's need to address both actions and thought patterns in the process of working through their issues or trauma with the group.

CRISIS-CENTERED GROUPS

A **crisis-centered group** is formed in direct response to a **traumatic precipitating event**. The event could involve a few individuals, or could be school-wide, such as a shooting or bus accident. The overarching purpose of a crisis-centered group is that of providing a controlled venue where students can express their feelings. In the case of an issue involving a few students, such as a disruptive conflict between students, an additional goal of the crisis-centered group is to facilitate resolution of the conflict. In this case, the group will form for the purpose of resolution, and will meet at least until the matter is resolved. In the case of a large population trauma, the group will form to assist the students in coping. In both of these instances, additional meetings could be held to work on personal development issues for the student members.

PROBLEM-CENTERED GROUPS

Problem-centered groups are often an outgrowth of crisis-centered groups, formed after the crisis has passed or been resolved. These groups are formed to address issues that either precipitated the crisis or could cause problems in the future. The students in these groups come together to focus on specific issues that may be hindering their academic progress or their general well-being. Some of the issues that are addressed in problem-centered groups are stress management, conflict resolution strategies, academic or career goals, and substance abuse. The effectiveness of the group depends on the openness of its members to resolution. Participation in problem-centered groups is usually an option chosen by the students involved. The members of these groups, which are usually smaller than crisis-centered groups, benefit from the support and input from other members in resolving an issue that may feel overwhelming when faced alone.

GROWTH-CENTERED GROUPS

Similar to problem-centered groups, **growth-centered groups** often form as an outgrowth of a previous group. For instance, if a crisis-centered group is formed to address situation by discussing anger management, the growth-centered group will instead address each individual student's issues and concerns, which may be peripheral or essential to the group topic. Under the umbrella topic of a common issue like anger management, students may be dealing with low self-esteem, stress as a result of poor time management, conflicting value paradigms, etc. The tone of the group is supportive and empathetic, allowing students to develop healthy responses to their situation. The group as a whole works on positive behavior dynamics. Growth-centered groups allow counselors to identify and address students on an individual basis.

FORMING GROUPS IN SCHOOL SETTINGS

Once a counselor perceives a need to form a group, based on input from teachers, parents, and/or students, the following parameters need to be explored and established:

- Topic and purpose of the group
- Group meeting schedules and the time allotted for sessions
- Proposed members of the group and total group size
- Established process and rubric for recruiting and screening potential members

The focus and purpose of these groups should be primarily for the benefit of the students, within the context of the therapeutic paradigm. Counselors should discuss the group's formation with teachers and other school personnel as appropriate before launching the group. Issues of confidentiality should be clearly and firmly established and communicated to students, parents, and school personnel. Although the groups are generally established for the benefit and well-being of the students, the provisions of confidentiality and other counseling ethics continue to apply.

DOVETAILING OF SCHOOL COUNSELING CURRICULUM TO STANDARD ACADEMIC CURRICULUM

While the **school counseling curriculum** is developed within the same parameters as the standard academic curriculum, there are distinguishing characteristics and processes. One of the differences is that the standard academic curriculum is generally developed to address grade- or age-based curricular goals, whereas counseling curriculum also incorporates behavioral strategies and expectations. Counselors can further augment curriculum with professional expertise and knowledge gleaned from professional journals or other resources. In terms of process, standard academic curriculum is often a collaborative product of committees that include parents, school staff, and administration. School counseling curriculum is generally developed by counselors and teachers. However, many schools have liaison committees available to assist school counselors in developing curriculum. Nonetheless, all school staff should be aware of the goals and strategies employed in school counseling curriculum, and counselors should align academic curricular goals with the school counseling curriculum.

STANDARDS FOR DEVELOPING SCHOOL COUNSELING CURRICULUM

There are both state standards and national models (from associations such as the ASCA) for the development of school counseling curriculum. These models address **expectations for grade and education levels**, as well as school guidance models targeting different regions and grade levels. A number of states have developed counseling programs that are derived from national recommendations, incorporating current literature and the success rates for particular models or strategies. When developing school counseling curriculum, counselors should follow these **national and state models** while continuing to consider recommendations from the school community. The **local school community** is often the best source for strategies to improve the academic, personal, and career development of the students. Collaboration with a school advisory group can also facilitate development of a counseling curriculum that best meets students' needs and the goals of the school community at large.

DESIGNING PROGRAMS FOR ALL STUDENTS THAT WILL ALSO BENEFIT THE COMMUNITY

Since schools are the **primary focal point for issues** relating to adolescents, counselors and educators often work with other community entities in discussing and developing strategies for addressing the needs of youth. Some of these entities include libraries, police departments, private schools, recreation centers, and other community-based programs as well as national- and state-based organizations. One of the ways that **counselors can work as liaison** between students and these entities is by dispelling the idea that the onus of at-risk behavior lies with the student. They can work with community representatives who feel that students are solely or primarily to blame for their behavior. Counselors can collaborate with educators to develop programs that are designed to address the needs of not only mainstream students, but also at-risk students. These programs can incorporate the needs and concerns of the larger community as well as academic goals identified for the student population.

FAMILY SYSTEMS THEORY

Family systems theory focuses on the particular context of the child's family. Whereas individual approaches may focus on modifying a particular behavior, or considering the personality traits of a student, systems theory attends to the **interactions of the child with parents, siblings, extended family members, and family history**. Theorist and practitioners like Murray Bowen and Virginia Satir recognized that individuals are under constant pressure in the family system to act in ways that maintain stability of the system—sometimes at great cost to the well-being of the individual.

Virginia Satir, who started working with families in 1951, was arguably the first family systems therapist in the United States. Satir identified the omnipresent characteristic of family homeostasis but also insisted on the lifelong potential of change for the better. Children are helped by addressing family interactions, and the entire family becomes healthier.

Satir also attended to the negative effects of low self-esteem on marital partners and how unhappy marriages create dysfunctional families. One dysfunctional process, triangulation (also researched by Murray Bowen), puts a child between the warring adults, perhaps as scapegoat, confidante, or go-between but always to the child's detriment.

SCHOOL COUNSELING ADVISORY GROUP

A school counseling advisory group can provide guidance counselors with the **comprehensive expectations of the school community** as well as a track record of current and previous school counseling models. Generally, these advisory groups are comprised of school staff, school counselors, parents, and community members. The overall focus of most counseling programs, and therefore their advisory groups, is often the development of curriculum that **addresses common and relevant issues** like sexual harassment, bullying, and social relationships. Counselors can refer to past discussions and studies to glean information about strategies that did or did not work, as well as areas that may have required particular attention. Advisory groups can inform counselors about pedagogical or counseling approaches that work best in their school environment. It is advisable for counselors to maintain ongoing communication with advisory groups and other school community members in order to keep apprised of current needs or problem areas.

CONSIDERATIONS WHEN GENERATING STUDENT OUTCOME EXPECTATIONS

Expected student outcomes should reflect the combined input of **state and national standards**, **current literature**, and **formal and informal needs assessments** conducted at the school or district level. Advisory groups, when undertaking the task of generating student outcome goals, should first amass the relevant information and resources. This will form the basis for future discussions and collaboration within the group and with the school counselors. Student outcomes should represent what students should know or be able to do upon graduation from high school. The National Standards for School Counseling Programs delineates 9 standards that incorporate academic, personal, social, and career development areas. Student outcome expectations should be broken down into smaller sequential goals. Counselors working with the district and school community can develop strategies and a rubric for addressing these sequenced student outcome goals.

Developing Instruction and Assessment

DESIGNING K-12 GRADE-BASED CURRICULA

Although counselors teaching at various grade levels are generally responsible for developing and delivering curricula appropriate to the level, it is recommendable to develop that curricula as an integral part of a comprehensive K-12 curriculum. For example, counselors who teach at the elementary level, while **delivering curricula appropriate for that grade level**, also should be cognizant of the **larger curricular goals** as well as the next phase of students' studies. It is important that students receive curricula that builds on previous learning foundations. Student learning within each classroom should not be an isolated experience, nor should it be unnecessarily redundant. Although some schools and districts operate within a paradigm that allows for quasi-isolated curriculum development within broad age groups, it is nonetheless usually recommended that all curriculum development be designed within a larger K-12 context.

FACILITATING STUDENT EXPANSION OF KNOWLEDGE

Counselors can and should encourage the furtherance of student knowledge, either through synthesis between disciplines, or through sequential learning within a particular discipline. Counselors and teachers can communicate and collaborate, both within a grade level and between grade levels, to develop lesson plans that encourage students to **form correlations between counseling curricula and academic curricula**. This can also extend to correlation between disciplines, such as between history and narrative or between math and music. Teaching in the classroom can include the Socratic approach, encouraging student curiosity about the connections between disciplines. Counselors can also work with students to strive for the next level of sequential learning within a particular discipline, by making those connections explicit within the lesson plans. Sequential learning strategies contribute to future student success as they move to higher grade and school levels.

LESSON PLAN COMPONENTS

Generally, regardless of the grade level or the discipline, most **successful lesson plans** will include three basic components. The first of these components is the **introduction**. In this part of the lesson, students are introduced to the general topic or the particular focus area of the lesson. Secondly, the lesson plan should include **activities that will serve to develop the lesson**. These activities can be performed by the counselor, a teacher, or can be participatory activities by the students. The third section of the lesson not only **concludes the lesson**, but also evolves into an **application portion**, whereby students are able to project the lesson into their daily lives. This portion of the lesson often also includes student discussion. The total effect of this kind of sequenced lesson plan is increased student engagement and a greater likelihood that students will remember and assimilate the lesson.

LESSON INTRODUCTION

Introducing a lesson topic serves several purposes in classroom teaching. Initially, it focuses students' attention on the topic to be addressed. In this sense, delivery of the introduction should be clear and compelling, **soliciting student interest and engagement**. It can also be valuable to let students know the planned learning goals or areas to be covered. Students can begin to develop a mental blueprint as the lesson progresses, and will be more receptive to each step of the lesson development, like a concert attendee following a program. It also helps to make connections with previous lessons or knowledge foundations, encouraging class participation. Lesson plans that are well introduced are more likely to result in comprehensive student understanding.

INCLUDING PREVIOUS KNOWLEDGE IN LESSON PLANS

Incorporating previous knowledge in a lesson plan imbues students with the self-confidence and orientation to the lesson to be more engaged. It also helps to establish a **participatory trust** between counselor-teacher and students. Students are more likely to feel that they already possess useful information, and the counselor is there to facilitate the expansion of their knowledge base. A useful strategy for incorporating previous knowledge in a lesson plan is to ask questions, to which students can positively respond. Building on this, counselors can introduce next sequences or facets of knowledge, possibly by asking relevant questions and volunteering the answers. Another valuable strategy is to reiterate previous knowledge, with which students are already familiar, and then to lead the class to the next phase of knowledge or skill development. Students whose previous knowledge is acknowledged are likely to be more receptive and participate more fully.

DEVELOPMENTAL ACTIVITIES IN LESSON PLANS

Counselors can also **incorporate previous knowledge** in the developmental activity portion of a lesson plan. Planned activities can address students' existing knowledge about a topic, giving them opportunities to express that knowledge, and then can lead the students to a new level of of understanding. It is important that counselors develop a **clear outline for planned activities**, cognizant of the strategies being utilized to reach the objectives. Additionally, a **rubric** should be established in order to clearly assess the effectiveness of activity strategies. A distinguishing characteristic of developmental activities is that they provide a vehicle for expression through multiple intelligences, further contributing to the collective benefit of the class. Counselors should be sensitive to individual strengths and needs, and should tailor activities accordingly. Developmental activities can provide another vehicle for student confidence and participation.

ELICITING RESPONSES THROUGH DIFFERENT INTELLIGENCES

Counselors can augment the traditional verbal/text-based classroom lesson plan with activities that engage students' artistic, spatial, logical, kinesthetic, and other learning modes. Counselors can **present lesson topics through various media**, including music and pictures. They can also ask students to respond experientially by drawing, writing a poem, playing drums, or possibly composing and performing a song or dance. **Multiple media responses** are particularly valuable when working with students on qualitative issues like problem-solving or personal crises. Counselors employing multiple-media and multiple-intelligence approaches to curriculum delivery provide students greater opportunity for engagement and expression. This increases the efficacy of the lesson, and is a more inclusive strategy for students with diverse learning styles. Counselors should be sensitive to the particular student group in the classroom, and the individual learning styles represented.

EFFECTIVENESS OF PASSIVE AND ACTIVE LEARNING STYLES

The **traditional lecture-based curriculum delivery style** is effective in terms of transmitting information, but only requires the student to participate in a very **limited, passive manner**. Students who simply hear the information are limited to a particular learning style and more subject to distraction. Complementing the lecture with videos or handouts can increase students' receptivity by adding visual stimuli. A more effective augmentation would be to include opportunities for students to actively participate and learn. Some examples of **active learning** include verbal question response, writing on the board, note taking, and other activities that require students to be engaged. Also, if students are asked to reiterate information through writing or other activities, they necessarily are focused on the lesson. Active learning strategies significantly increase the amount of data that students acquire.

CONCLUSION TO A DEVELOPMENTAL LESSON OR ACTIVITY

Although the **conclusion** is generally fewer than five minutes, there are several objectives to be accomplished in its various components. The conclusion is a time to reiterate what has been learned, and to give students the opportunity to **assimilate new knowledge**. Counselors can begin by repeating the knowledge that students brought into the classroom, and the increased knowledge that was obtained during the session. Students should be asked to give a **recap or response to the lesson**, to indicate that they have understood. Student response increases their receptivity, and gives the counselor an indication of how much the students have understood. This time can also be used to cite examples and applications for the lesson, further increasing students' assimilation of the lesson. Student participation and response is pivotal to this part of the lesson.

IMPORTANCE OF ASSESSING LEARNING OBJECTIVES

Counselors can **informally assess the effectiveness of a lesson** and the general level of student receptivity by listening to student responses during the lesson and at the conclusion. However, a more **formal assessment** can be advantageous for a few reasons. If a counselor develops a written rubric before presenting a lesson, this rubric can provide a real-time backdrop for counselors to both assess and guide the lessons toward its conclusion. Having a kind of inventory for lesson objectives can provide an outline for the discussion that can be at least informally shared with students, allowing them to realize their progress. In addition, a written rubric can provide the kind of quantitative, formal assessment vehicle that is very valuable in **building credibility** with the school community. With clear assessment information, counselors can experience increased collaboration and support from school staff, counselors, and parents.

DESIGNING AN ASSESSMENT RUBRIC

Designing an **assessment rubric** for school counseling classroom strategies begins with defining the learning objectives. Also included should be the demographics of the group, expected learning outcomes, and clear criteria for measurement. Once this rubric is clearly delineated, counselors can **target learning objectives** with specific planned activities. They can **assess the success of the activity** by comparing student responses with the rubric criteria. It is important that the components of the rubric be clearly defined before the commencement of the lesson, in order for the counselor to design and deliver activities that will elicit appropriate responses. All of this can be conducted during the normal course of a classroom lesson, with its introduction, activity, and conclusion. A clearly written rubric designed well before the lesson will ensure a successful, non-disruptive assessment.

> **Review Video: Learning Objectives**
> Visit mometrix.com/academy and enter code: 528458

ROLE OF ASSESSMENT IN DESIGNING LESSON STRATEGIES

Lesson plan assessment results can provide a **metric for the success of the lesson** as well as the **relevance of the learning objectives**. If student responses have met the criteria set forth in the rubric, counselors can be fairly assured that the lesson or activity was relevant and targeted the expected objective. However, if student behaviors or responses do not meet the rubric criteria, there are several possible explanations that should be considered, individually or in concert. An initial consideration is that of the lesson or activity, to review its **applicability to the group and to the objectives**. Another consideration is the objectives themselves. Counselors should determine whether the objectives were reasonable for the student group. The value of a rubric with clearly defined components is realized if some of the criteria are met, but others are not. Counselors can then adjust the lesson or activity according to the results of the assessment.

Technology and Counseling

ASCA's Ethical Guidelines in Relation to Counselors' Use of Technology

The technology a school counselor chooses to use must be both **applicable** to the student's needs and **ethical** in its implementation. The American School Counselor Association's (ASCA's) guidelines promote safe and confidential practices, emotional and social consideration, and equitable practices.

ASCA Ethical Guidelines (2016):

- Demonstrate appropriate selection and use of technology and software applications to enhance students' academic, career, and social/emotional development. Attention is given to the ethical and legal considerations of technological applications, including confidentiality concerns, security issues, potential limitations and benefits and communication practices in electronic media.
- Take appropriate and reasonable measures for maintaining confidentiality of student information and educational records stored or transmitted through the use of computers, social media, facsimile machines, telephones, voicemail, answering machines, and other electronic technology.
- Promote the safe and responsible use of technology in collaboration with educators and families.
- Promote the benefits and clarify the limitations of appropriate technological applications.
- Use established and approved means of communication with students, maintaining appropriate boundaries. School counselors help educate students about appropriate communication and boundaries.
- Advocate for equal access to technology for all students.

Potential Limitations in Virtual/Distance (Remote) School Counseling

Limitations in working with students remotely include the following:

- Emergency situations when the client needs someone in person and the counselor is not available—Counselors should assist clients to identify one or more trusted people living near the student: in an emergency, the student has backup support.
- Potential loss of confidentiality—Someone could enter the room (either the student's or the counselor's) room during a session. An email or voicemail could be accessed by someone who is not the counselor or client. Arranging student privacy in the session is important. Using a special, secure, school email server is one way to keep records of emails confidential while also assuring there's a reliable archive.
- There is always potential for misunderstanding, especially with the written word, as there are no nonverbal cues to interpret. Ideally, a backup plan for texting and emails would be to check in by phone or video call.

Use of Technology to Provide Services to Students Being Schooled in Remote Locations

Counselors can talk with students informally or schedule formal counseling sessions via phone, Skype, Facetime, WhatsApp, or other calling apps. Online learning programs give students access to emotional and cognitive skills development as well providing information on nearly anything— health, relaxation, college preparation tutorials, or stress reduction practices, for example—by way of videos. Online courses, e-books, or audiobooks can be purchased, and there are multitudes of free resources on YouTube.

Curating and sending links to students not only provides them with important information in an accessible format—it also sends the message that the counselor is working on behalf of the student, caring, even at a distance.

Limitations in technological client care may increase risk when a student is in crisis. Ideally, when someone is in real trouble, there's an actual person available to help. In crises such as potential or attempted suicide, the counselor may contact a local crises unit, call an ambulance, or arrange and pay for an Uber ride to a clinic or away from a dangerous situation.

Technology can't completely replace a face-to-face relationship, but it can make counseling possible in places or situations in which it would otherwise be impossible.

TECHNICAL REQUIREMENTS OF COUNSELORS

The ACES list encompasses the **technological requirements** involved in nearly every aspect of the school counselor's job from providing one-on-one services to mass communication and doing research to interpreting the research of others. Counselors need to be able to use software to build web pages, write letters, create spreadsheets and presentations, send emails, access databases, collect data, advance their own professional development, and help students use career, academic, and counseling-related resources.

Along with the nuts and bolts of knowing how to operate and maintain a computer, its software and associated printers, and other hardware, counselors also have to understand the potential pitfalls of technology use in terms of ethics and legalities. Like most professions, school counseling requires computer literacy, and counselors have the added mandate of showing students how to find the resources they need online. Familiarity with the Internet is also an important part of understanding, preventing, and stopping cyberbullying.

Chapter Quiz

Ready to see how well you retained what you just read? Scan the QR code to go directly to the chapter quiz interface for this study guide. If you're using a computer, simply visit the bonus page at **mometrix.com/bonus948/praxsccoun5422** and click the Chapter Quizzes link.

Assess

Transform passive reading into active learning! After immersing yourself in this chapter, put your comprehension to the test by taking a quiz. The insights you gained will stay with you longer this way. Scan the QR code to go directly to the chapter quiz interface for this study guide. If you're using a computer, simply visit the bonus page at **mometrix.com/bonus948/praxsccoun5422** and click the Chapter Quizzes link.

Research-Based Practice

EFFECTIVE OPERATION OF DATA-DRIVEN COUNSELING PROGRAMS

Counselors may find that many counseling programs or other student services models are **data driven**, meaning that statistics are routinely collected and used as the basis for institutional decisions. Counselors may discover that either the data being generated is incomplete, or that it is being organized and presented in a manner that does not reveal pertinent information about particular student issues. Data may describe the entire student body without focusing on groups of students in need. Counselors can apply system analysis to the data system with the goal of isolating the student needs that can be addressed by the counseling program. When the right students are placed at the center of the system, data regarding school, family, and community becomes more relevant. School counselors can also view the entire system, including the subsystems and the interconnectedness of those systems.

BENEFITS OF HOLISTIC COUNSELING IN SYSTEMIC, DATA-DRIVEN PROGRAMS

It is understood that the benefits of a data-driven counseling program include **quantifiable accountability** and assessment of professional review organizations. The ASCA describes these programs as clearly defined and sequential. They can also offer a **holistic, comprehensive assessment** of individual students. Counselors can combine the systemic overview and the needs of individual students by creating a data collection system that promotes holistic development in students. This includes nurturing individual qualities in students, and cultivating the particular goals and skills identified in the data. Using the data-driven system for the implementation of the program, counselors can partner with school members to develop a comprehensive program that identifies the needs of individual students and the student body as a whole. This type of program will help the students by giving them the confidence and leadership to pursue their dreams.

PROMOTION OF SOCIAL JUSTICE IN SCHOOL SYSTEMS

A campus that endorses and supports **social justice** does not differentiate on the basis of culture, race, economic status, special needs, sexual orientation or gender, religious background, appearance, or primary language. Counselors can encourage this kind of campus through their work with individual students, and by working with the particularities of the data system. All members of the community will expand their commitment to social justice and **educational equity** when the systemic data-driven approach is initiated at the school, which will increase the probability of all students having equal opportunities within the school counseling program. The counseling program in particular is a prime area in which to model equal access to resources by advocating for all students with no attention to personal characteristics that define each student. By promoting social justice, campuses provide a model for the surrounding community.

SCHOOL MISSION STATEMENT

Counselors should refer to the **school's mission statement** when developing or revising programs or data systems. A mission statement represents the **basic tenets, philosophies,** and **goals** of the school as a whole, which should be represented appropriately in its programs and practices. The mission statement can assist counselors in the development of programs or outreach efforts, so that the overall direction and mission of the school can be incorporated into the rationale for the proposals. Counselors may also be in a position to collaborate with school officials in developing or revising a mission statement, possibly to better serve a diverse population and/or the surrounding community. The statement should embody a collective result for all students, and should provide a clear and concise focus that will frame future program development and evaluation.

SYSTEMIC APPROACH

ASSESSMENT

When developing **assessment methods** for a systemic approach, counselors may first want to refer to existing data from school and district databases as well as **adequate yearly progress** (AYP) reports for a baseline representation of academic achievement or other pertinent information. Qualitative assessment from focus groups, interviews, and observations can provide a profile of key areas to be addressed. Counselors can then glean a basic understanding of what influences the access to resources and the academic achievement of students. Counselors may then want to choose the best format for assessment, incorporating best methods for garnering information, most comprehensive participation, and best feedback. They will want to look at those specific areas that will provide the clearest and most comprehensive picture of assessment of the program. Once the data is synthesized into a rubric, or other assessment vehicle, counselors can identify the students' needs more clearly.

GOALS

Counselors developing a **systemic approach** to counseling and assessment should first refer to the **goals** identified by the school, district, state and federal levels, so that the quantitative data can be tailored in accordance with recognized goals for which the school is accountable. Some of the identified goals are as follows:

- National goals: reduction of attainment and achievement gaps, attendance improvement, and likelihood of a drug-free school environment
- State goals: national goals, some of which are identified above, as well as state-specific goals such as improving the rates of literacy and post-secondary matriculation
- District goals: at the district level, there may be additional goals that address areas of particular concern to the region.
- Local goals: further focus on the needs of students and how those goals can be realized in students' lives

PROGRAM INTEGRATION

The effective data-driven approach to improving student achievement is a collaborative endeavor shared by educators, counselors, and other school personnel. Recognizing that each program strives for equal access, attainment, and achievement for the students, counselors can work with educators and other school staff toward a comprehensive data assessment system, and ongoing oversight and revision as needed. A holistic **systemic approach** utilizes inherent connections between programs. Education and counseling programs are connected by a related structure that allows for the alignment of content, delivery, and the reporting of results. The systemic data-driven counseling program is further connected to the school mission, inherently aligning it with the program goals, development, and evaluation of educational goals. All school-based programs are aligned with federal and state goals, and any counseling goals are aligned with ASCA standards that address goals and strategies to best target student needs. Through these combined efforts, students are helped toward their academic and career goals.

PROGRAMS AND PARTICIPANTS

Schools that are regulated and data driven nonetheless recognize that targeting the whole student can include not only classroom delivery, but also extracurricular activities. Since the school is also a social system, it includes a hierarchy of activities and relationships that incorporate the entire school community. **Standards-based educational programs** can generate protocols and competencies for classroom delivery, tutoring programs, extracurricular clubs, peer programs, mentoring programs, school sports, service learning projects, honor societies, and arts-music groups. The **comprehensive education program** can also include the contributions of parents, business collaborators, and pertinent outreach programs. The presence or absence of this kind of holistic inclusion can define a school culture in a way that either supports or hinders students' achievement. When developing a counseling program, counselors should endeavor to support and enhance existing educational program approaches, to the maximum benefit of students.

REPORTING OUTCOME ASSESSMENT TO SCHOOL COMMUNITY

As a member of the school community, counselors should report **outcome assessment** in a way that will be most accessible to the other members of that community. One of the ways that this can be achieved is by categorizing outcome results in alignment with the groupings established by the school. By presenting data that aligns with educational outcomes, the connection between the counseling and educational programs will be more clearly understood. Counselors may also want to provide access to outcome assessment to the larger school community. Results can be disaggregated to profile outcomes for grade levels, individuals, or subgroups on the school campus. Some counselors may also provide online access to outcome results for students, families, or community, in a report card or other user-friendly format. By providing reasonable access to easily understood data, counselors can further cultivate the integration of both educational and counseling goals.

ROLE OF ASSESSMENT DOCUMENTATION IN ADDRESSING EQUITY IN SCHOOL POLICIES AND PRACTICES

Well-documented assessment provides accountability for the success of the program in addressing student needs. **Assessment reporting** and **documentation** can also isolate and identify student groups that are not being served by current programs and policies. By disaggregating data, school counselors can reveal portions of the student demographic – such as those identified by race, ethnicity, socioeconomic status, and other defining categories – who are not being met. Counselors may also want to conduct **longitudinal studies** that will reveal the success or failure of various strategies within these subgroups. This kind of focused, delineated data can clearly point to underserved students, and can help prescribe revisions in policy or program development. The contemporary school counselor can serve as a leader in the creation and refinement of school programs that equally address the needs of all students. Documented assessment can provide tangible evidence to garner school support for policy changes.

IMPLEMENTATION OF DATA-DRIVEN PROGRAMS AT DIFFERENT SCHOOL SYSTEM LEVELS

Implementation of a data-driven program is delivered differently at each of the following levels within the school community:

- Individual levels focus on particular students, including crisis situations and student-specific situations, and can provide insight into issues experienced by the entire student body.
- Grade levels focus on age-specific experiences and may be best implemented by long-term planning.
- Classroom levels align the counseling program with the academic curriculum.
- School-wide levels call for coordination of interventions, in the interest of benefiting the entire school.
- Family levels involve parents and/or guardians as equal partners in the promotion of student achievement.
- Community levels involve members of the surrounding area to form partnerships toward the promotion of student achievement.

VALUE OF DATA-DRIVEN SYSTEMIC SCHOOL COUNSELING PROGRAMS

Counselors and other interested parties can view firsthand the **value that data-driven accountability** can add to the contributions of counselors toward student achievement. Data-based assessment that is designed around standardized categories can also assist state and national data management in **evaluating their goals** for equity in academic achievement. The information gleaned can help counselors identify which programs were successful, and which programs could be improved. Data revealed in well-designed systemic programs can isolate particular academic areas, student issues, or student populations that are not being well served. Counselors can implement strategies for **program improvement**, incorporating its assessment in the data system. As counselors are regularly able to evaluate and revise the process of setting goals and assessing their achievement, they can adjust the school counseling program to effectively and comprehensively serve the needs of the students, the school, and the community.

SCHOOL COUNSELOR'S RESPONSIBILITY IN DEVELOPING DATA-DRIVEN COUNSELING PROGRAMS

Counselors who do not adopt the data-driven model of program development place themselves out of the school and district accountability sphere. They may place the **program at risk** by not aligning it with the accountability paradigm. Counselors who are ethically responsible should reap the benefits of a data-driven system of planning and accountability. Counselors can embrace the systemic approach by utilizing the expertise of school counselors and district counseling resources. They can then serve as mentors for emerging school counselors. Counselors should take the time to research available information about data-driven programs and how they can best benefit the students and the counseling program. This includes learning how to analyze the data, apply it to existing strategies and programs, and revise intervention strategies accordingly. Although data-driven counseling does not replace individual counseling, it can provide valuable empirical oversight to assist the counselor in maintaining an effective and relevant program.

UTILIZING A DATA-DRIVEN PROGRAM

Counselors can apply the following steps to realize a program that embodies social justice with a mission of access and equity:

- Analyze data to identify need: for example, graduation rates may identify inequity between demographic groups
- Develop goals: for example, graduation for all students
- Align goals with school mission: for example, sequential-year plans for graduation involve all stakeholders
- Integrate interventions: for example, utilize existing educational programs toward the goal of graduation for all students
- Implement interventions at different levels: for example, incorporate interrelated and interdependent interventions at various levels.
- Collect data results: all levels of program intervention should be collected
- Analyze data and present it for evaluation: include goals met, goals not met, and potential strategies in response
- Revise programs if needed: make changes to program strategies in accordance with new data

COMPONENTS OF SCHOOL COUNSELING ACCOUNTABILITY

A proactive approach to school counseling accountability includes **clearly articulated parameters** for responsibilities and duties, well-defined **evaluation** and **assessment vehicles**, and **reporting the results** of the evaluation to stakeholders. The following components contribute to a dynamic accountability model:

- Identify and collaborate with stakeholder groups. Take a proactive, collaborative stance.
- Collect data and assess the needs of students, educators, and community.
- Set goals and establish outcomes as revealed by data.
- Implement effective interventions that address the goals and objectives of the program.
- Design and implement effective outcome assessment for the interventions.
- Utilize the results to improve the counseling program.
- Share the results with students, parents, educators, school counselors, school boards, school counselors and supervisors, and community leaders.

SERVING AS AMBASSADORS AND PROPONENTS OF DATA-DRIVEN COUNSELING PROGRAMS

Data-driven accountability for a school counseling program can provide counselors with ordered data and methodical strategies for strengthening appreciation for the program by the school community. Counselors can provide the following accountability information:

- Program evaluations or audits when asked about the comprehensive, standard-based program in place.
- Needs assessment results when asked about the specific needs of the student population based on the results of evaluations.
- Service assessment results when asked to provide examples of implementations that address student needs.
- Results or outcomes of studies when asked about the results of interventions.
- Performance evaluations when asked about counselor performance.

The school counselor must perform the tasks of needs assessment, program evaluation, test program management and interpretation of assessment results in order for the counseling program to be accountable to school boards, parents, or other members of the community who may be concerned about the value of the program.

ACCOUNTABILITY STUDIES
ADVANTAGES

Accountability studies can enhance counselors' overall knowledge and awareness about the effectiveness of strategies or programs, so that they can provide **valuable input** during the decision-making process involved in new programs or practices. Based on the results of these studies, counselors may become aware of professional development or staffing needs. The quantitative data from the studies can provide the tangible rationale for these requests. Counselors who are well versed on the assessment results of their program are better able to network with other counseling professionals to share program results and learn about new intervention strategies. Accountability studies can be a valuable **public relations vehicle** for informing educators and the larger community about the accomplishments of the school counseling program and the focus of the school system for its students. Counselors who engage in accountability studies demonstrate a personal and professional commitment to ongoing standards of quality and success.

DISADVANTAGES

Although **accountability studies** can provide valuable information for the school counselor, as well as the school community as a whole, there are inherent disadvantages associated with these studies. An obvious disadvantage is that the studies take time away from individual or group counseling, in order for the counselor to implement and assess the accountability model of evaluation. Although this time could be well justified by the overall benefits to the program and to the student body, these benefits can only be realized if the counselor is trained in utilizing the data and spends the time on research and evaluation to achieve any useful results. Counselors may have misgivings about utilizing accountability studies because they may produce **results that are counterintuitive** to implementation strategies that have proved successful in individual and/or group counseling. Some counselors may also be hesitant to perform accountability studies because of a perception of being micro-managed by the stakeholders requesting the data.

SCPAC
PURPOSE AND PARAMETERS

The **school counseling program advisory committee (SCPAC)** is generally comprised of counselors, parents, educators, and other members of the community, all of whom have a stake and influence in the school's decision-making. The school principal should always be included, particularly since he or she will need to be included in the discussion about proposed program improvements or recommendations, and will be instrumental in approving funding for these proposals. The SCPAC can serve as a sounding board during decision making and can assist the counselor in introducing needed program changes or requesting resources. The SCPAC can serve as a liaison committee with the larger community, and can include parent-teacher organizations by invitation or at least by communicating with them regarding relevant impending decisions. By including community input through the liaison SCPAC committee, counselors demonstrate their willingness to consider outside perspectives and additional sources for funding.

ROLE

Assuming that the **SCPAC** is active, ongoing and not undergoing significant changes, it is customary for the group to meet once each semester to discuss the needs and available resources of the counseling program, and to provide recommendations and endorsement for **proposed improvements**. The group can analyze assessment results, propose program modifications, and consider recommendations from staff members. Program proposals are generally based on the results of assessments. The group can identify potential funding sources, but the school principal should always be included in any funding discussions. The group can serve as a valuable resource for demonstrating support among the school community for program enhancement, and potentially for influencing the principal in funding and approval decisions. Counselors should consider the benefits and the potential impact of the SCPAC and should focus their attention and time on the group as needed.

NEEDS ASSESSMENT

Needs assessments serve to analyze and identify the needs of the school, the student body, and the community. An effective needs assessment will identify the **particular needs of specific subgroups**, and whether or not the needs of all groups and subgroups are being met. A **comprehensive needs assessment** will reveal areas to be addressed in the student body and its respective demographic subgroups, as well as in the school community, including parents, staff, counselors, local business, community organizations, and community members. Counselors can create effective, comprehensive counseling programs that will enable students to realize improvements in their personal and academic performance. Needs assessments can also assist counselors in better understanding the various needs of different subgroups and addressing the significant issues of the school community.

PROGRAM EVALUATION

The **purpose of process evaluation**, or program audit, is to determine if the program is appropriately implemented in all areas, and if that implementation is properly documented. The evaluation reviews whether there is implementation and sufficient documentation of all relevant facets of a comprehensive school counseling program. By providing an analysis of each component of the program, the audit identifies areas of strength and weakness within the program, and indicates how these areas compare with district or state mission statements. The following terms are used to evaluate areas of the program:

- None: not in place
- In progress: started but not completed
- Completed: possibly not implemented
- Implemented: fully in place
- Not applicable: areas where the criteria do not apply

SERVICE ASSESSMENT
EVENT-TOPIC COUNTS

Counselors may be required to **provide service assessment reports** to guidance supervisors, superintendents, and school boards. Although guidance supervisors may request general service assessments, school boards and superintendents may ask for more specific event-topic counts. These counts refer to how a counselor spends his or her school time. Counselors are asked to document each time a student is contacted, receives any type of counseling service, or interacts with the counselor in any capacity. The reporting of these counts may be in the form of a log or a simple count, and requires the counselor to maintain a weekly or monthly recording of how many students receive general counseling or individual sessions to treat depression, behaviors, anxiety, social skills, anger management, family changes, or conflict resolution. Counselors and school boards can appreciate the contributions of the counselor evidenced by quantified event-time counts.

TIME LOGS

The purpose of **time logs** is generally determined by the school, the district, or some other oversight entity. Time logs can provide valuable **compliance documentation** to counselors and school boards for funding purposes. Certain states and school counseling programs require the use of time logs in order to quantify the type of work being done in the school community and surrounding areas. Some school programs may require the counselor to spend a certain percentage of their time in meetings with students individually, in groups, or for guidance purposes. Counselors should set up the time log format in a manner that will best document the time spent in each capacity, and be categorized in a manner that will be most useful to the entity requesting the time log. The amount of time spent on any counseling-related activity should be documented and categorized as accurately as possible. Counselors may want to maintain daily time logs to effectively capture data regarding time spent.

OUTCOME ASSESSMENT

In contrast to a service assessment that quantifies time spent, a well-defined **outcome assessment** can provide a profile of the effectiveness of particular aspects of the program. Counselors should recognize that it is not intended as an evaluation of his or her performance, but rather as a useful assessment of the program itself. Counselors should focus on the two key features of outcome assessment:

- It is not a professional evaluation of the counselor, a limit to his or her ability to perform the job, a requirement for standardized tests or curricula, or a prescribed process with no capacity for expansion.
- The assessment is:
- A vehicle for garnering information on program-related questions.
- The responsibility of an accountable counselor.
- An ongoing and evolving process.
- A cooperative outreach to other SCPAC members and stakeholders.
- A path toward better education for all students.

ASSESSMENT TERMS

The following are assessment-related terms and their definitions:

- *Evaluation* implies a measurement of worth, indicating that the effectiveness will be judged.
- *Evidence* refers to all data that can be used to judge or determine effectiveness. It is either quantitatively or qualitatively derived.
- *Formative evaluation* describes specific feedback received during a program implementation.
- *Summative evaluation* refers to anecdotal feedback received during the evaluation process.
- *Stakeholder* refers to any person or persons who are involved in or benefit from the school counseling program.
- *Baseline* refers to data gathered at the onset of evaluation, to define a starting point.
- *Pretest* describes an administered measure given before an intervention.

- *Posttest* describes an administered measure given after the intervention has been completed.
- *Value-added assessment* refers to the timing and final result of the intervention.

> **Review Video: Formative and Summative Assessments**
> Visit mometrix.com/academy and enter code: 804991

PLANNING FOR OUTCOME ASSESSMENT IN RESEARCH DESIGN

When **designing research** or implementing new intervention strategies, counselors should consider outcome assessment in the initial stages of planning. Otherwise, they are reliant upon prescribed case studies, non-experimental design paradigms, or static-group comparison studies to analyze the effectiveness of the intervention. By planning for outcome assessment, counselors can **tailor the assessment to the intervention**. The optimal format for research design is random assignment of participants to treatment conditions. This will allow the counselor to implement true experimental designs. Otherwise, with little or no control over assignments, counselors must rely on the results of a quasi-experimental or non-experimental design. The completion of pretests and posttests is also optimal, although not all counselors require the dependent variable.

IMPLEMENTING AN ORIGINAL OUTCOME ASSESSMENT

There may be a time when a counselor chooses to develop an **original outcome measure** that directly addresses the application, or is more appropriate for the group. When posing questions to the group for responses to be used in the assessment, the **following considerations** should be incorporated:

- Use simple language and question the group members only on events or circumstances with which they are familiar.
- Each question should be specific, and any unclear terms should be specifically defined in the appropriate context.
- Counselors should always avoid yes-no questions.
- Counselors should always avoid double negatives since these can confuse the response group.
- Questions should be posed individually, and not in combination with another question.
- Topic-specific wording should be consistent with the wording used in the discipline.
- Counselors should be sensitive to cultural differences.
- Counselors should learn to handle difficult response groups effectively.
- Second-hand opinions should only be accepted if first-hand information is unavailable.
- Background information can be provided to remind the group members of a specific event or reaction.

DATA COLLECTION METHODS

Counselors can **collect data** through the **following methods:**

- Interviewing counselors, educators, or members of stakeholder groups in a structured, semi-structured, or unstructured manner.
- Observing students informally and formally.
- Distributing written questions, rating scales, and surveys containing open- and closed-ended questions requesting factual responses or anecdotal perceptions. This method may prove problematic for participants to complete in its entirety.

- Reviewing program records or schedules usually kept in a database format for easy retrieval and archival use.
- Quantitatively comparing the results of standardized tests with educator-generated tests to measure student performance.
- Analyzing performance indicators such as grade-point average, classroom grade, attendance, and daily behavior.
- Studying products and portfolios of student performance in the classroom.

CHOOSING AN APPROPRIATE ASSESSMENT METHOD

The following considerations should be incorporated when **choosing an assessment method**:

- How the test developer defines the construct that will be used, e.g. aptitude, achievement, etc. The counselor should not utilize the assessment in a context other than the original one, since the results could be misrepresentative. The technical manual should also be studied, in order to value the utility of the test as well as the reliability and validity of the scores.
- How other organizations reviewed the test. Professional literature is available that will provide reviews from other counselors and similar organizations.
- The key factors that should be considered. Counselors considering a quantitative or qualitative assessment should analyze if the baseline and original population are appropriate for the student and whether the instrument can indicate a direction for intervention.

NEED FOR CURRENT RESEARCH AND EVALUATING RELIABILITY OF SOURCES

School counseling is a relatively young field; it has been around only since the 1920s. Since its establishment, school counseling has changed in focus and added much to its foundation, but there is much left to be learned. It is important that school counselors be familiar with **current research** so they can understand the most effective counseling trends.

Because research drives practice, it is important to use only research that is reliable. The source of a study should be peer-reviewed, which assures the reader that several professionals have reviewed the study for **ethical quality**, potential **biases**, and **methodology** to ensure the results are valid and reliable.

Considering the **literature review** that founded a study may also be helpful because it can point the reader to other related and reliable sources. A school counselor should read research skeptically and not only read the abstract of a study but review the data to see if the study was large enough to signify trends. Small studies may be informative but are more prone to population and sampling biases.

ANOVA

Analysis of Variance (ANOVA) is statistical calculation that determines whether the new teaching strategy has enough of an effect on a dependent condition (e.g., children's math scores) to make using the strategy worthwhile. Researchers compare two groups of test scores. One group did not experience any new teaching: the other participated in the new math program. The more people in a study, the more you can account for individual differences that might get in the way of seeing if the teaching strategy is what is determining the change in test scores. ANOVA equations look at the difference between the non-taught students' scores and the taught students' scores and evens out the differences that are not accounted for by the teaching method. Finally, the F-test shows whether or not the test scores were statistically significant. If F is more than 1, it is considered significant, and the amount over 1 (e.g., an F could be 17) gives an indication of how strongly the new teaching

119

method is associated with the rise in test scores. A high F score indicates that there is a strong, positive relationship between the new

USE OF RESEARCH TO PROMOTE UNDERSTANDING OF NEED FOR SCHOOL COUNSELING TO COMMUNITIES

Counselors can use **research to inform the public**; for example, in newsletters to parents, a counselor might write a research-based article that describes the signs of cyberbullying.

Research studies can be used to create highly effective in-school programs informed by up-to-date findings. Well-established, recently re-validated assessments can be identified from professional journals before being offered to students.

Conducting thorough assessments of school counseling programs and presenting the findings to the greater community can help raise awareness of the usefulness of school counseling.

Action research is a trend in research in which educational professionals can bring research principles into their own practice to actively evaluate their own practice and provide information to expand the research base. Action research is used to identify weaknesses in one's own practice, become informed, and take recursive action in response.

CURRENT RESEARCH DATABASES

School counselors can use **databases** such as ERIC, PsycLIT, or PsycINFO to locate thousands of **peer-reviewed articles** published in a vast number of journals. For one seeking widespread information on a particular topic, databases provide the option of accessing scores of studies across hundreds of journals and decades of research.

Maintaining subscriptions to important peer-reviewed journals such as the *Professional School Counseling Journal* or *Journal of School Counseling* helps counselors stay abreast of current research and discussion in the field. Journals covering gender and cultural diversity aid in keeping important sociocultural issues in the forefront of the counselor's awareness.

Attending seminars and continuous education classes not only aids in the professional development of the counselor but also brings her or him into contact with current issues and discussions in the field.

Joining local groups of colleagues expands awareness of regional issues, creates opportunities to work together to implement relevant local change, and provides a forum of professional support.

Student Assessment

IMPORTANCE OF ASSESSMENT

Assessment of both the student and the situation in any counseling sessions is very important, in that it serves to provide the counselor with both treatment and methodology for that treatment. A counselor will consider each student's developmental stage and environment to determine the best method for approaching a particular circumstance or problem. In addition, school or district policy can affect the counselor's methods, as for instance whether to use formal methods or to be more informal and flexible in developing a treatment for a particular student. Assessment can be formal or informal, and can be rather individualized among counselors. A comprehensive assessment of student needs, the precipitating event or situation, and a careful choice of approaches and actions based on this assessment are very important factors in the success of a counseling relationship.

Distinguishing Characteristics of Effective Assessment Methods in Academic Setting

In contrast to the **assessment methods** used in a mental health institution, assessment in an academic setting is less formal and more geared toward establishing a trusting and collaborative relationship with the student. In a mental health setting, the counseling session might be well served if the counselor asks direct questions to the client, in order to assess the problems. However, in an academic setting, an effective counseling relationship depends not only on the student's cooperation, which is facilitated by a less direct approach to assessment, but also on the incorporation of student needs not readily divulged. A counselor in an academic setting needs to be aware of, for instance, a student's body language when assessing and treating the student. It is important for a counselor in an academic setting to listen and observe carefully, and to engage in non-intrusive inquiry.

Information Obtained During Assessment

Although a counselor may discover information over a period of time and through different methods, in the context of the counseling relationship he or she should strive to obtain the following information:
Precipitating situation or event: specifically the duration, intensity, manifestation, and triggers

- Developmental and environmental factors: for instance, socioeconomic and cultural settings, medical and emotional background, physical and emotional development, etc. This information can often be obtained from parents, teachers, and other people connected to the student.
- Relationship specifics: specifically relationships with family, classmates, and teachers, and how the student behaves in these relationships
- Academic performance: what are the student's successes and failures in school? Does the student have difficulty in particular subjects? Does the student have an identified learning disability?
- Personal attributes and affinities: favorite activities, favorite subjects, talents, and strengths, and how these are incorporated in the student's daily life

Informal Assessment

Informal assessment can occur in the classroom setting, in conversation with the student, or by observation. Although informal assessment does not lend itself to a standardized rubric, such activities as games or storytelling can provide a holistic profile of a student. Other strategies for informal assessment include role-playing, opportunities for decision-making, writing exercises, and prioritized lists. These activities can reveal a student's thought patterns and coping strategies, including those areas which a counselor identifies with specific treatment. Informal assessment can be particularly beneficial when working with an early or middle childhood student who may not be able to isolate and articulate difficulties. Counselors conducting informal assessment need to report their findings in a more comprehensive and less quantitative format than that of formal assessment.

Formal Assessment

Formal assessment is conducted with standardized instruments and can be beneficial in identifying specific areas and treatments for intervention. Formal assessment operates within a rubric, or set of rubrics, that incorporate behavior checklists, measurements of self-perception, value scales, and inventories of skills and interests. This type of assessment also provides the counselor with identification factors that are more targeted and specific than those of informal assessment. Formal assessment, because of its rubric-driven reporting, can sometimes provide counselors with a more objective evaluation of a student than would be gained from informal assessment. Counselors should be aware of, and trained in, an array of formal assessment methods. Results from a formal assessment may include data relating to significant behaviors or attributes that could be overlooked and therefore not addressed in an informal assessment.

RIASEC

John Holland observed that different people have different orientations and preferences to tasks and that certain tasks are associated more strongly with certain occupations. If you can ascertain the person's task preferences (or interests) and match them to a vocation, there is a better chance that person will find career satisfaction. Holland and others used traits to create vocational inventories (e.g., the self-directed search [SDS] and the Strong Interest Inventory [SII]) that could predict the type of work a person might be drawn to and succeed at. **RIASEC** (realistic, investigative, artistic, social, enterprising, conventional) is the acronym that stands for the personality types that fit into particular occupational categories—they are often called the Holland Codes. The theory is that by obtaining one's codes, one can identify careers of interest that fit into the interest of the person. After deriving a code from an inventory, students can use software programs or resources like the *Dictionary of Occupational Titles* or the *Occupational Outlook Handbook* to explore interesting careers they might not have been aware of before.

PARTICIPATING IN DEVELOPMENT AND IMPLEMENTATION OF STUDENT SERVICE PLANS

School counselors may be present from the beginning of a **service plan**, as when the parent of a new student states an already-identified need and asks for help or when a teacher sees the student struggling and consults with the counselor to find out why. The school counselor is in the unique position of being able to help at every stage of the process, from identifying a problem, arranging needs assessments and interpreting outcomes, and consulting with other professionals (such as psychologists, psychiatrists, speech pathologists, etc.) to making sure the student's academic schedule is modified to the best possible fit. The school counselor can check in regularly with the student, teacher, or other direct-service providers, track progress, and collaborate with others to provide counseling and other learning services. The school counselor stays in touch with the parents as well and may act as mediator if problems arise in service teams. Along the way, the counselor can provide the student with individual-based advocacy, support, and encouragement.

STRONG INTEREST INVENTORY, MMPI, WAISC-II, AND BECK DEPRESSION INVENTORY

The assessments listed are measuring different aspects of a person's makeup—they're used for different purposes. The Strong Interest Inventory is a career inventory, usually administered to students in high school, that gives the taker an idea of his/her inclinations in the vocational arena. The **Minnesota Multiphasic Personality Inventory (MMPI)** is usually given to people for whom there is a suspicion of personality problems that run deeper than the average neuroses: a student who shows signs of psychopathology, such as schizophrenia, may take the MMPI before school personnel begin to investigate a possible diagnosis of serious mental illness.

The **WAISC-II** is an IQ test that many students will take at some point in their education. The results may tell those who interpret it at which level a student should be placed in academic coursework. IQ tests can also help reframe behavioral problems: a student may be acting out because the material is too difficult or out of boredom if the student's intellect is not being sufficiently challenged. The **Beck Depression Inventory** would not normally be administered to a student unless there is some concern that the student is suffering from depression.

ACHIEVEMENT TESTS AND INTELLIGENCE TESTS

Intelligence tests provide a score for an individual student, and because intelligence is considered a stable quality, it rarely changes significantly across a lifetime. The student is primarily affected by IQ scores, which can determine whether he/she may be placed in an ordinary classroom, in special needs education, or in a gifted program. Because IQ is seen as fairly immutable, there is no particular attempt to increase IQ by way of additional coursework or special programs. The person affected by IQ assessment results is the test taker: no one is held accountable for a student's IQ score.

Achievement tests, also called high-stakes tests affect more than the individual test taker, although they also have an enormous effect on a student's career. The Stanford Achievement Test and the ACT determine whether a student will graduate high school, go to college, and which college will accept him/her. But achievement tests are also used to evaluate teacher performance and overall school ratings (hence the high stakes). The aggregate of students' achievement test scores can affect the funding or teacher allocation—the life or death of the entire school.

INTERPRETATION OF IQ TESTS

IQ tests are formal, norm-referenced assessments that help educators understand where a student's academic intelligence falls on a continuum. IQ scores help establish students' correct placement in academic courses and can help identify whether there are unusual circumstances (developmental disability, learning-related neurological problems, or giftedness) that require different types of learning support. IQ tests are standardized, with a mean (average) score of 100 and a standard deviation of 15. The standard deviation is the average amount of error (hence, deviation) around the mean of a given population.

Because the tests are standardized, a student's derived IQ score is associated with a percentile: it can be plotted on a normal curve, using the standard deviation to determine where the score falls in comparison to the norm. It's possible to state with high confidence that a score of 130, for example, is two standard deviations above normal and places the student in the upper 95% of IQ scores. A score of 85 is an indicator of low IQ or borderline intellectual disability—far enough below normal to warrant special attention from the educational team.

CAUSATION AND CORRELATION

In scientific assessments, many different statistical factors may be related to an issue in question, usually indicating a **correlation.** Correlations between factors do not indicate which is an independent versus dependent variable, and often, correlations can be coincidental with no relation. There are often more than two factors to consider, which leads to other issues in identifying the cause. Statistical analysis can demonstrate only correlation strengths between two variables, but **causation** comes down to inference and logic. For instance, there is a correlation between ice cream melting when it is hot outside because hot days and ice cream melting coincide. The correlation is very strong in this example; however, causation is not indicated by statistical overlap alone. In the same way, school counselors should be wary of assuming the causation of an effect in a student's life and instead look at the problem from multiple directions before implementing a solution.

RELIABILITY

TEST CONDITIONS

Reliability is a measure of how often a particular score will be derived under the **same conditions**. Another word for reliability is **consistency.** The importance of conditions can't be overestimated. If you measure the height of a tree using a digital laser tape measure, assuming you use it correctly, you'll get the same height every time. If you climb the tree and measure it with a shoelace, chances are you'll get different numbers each time. If you have three glasses of wine, climb the tree, and measure it with your thumb, chances are you'll fall off before you get halfway up the tree—and if you do manage the climb, your numbers will be wildly inaccurate.

Reliability uses deviations in measurement to ask, "If we gave this test again under the same conditions, would the same test taker get the same score, and if not, how different would that score be?" A highly reliable test will give a very similar score under the same conditions.

> **Review Video: Assessment Reliability and Validity**
> Visit mometrix.com/academy and enter code: 424680

RELIABILITY IN ASSESSMENT

The Stanford-Binet, the WAIS, and the WISC have been in use for many years, been given millions of times, and been revalidated many times over the years. Recent studies on the WAIS-IV show test-retest reliability scores of .70 to .90 on tests repeated between 2 and 12 weeks. (Test-retest reliability is reported on a scale of 0 to 1.0. A score of 1.0 would mean that the person taking the test would get the same score every single time.)

Internal consistency reliability measures whether items that purport to measure a construct actually do so. Items supposedly measuring the same thing are measured in terms of how highly they correlate with each other. In this measure of reliability, researchers aren't looking for extremely high scores (such as a Cronbach's alpha of .95+), indicating item redundancy. Low correlation between items (such as $\alpha < .30$) indicate that items are actually measuring different constructs—and have poor reliability.

Inter-scorer reliability determines how closely two scorers would grade the same essay, for example: obviously, if one scorer gives an essay 95% and another scorer gives it 30%, there is low inter-scorer reliability. The scoring system itself must also be reliable.

VALIDITY

Validity asks, "Is this test measuring what it claims to measure?" Early IQ tests, for example, often measured whether a student was male or female, rich or poor, or black or white: wealthy, white male students invariably got higher IQ scores than other students. With rising consciousness of diversity, tests were reformulated, with items and subtests measured for construct validity. Some cultural biases will always exist (the expectation that we can measure intelligence with a written exam is one such bias), but with time, more and more test-taker diversity is included in the more valid tests.

Content validity determines whether individual items actually measure the construct. If, for example, an IQ test item actually measures preference for the color blue, and we know that liking blue isn't related to one's intelligence, that item diminishes the content validity of the test.

Criterion and concurrent validity measures whether the measure (test) is highly correlated with other measures of the same construct. For example, does a high IQ test score predict academic success (criterion), and does it correlate highly with the score of the same student on another IQ test (concurrent)?

ETHICAL REQUIREMENTS RELATED TO ADMINISTRATION OF ASSESSMENTS

Confidentiality is an important consideration for the **administration of assessments** of groups and of individuals. In administering a group test, students will naturally know who took the test, but in cases in which an individual student is taking an assessment, it is preferable to plan the test taking to be as private as possible, so the student doesn't feel singled out and other students don't notice. Confidentiality of scores and interpretations is a vital part of protecting students as well.

Ethical guidelines remind counselors not to overstep the scope of their competence: if one has not been trained in the administration and/or interpretation of a particular assessment, a more experienced professional should be chosen.

Choosing well-constructed assessments is an ethical responsibility as well: school counselors should investigate assessments in terms of their cultural, economic, or gender biases before assuming the assessments fairly measure students from diverse backgrounds.

NONACADEMIC FORMAL AND INFORMAL ASSESSMENTS

Assessments should never be given in the absence of a reason. If a child is having trouble that seems to be related to poor academic performance or is clearly personal, assessments may be used before deciding on interventions to try to determine where the problem lies. Students who are bullying or being bullied or who are showing signs of stress, depression, anxiety, or substance abuse may be candidates for **formal and informal assessments** covering nonacademic life factors. Some formal assessments of personality, emotional, and behavioral conditions may include the Meyers-Briggs Type Indicator (MBTI), Lazarus's BASIC ID, and Cameron and Turtle-Song's SOAP notes.

Components of the BASIC ID assessment help the counselor see the client holistically through the following categories: behavior, affect, sensation, imagery, cognition, interpersonal relationships, drugs and diet. **SOAP** notes are organized to help with case conceptualization:

- **S**ubjective observation—client reports and school counselor's observations
- **O**bjective observation—client orientation, physical appearance, and behaviors in face-to-face sessions
- **A**ssessment—a general idea of the client's current thinking, feeling, and social interactions
- **P**lan—treatment plans, including possible referrals

IQ SCORES OF CHILDREN CONSIDERED FOR SPECIAL NEEDS EDUCATION, REGULAR CLASSROOMS, OR GIFTED CHILD PROGRAMS

IQ scores below 85 are one standard deviation below the norm. Although no one would recommend basing a move to a special needs program on one IQ test score, a score below 85 would ring alarm bells and indicate a need for further investigation. A score between 85 and 100 might make a school counselor pay attention to whether the student has physical, intellectual, emotional, or social needs that aren't being met or is experiencing life stressors that are seriously affecting the ability to concentrate or retain information. The "normal" IQ range is between 100 and 115, and students with scores over 115 may be considered for inclusion in gifted programs. Students who experience behavioral problems but obtain high IQ scores may need to be moved to more challenging coursework, or to life situations that ask more of them, to prevent boredom and burnout. But whatever a student's IQ score, school personnel should keep in mind that IQ tests don't necessarily measure emotional intelligence or other forms of intelligence beyond the traditional language and math skills. Extremely bright students may lack vital intelligences in terms of communication, social skills, or empathy that less "intelligent" students may have.

Chapter Quiz

Ready to see how well you retained what you just read? Scan the QR code to go directly to the chapter quiz interface for this study guide. If you're using a computer, simply visit the bonus page at **mometrix.com/bonus948/praxsccoun5422** and click the Chapter Quizzes link.

Praxis Practice Test #1

Want to take this practice test in an online interactive format?
Check out the bonus page, which includes interactive practice questions and
much more: **mometrix.com/bonus948/praxsccoun5422**

1. Solution-Focused Brief Counseling consists of what six steps?

    a. Define problem, determine goals, develop intervention, assign strategic tasks, emphasize positive behavior, terminate counseling

    b. Define problem, determine goals, develop intervention, revisit goals, develop a second intervention, terminate counseling

    c. Conduct psychoanalysis, determine underlying problem, develop group intervention plan, reinforce behavior, assign strategic task, terminate counseling

    d. Identify prevention steps, define problem, determine goals, develop intervention, assign strategic task, terminate counseling

2. Which of the following school counselor activities does NOT take place within the Manage component of the ASCA National Model?

    a. Completing a use-of-time assessment

    b. Analyzing a results report

    c. Creating a closing-the-gap action plan

    d. Writing a mission and vision statement

3. What forms can professional development take?

    a. Continued education

    b. Evaluating and reporting on program outcomes

    c. Presenting research at professional conferences

    d. All of the above

4. Mrs. Mason is a high school counselor who has been working with a 9th-grade student in individual counseling for a month. During their first three sessions together, it becomes clear that the student has significant depression and has not experienced any improvement during the course of individual counseling thus far. Which of the following is the most appropriate next step for Mrs. Mason?

    a. Sign up for a webinar about depression to learn new strategies to help the student.

    b. Call a local mental health facility for a crisis evaluation on the student.

    c. Seek professional advice from another school counselor in the district.

    d. Work with the student and their parent to refer the child to an outside mental health provider.

127

5. Which of the following topics or tasks would not be addressed in the group selection process for school-age children?

    a. Informed consent
    b. Voluntary participation
    c. Parent permission
    d. Allaying anxiety

6. There is little parent involvement in many schools due to large numbers of working parents. What is one strategy to use to increase participation?

    a. Offer incentives for participation
    b. Focus on the unemployed parents to work with
    c. Suggest holding meetings and events on the weekends
    d. Offer opportunities at various times during the week

7. A student comes into your office with a referral from her English teacher. This is typically a straight A student; however, her grades have been slipping lately. She states that she has been "stressed out" but that nothing serious is going on. What issues might you want to ask about in order to determine the reason for her lower grades?

    a. Self-esteem issues
    b. Problems with a friend or boyfriend
    c. Difficulty level of her classes
    d. Mental health history

8. Grace is a high school student who asks her school counselor for support in choosing a career path. Using Frank Parsons' career counseling approach, what would be the first step Grace's counselor should take in beginning the career counseling process?

    a. Having a conversation with Grace about her goals, interests, aspirations, and personality
    b. Having Grace complete several tests in order to collect data about her personal traits
    c. Having Grace research careers that interest her to identify possibilities
    d. Having Grace complete the Self-Directed Search to determine her personality type

9. Cultural identity is:

    a. Primarily influenced by race and ethnicity
    b. Fully developed by early adulthood
    c. Stable across changing contexts
    d. Dynamic and constantly evolving

10. A school counselor is part of a school team tasked with developing an intervention plan for a 7th-grade student with severe social/emotional deficits and behavioral concerns. The team decides that, in order to understand the student's behavior, they must conduct an evaluation of the student's functioning in a variety of settings, including at school, at home with the immediate family, and in the community. The team's approach to evaluation best represents which of the following theories?

    a. Bronfenbrenner's ecological systems theory
    b. Bowen's family systems theory
    c. Vygotsky's social development theory
    d. Piaget's cognitive development theory

11. Adam is a 4th-grade student whose grades have been low for several months. His teacher reports that he seems to have a hard time grasping the content being taught in class and has foundational gaps in content knowledge. The school's intervention team convenes an initial meeting to discuss a plan of intervention for Adam. Which of the following would NOT be an appropriate stakeholder to invite to this meeting?

a. Adam's parents
b. The classroom teacher
c. The school psychologist
d. The school counselor

12. Which of the following describes a classroom accommodation which is likely to be the most beneficial for a student who has difficulty seeing written content on the board?

a. Preferential seating
b. Extended time
c. Wearing glasses
d. Small group instruction

13. A middle school counselor is planning classroom guidance lessons about career options. Which of the following would be the best use of technology in order to increase student knowledge of various careers?

a. Using a survey platform to gather pre-lesson data about careers that interest students
b. Having students utilize a search engine to research a career of interest
c. Having students create a presentation about a career of interest
d. Using a career search such as O*NET to connect careers to skills and interests

14. A school counselor is working as part of a team to evaluate a student for possible learning disabilities. Which of the following methods of data collection would NOT be appropriate for gathering background information to support the team in selecting appropriate assessments and evaluating the student?

a. Collecting intervention data
b. Reviewing academic records
c. Collecting teacher surveys
d. Gathering a health history

15. Which of the following is true about brief solution-focused therapy?

a. In brief solution-focused therapy, the counselor must understand the client's problem before beginning to work on solving it.
b. Brief solution-focused therapy is appropriate when the client is unable to articulate their desired goal.
c. Brief solution-focused therapy requires the client to make major changes in their daily lives.
d. Brief solution-focused therapy does not require the client to have a mental health diagnosis to begin counseling.

16. Joshua is a 5th-grade student who is frequently disruptive and explosive in the classroom. Schoolwide and classroom-wide interventions, such as positive recognition, class-based rewards, and modifying classroom procedures to reduce opportunities for inappropriate behavior have not resulted in an improvement in Joshua's behavior. Joshua's school counselor is working with the administrative team to develop a behavior plan for him. What would be the best method for collecting data to support the development of this plan?

   a. Asking Joshua's teacher to write a narrative about his behavior throughout the school year and the interventions put into place
   b. Collecting all of the discipline incident reports generated when Joshua was suspended throughout the year and looking for patterns
   c. Asking Joshua's parents to complete a behavior checklist, indicating the behaviors they are most concerned about
   d. Conducting a functional behavior assessment to determine the purpose of Joshua's behavior and factors contributing to it

17. What is the benefit of continued assessments?

   a. Student progress is monitored.
   b. Areas of weakness are identified.
   c. Learning styles and goals can be modified.
   d. All of the above

18. If a school counselor has a private practice, why would she refer a student in need of intensive counseling to someone else rather than seeing the client at her private practice?

   a. She cannot see a client more than once a week.
   b. She does not offer the counseling that this student needs.
   c. She must have a full case load with her private practice.
   d. She cannot use her position within the school to benefit her private practice.

19. A new school counselor is working with his administrator to finalize the comprehensive school counseling program for the upcoming school year. The administrator has asked him to identify the components of the counseling program in terms of tiered interventions. Which of the following activities would best fit tier I of a tiered intervention model?

   a. Classroom guidance curriculum
   b. Small group counseling
   c. Individual counseling
   d. Closing-the-gap action plan

20. On which of the components of a comprehensive counseling and guidance program should a counselor ideally spend the majority of their time?

   a. Foundation
   b. Management
   c. Delivery
   d. Accountability

21. Mrs. Harris, a school counselor, is approached by a teacher at her school who asks her if she has a moment to talk. The teacher then shares with Mrs. Harris that she is having conflict in her family and is struggling mentally and emotionally with her situation. She asks Mrs. Harris if she can provide individual counseling to help her through this difficult time. What would be an appropriate next step for Mrs. Harris?

   a. Mrs. Harris should listen empathetically but ultimately provide the teacher with a list of referral resources to find a counselor outside of school.
   b. Mrs. Harris should listen and set up regular times to meet with the teacher to talk because the teacher's mental health impacts students.
   c. Mrs. Harris should steer the conversation away from the teacher's personal problems and should only discuss academic concerns with her.
   d. Mrs. Harris should discuss the teacher's situation with HR because they can provide information about the school's mental health insurance benefits.

22. A counselor has developed a comprehensive developmental counseling program in a large school. This program consists of daily meetings and programs to address the various needs of students. In order to avoid burnout, how might the counselor effectively manage so many meetings and programs?

   a. Schedule meetings a few hours after school ends so she or he can take a break
   b. Recruit the help of teachers and peer mentors to assist with the programs
   c. Try to combine groups so that there are not so many
   d. Rely on consultants to run the programs that are scheduled for after school

23. Researchers examining teen dating and relationships consider peer influences, personal beliefs, and environmental factors. This is known as:

   a. The zone of proximal development
   b. The pleasure principle
   c. Reciprocal determinism
   d. Psychological hedonism

Refer to the following for question 24:

> You work in an inner-city school where students are subject to a number of risk factors. The rate of violent incidences is above average, as are the numbers of drug offensives and teen pregnancies. The school currently has various in-house prevention and intervention programs offered on a volunteer or referral basis to all students. However, even the most successful of these programs yield few positive results. As the counselor, you decide to restructure the programs in an attempt to increase their effectiveness by collaborating with the community.

24. It comes to your attention that some of the teachers in this school are treating students in drug intervention programs differently. As the school counselor, what should you do to stop this behavior?

   a. Conduct training for the teachers on discrimination and diversity in the schools
   b. Report these teachers to the proper superiors
   c. Nothing, your job is to deal only with the students
   d. Speak to each teacher individually about the effects of their negativity

25. Self-control procedures include all of the following EXCEPT:

    a. Self-monitoring
    b. Self-punishment
    c. Response control
    d. Stimulus control

26. A school counselor would like to observe the social skills of a newly referred third grader. Prior to the intake, the counselor observes the student during physical education and later during lunchtime. This type of observation is advantageous over a formal observation because:

    a. There is a decreased likelihood for the Hawthorne effect.
    b. There is a decreased likelihood for confirmation bias.
    c. Interrater reliability values are higher.
    d. Threats to internal validity are minimized.

27. A student's standardized score report for academic assessment indicates that their stanine score is 8. Which of the following is a correct interpretation of this information?

    a. The student's score is far below average.
    b. The student's score is below average.
    c. The student's score is average.
    d. The student's score is above average.

28. Mr. Dean, a school counseling student in a graduate program, is applying for internship positions for the upcoming school year and is required to carry professional liability insurance. What is the best method for Mr. Dean to acquire a complete professional liability policy?

    a. Contact his university field experiences office
    b. Contact the local school district to be added to their district policy
    c. Join the National Board for Certified Counselors
    d. Join ASCA as a student member

29. A school counselor presents data about their school counseling program to their principal. Which of the following would the counselor be most likely to advocate for using process data from the previous school year to support their requests?

    a. An appropriate counselor-to-student ratio in accordance with ASCA recommendations
    b. Additional professional development about working with students with anxiety
    c. The reassignment of inappropriate duties to other professionals within the school
    d. Time during the year to train teachers and other staff on student mental health

30. Frank Parsons, "The Father of Guidance," is best known for his contributions to the school counseling profession focusing on which counseling role?

    a. Therapeutic counseling
    b. Vocational counseling
    c. Promoting systemic change
    d. Advocating for the profession

31. A high school student experiences the death of their sibling a few days before they are scheduled to take the SAT. If the student takes the test as scheduled, which of the following is true?

a. Their test score will not be affected since the SAT is a validated assessment.
b. Their test score may not be reliable due to their emotional state.
c. Their test score may not be valid due to their emotional state.
d. Their test score will not be affected since the SAT does not measure social-emotional skills.

32. Ms. White, a high school counselor, is planning a small group focused on improving study skills. As part of the group, she plans to have students complete an electronic survey describing their independent use of various study skills in both the first and last meetings of the group. Which type of data is Ms. White collecting with this survey?

a. Process data
b. Perception data
c. Outcome data
d. Quantitative data

33. Which of the following is NOT true about most commonly-used intelligence tests, such as the Stanford-Binet or Wechsler?

a. Intelligence test scores are measured based on a standard bell curve.
b. The average intelligence score is 100, based on the individual's age group.
c. Intelligence tests are statistically valid and reliable.
d. Intelligence tests are valid across different cultures.

34. Which stage of the group counseling process represents the majority of the group's time?

a. Initial/forming
b. Transition/storming
c. Working/norming
d. Termination/adjourning

35. What is one of the primary reasons why counselors have a difficult time getting support from immigrant parents?

a. Immigrant parents do not challenge school authority.
b. Immigrant parents are oftentimes unfamiliar with American school systems.
c. Immigrant parents do not have time to talk with school counselors.
d. Immigrant parents have to work during the day.

36. A school counselor is conducting a small group focused on developing social skills. During a group session, a student begins discussing the misbehaviors of another classmate who is not in the group, making many comments about the student's lack of social skills. Which technique would be appropriate to use in response to these comments?

a. Clarification
b. Blocking
c. Linking
d. Active listening

37. A state requires all of its students to take an assessment each year that measures mastery of grade-level content standards taught during the year. This type of assessment is best described as which of the following?

  a. Achievement test
  b. Aptitude test
  c. Placement test
  d. Norm-referenced test

38. When dealing with middle school students, it is important for a counselor to understand the developmental relationship between Industry and Inferiority. This is an example of a theory of development based on the work of what psychologist?

  a. Freud
  b. Piaget
  c. Erikson
  d. Bandura

39. An elementary school has two school counselors. They each maintain their own caseload for classroom guidance, individual counseling, and small groups. Each year, the two counselors plan and implement a schoolwide career day, sharing equally in the planning and other tasks. Which of the following school counselor roles are the counselors demonstrating in the planning of career day?

  a. Consulting
  b. Collaborating
  c. Evaluating
  d. Counseling

40. A school counselor conducts a needs assessment with students and staff. Using the data gathered from the needs assessment, the counselor could do all of the following EXCEPT:

  a. Identify small-group counseling topics
  b. Design classroom guidance curriculum
  c. Identify individual student needs
  d. Evaluate the previous year's program

41. An educational trend that directly impacts the role of school counselors is the multi-tiered systems of support (MTSS) framework. Which of the following describes an appropriate role for school counselors in implementing MTSS?

  a. Coordinating referrals for students into the intervention process as well as maintaining appropriate data collection
  b. Coordinating standardized testing programs in order to help identify appropriate interventions
  c. Delivering standards-based academic, social/emotional, and career curriculum to all students
  d. Providing individual counseling to all students identified as tier III students

42. A school counselor is tracking graduation rates over the course of several years to determine if a program created to increase the four-year graduation rate is creating the desired result. In analyzing the data, the school counselor is specifically examining which of the following?

a. Trend
b. Mean
c. Mode
d. Standard deviation

43. Elementary school counselors must have a strong understanding of what?

a. Child development
b. Continued education options
c. Relationship building
d. Adjustment and coping mechanisms

44. A school counselor has several students with anxiety disorders. The counselor would like to provide support for those students in school and is considering small group counseling. Which of the following would NOT be a benefit to utilizing small group counseling for this purpose?

a. Meeting with more students at one time
b. Opportunities for peer modeling
c. Lower anxiety levels in a group setting
d. Opportunities for social exposure

45. Which major component of a comprehensive school counseling program most directly allows a school counselor to demonstrate school-level leadership?

a. Counseling curriculum
b. Individual student planning
c. Responsive services
d. System support

46. The counseling theory focusing on feelings of inferiority vs. superiority and the birth order of the client is based on whose work?

a. Erik Erikson
b. Alfred Adler
c. Sigmund Freud
d. Erich Fromm

47. Which of the following documents provides an outline of objectives that can be used in planning a classroom guidance curriculum?

a. ASCA Ethical Standards for School Counselors
b. ASCA Mindsets & Behaviors for Student Success
c. ASCA National Model
d. Recognized ASCA Model Program

48. Ms. Howell is a first-year counselor at an elementary school. In preparation for the upcoming school year, she works with her building principal to draft mission and vision statements for the counseling program. Writing a mission and vision statement most closely aligns with which component of the ASCA National Model?

    a. Define
    b. Manage
    c. Deliver
    d. Assess

49. Counseling program evaluations serve a variety of purposes for both the school counseling program and the profession as a whole. Which of the following is NOT a purpose served by school counseling program evaluations?

    a. Sharing results with stakeholders
    b. Advocating for the needs of the counseling program
    c. Identifying future program goals
    d. Advocating for a pay raise

50. An individual has begun to compare their accomplishments to those of their peers and feels a sense of pride in how they compare to others. According to Erik Erikson, this individual is in which stage of development?

    a. Autonomy vs. shame (ages 2-3)
    b. Initiative vs. guilt (ages 3-6)
    c. Industry vs. inferiority (ages 6-12)
    d. Identity vs. role confusion (ages 12-18)

51. Which of the following is NOT an example of a criterion-referenced assessment?

    a. End-of-grade exams
    b. End-of-unit assessments
    c. AP exams
    d. The SAT

52. Which of the following school counselor roles is considered a direct service?

    a. Consulting
    b. Collaborating
    c. Evaluating
    d. Counseling

53. In which of the following scenarios might a personality assessment, such as the Myers-Briggs Type Indicator (MBTI), be an appropriate tool?

    a. Determining placement in honors coursework
    b. Evaluating students for special education services
    c. Identifying careers that may be of interest
    d. Diagnosing an individual with a personality disorder

54. Alex is a middle school student who struggles with focus and attention in class. Alex's difficulties frequently result in incomplete work and poor grades on assessments. Alex's 504 team determined that he would benefit from preferential seating and extended time on assignments. Which of the following terms best describes preferential seating and extended time?

a. Intervention
b. Accommodation
c. Modification
d. Instruction

55. Studies have suggested that training in social skills benefits gifted and special needs students. What specific factor does such training address?

a. Self-esteem
b. Sociability
c. Attendance rates
d. Family risk factors

56. Mrs. Black is holding the first of six group counseling sessions. Which of the following is NOT an appropriate goal for this stage of the group counseling process?

a. Explaining the purpose of the group
b. Establishing behavioral and confidentiality expectations for group members
c. Encouraging the development of group cohesion
d. Addressing conflict between group members

57. Jim, a member of a counseling group focused on overcoming social anxiety, shares his recent success with utilizing skills learned from the group to navigate a tricky social situation. Jim is excited about his success and how the skills he learned helped him in that situation; the other members of the group are excited for him as well. Which benefit of group counseling would be directly demonstrated by this scenario?

a. Installation of hope
b. Universality
c. Group cohesiveness
d. Imparting information

58. Sarah is a 4th-grade student who, for the past seven months, has demonstrated restlessness and an inability to focus at school. She is frequently irritable and snaps at her classmates, which has resulted in difficulty maintaining friendships. She complains of frequent headaches and stomach aches and often seems tired. Sarah's mother shared with the school counselor that Sarah has difficulty sleeping at night and there is no known medical cause for her headaches or stomach aches. Which of the following disorders could Sarah's symptoms be consistent with?

a. Generalized anxiety disorder
b. Autism spectrum disorder
c. Oppositional defiant disorder
d. Attention-deficit hyperactivity disorder

59. When would a formative assessment be conducted?

  a. Prior to an intervention
  b. During an intervention
  c. After an intervention
  d. Only if the student refuses an intervention

60. Mrs. Jones is a high school counselor working with a student in individual counseling. The student is struggling with math class, and recently received a failing grade on an exam. In the counseling session, the student makes the statement, "I failed my math test. I am so stupid!" If Mrs. Jones is taking a cognitive behavioral therapy-based approach with this student, which of the following would be an appropriate response to the student's statement?

  a. Challenging the student's irrational belief that they must be stupid if they received a failing grade on a test
  b. Asking the student about their previous experiences with math tests to explore the root of the student's struggles
  c. Asking the student if there has been a math test they performed well on and trying to identify what the student did differently on that test
  d. Reflecting the student's statement, validating their feelings, and demonstrating unconditional positive regard for the student

61. A counselor who assesses a student according to his or her microsystem, macrosystem, and exosystem will have a complete picture of the student's cultural and racial identity. What is this model called?

  a. Systems model
  b. Ecological model
  c. Cultural assessment model
  d. Full overview model

62. A counselor is working individually with a student toward their goal of developing friendships and feeling more connected at school. According to the theory of brief solution-focused therapy, how would the counselor approach termination of the student's individual counseling sessions?

  a. Wait until the student reports that they are at a 10/10 on the scaling question
  b. Terminate after six sessions, as anything longer is not "brief"
  c. Ask the student how they will know when they no longer need individual counseling
  d. Wait until the counselor observes that the student has achieved their goal

Refer to the following for question 63:

> You work in an inner-city school where students are subject to a number of risk factors. The rate of violent incidences is above average, as are the numbers of drug offensives and teen pregnancies. The school currently has various in-house prevention and intervention programs offered on a volunteer or referral basis to all students. However, even the most successful of these programs yield few positive results. As the counselor, you decide to restructure the programs in an attempt to increase their effectiveness by collaborating with the community.

63. You would like to enhance your school's drug prevention programs. Which community agency will you most likely collaborate with?

   a. Local police department
   b. Local courthouse
   c. Local jail
   d. Local AA group

64. Which of the following school counselor roles is NOT appropriate in relation to standardized testing?

   a. Disaggregating test results in order to drive instructional and programming decisions
   b. Providing classroom guidance for students designed to reduce test anxiety
   c. Coordinating the school's testing program, including accommodations for students with disabilities
   d. Advocating for standardized tests to be culturally and linguistically unbiased

65. A school counselor completes a school data profile in order to plan their school counseling program. In analyzing the data gathered, the counselor notes that the school's graduation rate has gradually decreased over the last few years among students with disabilities. Based on the available data, what ASCA National Model document should the counselor use to address this concern?

   a. Curriculum action plan
   b. Small group action plan
   c. Closing-the-gap action plan
   d. Lesson plan

66. A recent transfer student came from an inner-city school to your rural school. She is having difficulty adjusting to the area and the school. As the counselor, what steps can you take to ease this student's transition?

   a. Announce that there is a new student and ask volunteers to show her around the school
   b. Create a support team with the help of other students, teachers, and the new student's parents
   c. Provide Solution-Focused Brief Counseling to the student to find out the underlying problem
   d. Provide information about making friends and offer this information to the student and her parents

67. A school counselor is leading a small group focused on improving study skills. One group member continually asks other students if they are doing their homework, using their study skills, and focusing in class. This student reminds their peers that they are supposed to be doing their assignments and studying regularly. Which group role is this student demonstrating?

 a. Scapegoat
 b. Gatekeeper
 c. Energizer
 d. Interrogator

68. What is one strategy a counselor can use to increase job experience and skills that would require community collaboration?

 a. Creating an on-the-job training program
 b. Finding part time jobs for students
 c. Offering more career-based or skill-improvement courses, such as auto shop and computer applications
 d. Offering programs that focus on resume writing and interviewing skills

69. A 14-year-old client is involved in a neighborhood gang, is truant, and is using drugs on a daily basis. Which treatment program would be most efficacious for this client?

 a. The Incredible Years
 b. Parent-implemented intervention
 c. Self-help (e.g.,12-step groups)
 d. Multisystemic therapy (MST)

70. Unrealistic demands on time and job duties refer to what?

 a. Role ambiguity
 b. Role conflict
 c. Role mutations
 d. Role confusion

71. Mrs. Johnson is a middle school counselor who has been working with a 7th-grade student in individual counseling. The student was diagnosed by an outside therapist with an anxiety disorder and regularly earns failing grades on tests despite excellent classwork and homework grades. Mrs. Johnson convenes a team meeting to discuss appropriate accommodations for the student under Section 504. Which role of the school counselor was Mrs. Johnson primarily demonstrating in this situation?

 a. Advocate
 b. Collaborator
 c. Leader
 d. Consultant

72. A school utilizes a reward system in which students can exchange tickets for small prizes. A student at the school has been demonstrating the behavior of blurting out answers instead of raising his hand. When he raises his hand before blurting out an answer, his teacher gives him a ticket for a prize. According to B.F. Skinner's operant conditioning theory, the ticket represents which type of operant?

    a. Positive reinforcement
    b. Negative reinforcement
    c. Punishment
    d. Neutral operant

73. What is one strategy that a high school counselor can implement to increase parent participation in their children's academics?

    a. Provide training sessions that teach parents to be tutors for their children
    b. Require parents to sign a form confirming that students have completed outside reading assignments
    c. Suggest that parents help students with homework every night
    d. Offer regular reports and information on student performance, as well as school events and programs

74. A counselor is researching best practices for working with a family whose children witnessed a violent crime and are now experiencing anxiety, having difficulty focusing, showing physical illness, and displaying inappropriate behavior. Which of the following research-based approaches would this counselor most likely consider in working with these children?

    a. Family system therapy
    b. Trauma-informed practices
    c. Multi-tiered systems of support
    d. Positive behavior intervention and support

75. A middle school counselor is planning an anti-bullying curriculum for classroom guidance lessons. Which of the following statements is NOT true about middle school students and bullying?

    a. Middle school girls are more likely to experience social bullying than physical bullying.
    b. Middle school students are likely to experience or participate in cyberbullying.
    c. Middle school students who are "bystanders" are encouraging bullying to continue.
    d. Middle school boys do not experience or participate in social bullying, only girls.

76. Mr. Lowe, a classroom teacher, meets with the school counselor to discuss a student, Erin. Erin has a diagnosis of generalized anxiety disorder (GAD), and Mr. Lowe is seeking information about how to help mitigate the impact of anxiety on Erin's classroom behavior. During their meeting, the counselor shares general information about GAD as well as common strategies and techniques classroom teachers use to support students with this diagnosis. Their meeting could best be described as which of the following?

    a. Consultation
    b. Collaboration
    c. Professional development
    d. Referral

77. Ms. Joseph has been working with an anxious student individually for several weeks. It is clear that the child's needs are significant and the anxiety is interfering with his ability to attend school. Ms. Joseph recognizes that her training is not adequate for the needs of the student. What is Ms. Joseph's ethical obligation in this scenario?

a. Ms. Joseph should seek additional training and development in this area in order to better support the student.

b. Ms. Joseph should refer the child's parents to a counselor she knows who has been effective with other anxious students in the past.

c. Ms. Joseph should stop seeing the child and tell his parents that he should see an outside counselor.

d. Ms. Joseph should provide the child's parents with a list of referrals and continue working with the child in the meantime.

78. According to the ASCA National Model, which of the following tasks related to assisting students with post-secondary plans is an appropriate activity for a school counselor?

a. Calculating class rank and grade point average

b. Coordinating schoolwide SAT testing

c. Assisting students with understanding course selections

d. Copying records needed for college applications

79. As a high school counselor, you observe that the numbers of pregnant teens on campus have been increasing over the past few years. What steps can you put into place to address this issue?

a. Continue to focus on student academics

b. Allow pregnant students to have a lighter course load in order to focus on their health and the pregnancy

c. Develop prevention and intervention programs to address this issue

d. Counsel students on the difficulties of having a child at this age and assist with federal aid paperwork

80. A school counselor is completing a curriculum results report to evaluate the effectiveness of their classroom guidance program. Which of the following does NOT correctly describe a type of data the counselor would utilize in completing this evaluation?

a. Process data describing the number of classroom guidance lessons completed and the dates of each lesson

b. Perception data collected through feedback surveys after classroom guidance lessons

c. Outcome data describing the number of students who completed each classroom guidance lesson

d. Outcome data describing the improvement in academic achievement as a result of classroom guidance lessons

81. Which of the following statements about English language learners (ELLs) is NOT true?

a. Typically, ELLs lag behind their English proficient peers in reading.

b. ELL students are not eligible for special education services with an IEP.

c. Spanish is the most common home language for ELLs nationwide.

d. Urban schools typically have a higher percentage of ELLs than suburban areas.

Refer to the following for question 82:

> A 5-year-old boy continues to attempt to play with children who openly ridicule him and leave him out of games. His persistence with this group of children has recently resulted in a number of fights on the playground. After being referred to your office, you learn that he has an unsupportive home life. His parents were divorced last year. He lives with his mother who works at night, and he does not see his father. He is often left at home alone; however, a neighbor watches him from time to time.

82. According to Pavlov's theory of development, what would you expect to occur in terms of this child's learning and behavior?

a. Nothing, he would naturally continue to try to fit in.
b. The child would become conditioned to the negative response and avoid the situation.
c. The child would take cues from his social environment and act accordingly.
d. The child would grow out of this stage and soon make friends.

83. In peer mediation programs, students are trained to guide peers through a conflict resolution process based on which of the following conflict resolution styles?

a. Competing
b. Collaborating
c. Avoiding
d. Accommodating

84. Ms. McCoy is leading a counseling group for children whose parents are going through a divorce or separation. Which of the following would NOT be a goal of this type of support group?

a. Allowing children to share their feelings about their family situation
b. Allowing children to discuss the changes that are happening in their family
c. Allowing children to be reassured and feel hopeful about their situation
d. Allowing children to practice conflict resolution strategies and communication skills

85. Mrs. Martin, a school counselor, is analyzing data about her school counseling program to identify areas for program improvement. She is reviewing perception data from a series of classroom guidance lessons delivered to 5th graders. Which of the following questions could be answered by analyzing this data?

a. Did all students receive the same curriculum?
b. What impact did the lessons have on student GPAs?
c. Did the pre- and post-tests indicate an increase in knowledge related to the lesson objectives?
d. Were the lessons delivered as planned?

86. Which of the following is NOT true about mentor-mentee programs for students?

a. Mentor-mentee programs have a positive impact on student academic achievement.
b. Mentor-mentee programs are a tier I intervention for students at risk.
c. Mentor-mentee programs require parent permission for students to participate.
d. Mentor-mentee programs have a positive impact on the number of disciplinary referrals.

87. Counselors have a professional responsibility to provide parents with what type of information?

   a. The details of sessions with their children
   b. Objective reports with respect to ethical guidelines
   c. Subjective reports on their child's progress
   d. Positive parenting information

88. When developing a school's counseling programs, a counselor should consider what students would like to gain from the programs. Which of the following are factors important to students in regard to school counseling?

   a. Academic counseling
   b. Available resources and personnel
   c. College-preparation assistance
   d. All of the above

89. The school data profile is a spreadsheet template that school counselors can utilize to track which of the following data points?

   a. Disaggregated achievement data
   b. Attainment of competencies data
   c. Counseling process data
   d. Needs assessment data

90. Which of the following would be considered an educational group?

   a. A group focused on processing grief and loss.
   b. A group focused on teaching parenting skills.
   c. A group focused on planning a school event.
   d. A group focused on overcoming test anxiety.

91. Cognitive behavioral therapy relies on Albert Ellis's ABC model (originally developed as part of rational-emotive behavior therapy). What is the counselor analyzing when using the ABC model?

   a. The client's environment
   b. The client's emotional state
   c. The client's thoughts or beliefs
   d. The client's behaviors

92. Which of the following is true about the role of a School Counselor Performance Appraisal in an ASCA National Model program?

   a. The School Counselor Performance Appraisal is not part of an ASCA National Model program, but is a licensure requirement in many states.
   b. The School Counselor Performance Appraisal is a self-evaluation completed by the school counselor once a year.
   c. The School Counselor Performance Appraisal is conducted by an administrator once a year using school, district, or state guidelines.
   d. The School Counselor Performance Appraisal is based on an administrator's observations of the school counselor.

93. Mrs. Simon is in her second session of individual counseling with a student who wishes to improve her grades. In their first session, the student identified her goal as completing her homework each night and turning it in each day without skipping any assignments; previously, the student had a very poor homework completion rate. Based on brief solution-focused counseling theory, which of the following would Mrs. Simon use to begin their second session?

    a. Asking the student what challenges she faced in meeting her goal over the last week.
    b. Asking the student what is going better since they met last week.
    c. Asking the student what she was thinking as she completed her homework each night.
    d. Printing off the student's online grade book and highlighting missing assignments.

94. According to ASCA, which of the following is an appropriate use of standardized testing results?

    a. Using standardized test scores to determine students' eligibility to enroll in advanced coursework
    b. Disaggregating standardized test scores to guide programming and instructional decisions
    c. Basing promotion and retention decisions on standardized test scores
    d. Determining a student's eligibility for Section 504 services based on their standardized test scores

95. Mr. Golden is a school counselor whose religious beliefs discourage same-sex relationships. A student shares in individual counseling that he is in a same-sex relationship. What is Mr. Golden's ethical obligation in working with this student?

    a. Mr. Golden should refer the student to a different counselor within the school due to the bias his religious beliefs create.
    b. Mr. Golden should share his bias with the student so that the student has a full understanding before giving informed consent.
    c. Mr. Golden should seek training and development in this area to help him provide comprehensive services to the student.
    d. Mr. Golden should terminate the counseling relationship with the student as his beliefs are constitutionally protected.

96. Which of the following is NOT a type of results report completed as part of a school counseling program evaluation?

    a. Curriculum results report
    b. Individual results report
    c. Small-group results report
    d. Closing-the-gap results report

97. There are generally six levels of parent participation. Which of the following is not considered a level of parent participation?

    a. Parenting
    b. Communication
    c. Continued Education
    d. Volunteering

98. A counselor initiating a school-family curriculum program will probably structure the program in what way?

   a. Take-home activities for students and their parents
   b. Group discussions
   c. Surveys for parents
   d. Counseling sessions for those in need of cultural diversity education

99. Young girls who experience abuse in the home or in a relationship have increased risk factors including:

   a. Drug abuse
   b. Teen pregnancy
   c. Poor grades
   d. All of the above

100. A counselor begins seeing a student who has issues with low self-esteem. This student is of Chinese descent but was adopted by an African American family as a baby. What responsibility does the counselor have toward the student regarding culture?

   a. Provide the student with information on her Chinese heritage and encourage her to embrace it
   b. Suggest she join the Chinese American Club at school
   c. Question her feelings of being of Chinese descent but being raised in an African American home
   d. Respect the student's cultural identity as it is and assist her instead with the problems she brought to the attention of the counselor

101. A school counselor is creating a spreadsheet of student achievement data that includes end-of-grade test scores, graduation rates, and enrollment in honors courses. The counselor disaggregates the data by student subgroup. The counselor is most likely compiling this data for which of the following tasks?

   a. Creating a closing-the-gap action plan
   b. Creating a small-group action plan
   c. Preparing the annual agreement
   d. Conducting a needs assessment

102. A school counselor implements a classroom guidance program aimed at improving graduation rates. During the annual program evaluation, the counselor analyzes a variety of data to determine the effectiveness of the program and implement changes for the following year. Which of the following pieces of data gathered by the counselor represents perception data?

   a. 450 students in grades 9-12 completed three classroom lessons with their counselor.
   b. 120 9th-grade students submitted complete four-year graduation plans to their counselor.
   c. 135 students indicated they feel "very prepared" to complete high school in four years.
   d. The school's current four-year graduation rate is 83%, an increase of 7% over last year.

103. Collaboration with other teachers is a good way to incorporate positive behaviors and communication throughout the school. How can a teacher advisor program assist in this collaboration?

    a. Provides all-around support to the students
    b. Makes the teacher feel important and more willing to work with the counselor
    c. Provides more watchful eyes for bad behavior
    d. Gives students more opportunities to get help with their school work

104. Rather than requiring students who disobey the rules on fighting to serve a silent detention, you suggest conducting a problem-centered, structured intervention group. What issues should you focus on during this group?

    a. Self-actualization
    b. Aggressive behaviors
    c. Safety
    d. Physiological issues

105. What is the purpose of demographic information on survey assessments?

    a. No real purpose
    b. This information should not be included.
    c. Identify differences
    d. Identify similarities

106. Which of the following questions is answered by the school counseling program evaluation?

    a. "How are students different as a result of the school counseling program?"
    b. "What measurable progress have students made toward counseling program objectives?"
    c. "How effective is the school counseling program in achieving its stated goals?"
    d. "What impact has the school counseling program had on academic achievement?"

107. In designing and implementing a comprehensive school counseling program, which of the following is NOT a type of action plan utilized by the ASCA National Model?

    a. Curriculum action plan
    b. Small-group action plan
    c. Closing-the-gap action plan
    d. Use-of-time action plan

108. What is the best strategy for choosing teacher advisors for students?

    a. Divide the students alphabetically by last name
    b. Obtain a list of students each teacher would like to advise
    c. Obtain a list of preferred teacher advisors from the students
    d. Obtain a list of preferred teacher advisors from the parents

109. Mrs. Kim is planning to conduct a social skills group for students who demonstrate difficulty with peer interactions and aggressive behavior. She begins her group selection process by asking teachers to identify which students they feel would benefit from the group. What would be the next step in the group selection process?

    a. Conduct a brief individual interview with each of the students to determine if they have the social skills to participate in the group effectively

    b. Ask the identified students what they would like to achieve as part of their group participation

    c. Send home permission slips to the parents of the identified students to gain parental consent for group participation

    d. Conduct an individual counseling session with each of the identified students to practice the skills needed to participate in the group

110. A school counselor working to create an academic intervention plan for a student is most likely to utilize which of the following approaches to develop the plan?

    a. Strengths-based focus

    b. Problem identification

    c. Cognitive behavioral therapy

    d. Family therapy

111. Which of the following serves as an initial coping mechanism when experiencing grief and loss?

    a. Anger

    b. Depression

    c. Denial

    d. Bargaining

Refer to the following for question 112:

In survey type assessments, a Likert-type scale is often used. These scales use either an even or an odd number of responses. For scales using an even number of responses, there is no neutral answer, and the individual must choose either a negative or a positive response. For scales using an odd number of responses, the individual has the opportunity to choose a neutral or undecided response.

112. A student is given a 5-point Likert-type scale and selects all Neutral responses. What would a counselor determine from these results?

    a. The student is laid back and easy going.

    b. The student did not want to share his own thoughts and wanted to get the assessment done as quickly as possible.

    c. The student did not understand the task.

    d. The student is in need of intervention for indecisiveness.

113. Hanna is a new kindergarten student who is legally blind. Her parents talk to the school counselor during the enrollment process and ask for information about the services and supports their daughter will be able to access in school. Which of the following laws or programs would the counselor refer to in order to provide guidance about Hanna's situation?

- a. IDEA
- b. Section 504
- c. FERPA
- d. ESSA

114. A school counselor is planning a classroom guidance lesson on career development. Based on psychological career theory, what would be an appropriate first activity to include in this lesson?

- a. Having students research careers they are already interested in
- b. Having students complete a survey to determine their personality type
- c. Taking a field trip to visit a real-life work setting
- d. Having students research the skills and abilities needed for various careers

115. A middle school counselor receives a phone call from a case manager at a community agency. The agency provides tutoring and enrichment opportunities for low-income students, and the case manager tells the counselor that they are working with several students at the counselor's school and would like to know how they are progressing academically as a result of their tutoring. Which of the following would be the most appropriate way for the school counselor to work with this agency?

- a. Tell the case manager that they will have to ask the students' parents for this information, as FERPA prohibits the counselor from sharing academic information with an outside agency.
- b. Provide the students' parents with a release of information form which, once signed, will permit the counselor and case manager to share certain information with each other.
- c. Share basic information with the case manager as asked because they represent a stakeholder with a "legitimate educational interest" in the students.
- d. Send printed copies of the information with the students to provide to the agency so that they can decide what they would like to share.

116. A supervisor for a counseling program collects outcomes data for all clients who received services last year. When plotting the distribution, the supervisor notices that clients younger than age 12 have measures skewed to the left. Which of the following is true of distributions skewed to the left (i.e., negatively skewed)?

- a. The mean is less than the median.
- b. The mean is greater than the median.
- c. The mean and the median are the same value.
- d. The mode is the lowest value.

117. Which of the following statements is true regarding electronic communications according to the ASCA Ethical Standards for School Counselors?

    a. Electronic communication between the school counselor and other individuals represents a form of privileged communication and is confidential.

    b. Electronic communication between school officials about an individual student can create an official school record under FERPA.

    c. Electronic communication about an individual student does not create an official school record under FERPA as long as the student's name is not used.

    d. The only form of electronic communication that constitutes an official school record is that which takes place within the official student information system (SIS).

118. Classroom guidance is most often considered to be which type of counseling activity?

    a. Prevention

    b. Intervention

    c. Outreach

    d. Academic

119. What are three essential developmental skills?

    a. Self-concept, self-esteem, self-respect

    b. Ego, Id, Super-ego

    c. Operational thinking, concrete thinking, abstract thinking

    d. Thinking, feeling, relating

120. Which of the following types of data would be best utilized to identify areas for program improvement in an annual school counseling program evaluation?

    a. Closing-the-gap action plan

    b. School data profile

    c. State testing results

    d. Program outcome data

Answer Key and Explanations

1. A: Beginning a Solution-Focused Brief Counseling session involves having the student define the problem and determine his desired goals of the counseling. With the assistance of the counselor, the intervention or behavior change is both determined and initiated by the student. Strategic tasks are assigned by the counselor and involve a direct behavior change. For example, if a student is having difficulty with academics and has a goal to raise his grades, then a strategic task would be for him to study for one hour every night. In subsequent counseling sessions, the counselor would offer support and positive feedback in order to encourage the student to reach his academic goals. Once the goals for that particular problem have been reached, the sessions are no longer required and counseling is terminated.

2. B: Analyzing a results report is part of the Assess component of the ASCA National Model, not the Manage component. Results reports are used to evaluate the effectiveness of classroom instruction, small-group services to students, and closing-the-gap action plans. Completing a use-of-time assessment, creating a closing-the-gap action plan, and writing a mission and vision statement are all part of the effective management of a comprehensive school counseling program. These activities help counselors clarify the needs of their school and students and define priorities for their program.

3. D: Continued education is required for professional licenses. Depending on the state board of education, a counselor will have a specific number of hours in continued education to complete. This education is intended to provide the counselor with the latest counseling information and practices. Additionally, by evaluating and reporting on programs, counselors are able to learn about the success of specific programs as well as areas of improvement. By reporting on the outcomes, counselors are educating the community about the school and its counseling programs. Giving presentations at professional conferences allows the counselor the opportunity to share different counseling practices and strategies with other professionals. The sharing of information promotes professional development and is highly recommended in the counseling profession.

4. D: In any circumstance where a student requires long-term individual counseling or has significant mental health concerns beyond the scope of the school counselor's training, working with the parent (and student, if appropriate) to seek an outside mental health referral is appropriate. School counselors should not provide long-term mental health counseling in a school setting. Because nothing indicates a risk of crisis, an immediate crisis evaluation without parental permission would not be appropriate. While webinars for professional development and consultation with fellow professionals could help the counselor support the student in school, ultimately an outside referral is most appropriate for this situation due to the suspected mental health concern and need for long-term counseling.

5. D: Each of the first three answer choices describes a topic or task that would be addressed in the group selection process. Informed consent, parent permission, and voluntary participation would all be established in the individual interview and invitation to the group. Allaying anxiety is typically addressed in the initial group meeting or "forming" stage of the group.

6. D: Oftentimes, schools get into the habit of holding meetings at the same times year after year. In the case of parent-teacher conferences, which are often held during the day, working parents may have to take off work to attend. Additionally, many school council and PTA meetings are held in the evening. While this may be more convenient for working parents, busy families often find it difficult to participate in these events. By offering various times and days of these meeting and events, a school can maximize the participation of the parents.

7. B: There are a number of factors that can affect students, especially during middle and high school. In this case, it would be wise to discuss problems with friends or a boyfriend with this student. Social problems are often a cause of problems in school, including a marked drop in grades. If this student is having problems with a boyfriend, it may be important to determine the seriousness of the problems, as abusive relationships in schools do occur. Since this student typically does well in school, the difficulty level of the classes would not be the major concern, unless she recently began new advanced courses. Additionally, there is nothing in this student's history to indicate that she may have problems with self-esteem or mental health issues.

8. B: Frank Parsons developed the trait-factor approach to career counseling. The trait-factor approach utilizes data from tests to match an individual with one best career. Therefore, a strictly trait-factor approach would begin with testing to determine Grace's traits. Trait-factor approaches do not rely on objective data from conversations. The Self-Directed Search from answer choice D refers to a tool used in John Holland's personality theory of career counseling.

9. D: Cultural identity is dynamic and constantly evolving. Cultural identity is multifaceted and is impacted by race, ethnicity, gender, religion, spirituality, socioeconomic status, profession, and sexual orientation. One's cultural identity is a social construct and continues to be formed through social interactions and is impacted by historical and political contexts.

10. A: Bronfenbrenner's ecological systems theory proposed that, as children grow, the various environments (systems) in which they function interact to influence their development. Therefore, in order to understand a child's development, all of the systems must be evaluated. Bronfenbrenner proposed the following five ecological systems ranging from the most intimate to the broadest: microsystem, mesosystem, exosystem, macrosystem, chronosystem.

11. C: In most schools, the school psychologist is an appropriate member of a team when a child has progressed through the initial stages of intervention and is being considered for a special education evaluation. In the scenario described with Adam, the team is conducting an initial intervention meeting, so psychological or educational testing would not yet be appropriate and the school psychologist would not yet be involved.

12. A: Preferential seating is a classroom accommodation which allows for a child to be seated in an area of the classroom which best addresses their needs; in this case, preferential seating may include the child sitting near the board for the best chance at seeing what is written. Extended time is a classroom accommodation, however, the connection between difficulty seeing what is written on the board and providing extended time is not clear. Wearing glasses would probably help, but this does not describe a classroom accommodation as glasses are not provided in the classroom. Cues or reminders to wear prescription glasses may be a good strategy for the student described, but only if forgetting to wear glasses is an issue. Finally, small group instruction describes an intervention or instructional strategy, not a classroom accommodation. In addition, the link between not being able to see the board and small group instruction is not very clear.

13. D: There are a variety of ways in which a school counselor can incorporate technology into classroom guidance lessons. When making choices about technology use in classroom guidance, it is important to consider the objective of the lesson and how technology supports the objective. In this scenario, the goal was to help students learn about various careers, so a career search engine such as O*NET would provide a wide variety of information and help students discover careers they may not have previously known about. The other answer choices only help students in reference to the careers they already have knowledge of or interest in, so they do not support the objective of "increasing student knowledge of various careers."

14. C: Evaluating a student for a learning disability requires a review of a variety of existing data from a variety of sources. In addition, reviewing this data can be useful in selecting appropriate assessments for the student. For example, if a review of the child's academic record indicates a consistent difficulty in mathematics, then there is a reason to assess the child for a learning disability in mathematics. The review of existing data must be based on objective information and measurable objectives, so teacher surveys would not be appropriate.

15. D: Brief solution-focused therapy is, as the name implies, focused on solutions to the client's problems. Therefore, the deep analysis and exploration of the client's problems, past history, or mental health diagnosis are not necessary to begin counseling. In brief solution-focused therapy, the client is the expert, articulating their own goals and desired outcomes; the counselor is a guide who helps the client notice changes and improvements toward the desired outcome. Changes do not need to be major to be significant. The solution-focused counselor is an expert at noticing the small changes that are making a difference in the client's goal progress. There is a great deal of research supporting brief solution-focused counseling in a variety of client scenarios. However, a client who is unable to articulate their desired goal (such as one who has a severe intellectual disability or one who is experiencing extreme psychosis) would not be a good candidate for brief solution-focused counseling.

16. D: In this scenario, the student has progressed through schoolwide and classroom-wide interventions, and targeted individual intervention is appropriate. A functional behavior assessment (FBA) is a detailed method of collecting data about a student's behavior in order to develop an appropriate plan for changing inappropriate behaviors. While anecdotal evidence and historical data can be helpful, the FBA will provide the most detailed information to create an effective plan.

17. D: Continued monitoring and assessment of the learning environment can be beneficial in many ways. This process provides the counselor, teacher, student, and parents an ongoing progress report. Additionally, regular assessments allow problems to be identified sooner rather than later. This will ensure that the student is not falling behind his classmates or his intervention goals. Ongoing monitoring and assessment also allow the counselor to update and to modify goals and target dates. When considered a fluid process, assessments, goal monitoring, intervention modification, and encouragement will ensure that students are progressing at a comfortable and successful rate.

18. D: It is considered an unethical professional practice for a counselor to use the school as a place to gain private practice clients. While many issues can be resolved within the capacity of a school counseling program, there may be times when a counselor feels a student needs additional therapy or support. In these cases, the counselor should discuss these options with the student and the parents while keeping in mind rules of confidentiality. Additionally, after a referral is made, the school counselor does not have a right to information that the new counselor and student share. In certain circumstances, the school counselor may be asked to consult on various issues. If this occurs, the school counselor and the private practice professional must discuss the case only in factual, objective ways.

19. A: A tiered intervention model layers interventions from tier I (broad, whole-school or whole-class interventions), to tier II (more intensive, small-group interventions) and tier III (highly individualized, intensive interventions). Tier I can also be thought of as high-quality instructional practices provided to all students, while tiers II and III are layered on top of tier I. Because the classroom guidance curriculum is high-quality instruction provided to all students, it would be considered a tier I intervention. Small group counseling could be considered tier II and individual counseling could be considered tier III in terms of the levels of individual attention and intensity of interventions described by the tiered intervention model. A closing-the-gap action plan could certainly be part of a school's intervention planning, but it is not an intervention in and of itself; the action plan would describe interventions to be implemented for at-risk groups of students.

20. C: The Delivery component of the comprehensive counseling program includes all of the types of direct student services, which ideally make up 80% of a counselor's time. The Delivery component includes the comprehensive guidance program, individual student planning, and responsive services; these services are delivered through individual counseling, small group, and classroom guidance formats.

21. A: The ASCA Ethical Standards are clear when it comes to dual relationships. In this case, by providing individual counseling to a teacher, Mrs. Harris puts herself in a situation where she is creating a dual relationship that could negatively impact students. For example, if a student comes in later to discuss the problems they are having in that teacher's class, it would be difficult for Mrs. Harris to remain neutral because she has been providing individual counseling regarding personal concerns with the same teacher. The teacher's mental health indeed impacts students, but providing mental health counseling to the teacher is beyond the scope of the school counselor's role. Of course, Mrs. Harris should still maintain confidentiality regarding the teacher's concerns and should not approach HR on behalf of the teacher.

22. B: Proper delegation of responsibilities will lead to more effective counseling programs. There are many opportunities for teachers and students to participate in leading programs. For example, developing a teacher advisor program increases participation from teachers and offers students a larger support system. Peer mentoring programs allow mentors the ability to increase their leadership skills and allow mentees the opportunity to widen their network of support systems. Counselors who encourage the assistance of teachers and students with various programs will foster a cohesive school that works together toward a common goal. This cohesiveness will provide all students with the best possible learning environment.

23. C: The influence of peer relationships, personal beliefs, and environmental factors is known as reciprocal determinism. Reciprocal determinism is the foundational concept of Bandura's social learning theory, or social cognitive theory (SCT). SCT has been used along with attachment theory, interpersonal theory, and feminist theory to study factors related to adolescent dating and relationships. Lev Semyonovich Vygotsky used the term zone of proximal development to describe the difference between what a child does independently and what they can do with help. This concept is used to explore ways to teach reading, writing, and other language skills. Sigmund Freud used the term pleasure principle when explaining the role of the id in personality development. Psychological hedonism states that all human behavior is dictated by actions directed toward attaining pleasure or avoiding pain.

24. A: Students in drug intervention programs may be experience a number of feelings and barriers as they attempt to stop using drugs. Teachers must be aware of these issues, along with the recovery process. It will be important for those students in intervention programs to receive support from all staff members to ensure success. As a counselor, you may offer training for teachers and other staff members. This training can include information about the specific intervention programs offered at your school, the recovery process, and sensitivity training specific to this population of students.

25. C: Self-control procedures do not include response control. Self-control procedures include self-monitoring, self-punishment, stimulus control, and self-reinforcement. Counselors using self-monitoring encourage clients to record information about the frequency and duration of specified symptoms. Self-punishment and self-reinforcement help clients self-administer the consequences of the targeted behavior, so that it can be modified. Stimulus control includes behavior that is controlled by associated consequences. Stimulus control techniques include narrowing, cue strengthening, and fading.

26. A: This type of observation (i.e., an informal observation) is advantageous over a formal observation because it decreases the likelihood of the Hawthorne effect. The Hawthorne effect presumes that a subject is more likely to modify their behavior based on knowing that they are being observed. Because the student was not a current client, the student lacked an awareness of being observed. Confirmation bias occurs when a counselor seeks information to confirm an initial hypothesis despite encountering information that may refute that hypothesis. Unstructured observations are at greater risk for confirmation bias than formal observations. Interrater reliability values are likely to be lower rather than higher. Likewise, threats to internal validity are not minimized.

27. D: Stanine measurements divide a standard bell curve into nine equal groups, and a stanine score places an individual score within one of those nine groups. A stanine score of 5 is the mean, or average, with stanine 1 being far below average and stanine 9 being far above average. Stanine scores allow an individual to interpret their score in relation to the rest of the group.

28. D: One major benefit of ASCA membership, even for school counseling students, is the availability of professional liability insurance. University field experiences offices or local school districts may add interns to their policies, however, this varies widely. ASCA is the best option for Mr. Dean. The National Board for Certified Counselors is not an option for school counseling students who have not yet earned their degree.

29. A: Process data describes the school counseling program in terms of who was served and how. In other words, process data tells when and how often programming occurred and how many students participated. This type of data would be supportive for a counselor advocating for an appropriate student-to-counselor ratio, especially if their process data demonstrates that they are unable to reach all of the students on their caseload equally or their caseload is much larger than the recommended 250:1. Outcome and perception data is more likely to be utilized to support a request for professional development for counselors or teachers. Other types of data, such as the use-of-time assessment or published research on the training and impact of school counselors, could be used to advocate for reassignment of inappropriate duties.

30. B: Frank Parsons was the author Choosing a Vocation and the leader of the vocational counseling movement. A focus on the role of the counselor in a therapeutic role did not occur until later, with Carl Rogers' contributions to the profession. Systemic change and advocacy roles came much later with the introduction of ASCA.

31. B: Test reliability indicates how consistent a test is. Test validity means that the assessment measures what it is intended to measure. The SAT is a valid and reliable assessment, meaning that it measures what it is intended to measure and individual test-takers should receive the same or similar scores on repeated administrations. Individual circumstances, however, such as a recent death in the family, may mean that an individual's test score is not reliable for that administration. If that student were to repeat the test at a later date when their emotional state was not as heightened, they may perform differently.

32. B: Pre- and post-test data is a type of perception data that is used to measure gains in knowledge or changes in perspective. Perception data measures what people think they know, believe, or can do. Because of their subjective nature, surveys are commonly used to collect perception data, but not process or outcome data. Process data measures what a school counselor does and for whom, so subjective measures such as a survey are not applicable. Outcome data measures the impact of school counseling activities and is much more objective in nature, so this information is typically pulled from the SIS.

33. D: Commonly used intelligence tests are frequently criticized for having cultural biases which impact an individual's outcome; in addition, intelligence tests are known to measure a very limited type of intelligence. Even with these limitations, intelligence tests can be a helpful tool when utilized as a part of a broader assessment of an individual. For example, when evaluating students for special education services, a child's score on the Wechsler Intelligence Scale for Children may indicate relative strengths and weaknesses in different measurements of intelligence, which can help pinpoint specific learning disabilities. It is important, however, to keep in mind the criticism of these tests for being culturally biased and understand that they may not measure intelligence in the same way across different cultures. Like most assessments, intelligence tests should not be used as a single data point for decision making.

34. C: The working or "norming" stage of the group counseling process is where the majority of the group's time is spent, usually about 50% of the time. This is where the majority of the group goals are addressed and the true "work" of group counseling is accomplished. The initial or "forming" stage is when the group first comes together, goals and group rules are established, and the facilitator tries to alleviate members' anxiety about the group counseling process. The transition or "storming" stage is when the group begins to transition to the actual work of the group counseling process. This stage is characterized by conflict and group members challenging the facilitator. If conflicts are not resolved in this stage, the result can be difficult for the remainder of the group counseling session. Finally, termination or "adjourning" is the closing of the group, sometimes characterized by the grief of group members, and is focused on transferring new skills or experiences to the outside world.

35. B: Immigrant parents have many challenges when sending their children to school in America. Oftentimes, the parents do not speak English and are unfamiliar with the American school system. While language barriers often result in parents not participating in their children's education, a counselor can easily offer translators and other educational opportunities to overcome these barriers. However, if parents continue to be unclear about the needs and expectations of the school system, immigrant parents will continue to be inactive. This can be overcome by providing a supportive environment for both the parents and the students. Counselors in school systems with a high immigrant population will need to serve as "school-home-community liaisons" in order to promote the needs of the students and their families.

36. B: In this situation, the counselor's goal should be to stop the inappropriate conversation. Gossiping about others who are not in the group is not helpful to the group or appropriate in the context of the group. Blocking is a strategy for stopping a hurtful behavior. Clarification, linking, and active listening would all be inappropriate choices in this scenario because they would invite the student to continue their line of discussion.

37. A: Achievement tests measure how well the test-taker has mastered specific skills or objectives. End-of-grade or end-of-course tests, as required by many states and school districts, are examples of achievement tests because they measure a student's mastery of the content objectives or skills that are generally expected to be taught during that grade level or course. While some schools may use data from these achievement tests to make placement decisions for future courses, that is not what these types of tests are designed for. Aptitude tests are a different type of assessment that attempts to predict the test-taker's aptitude or future success in a specific area, while placement tests measure the test-taker's skill level in a specific content area in order to determine their current level for course placements. Norm-referenced tests measure the individual test-taker's or group of test-takers' results against another group of test-takers, while criterion-referenced tests measure the individual test-taker's results against a specific set of standards. For example, a norm-referenced test may indicate that a student's mathematics ability is more or less advanced than a group of their same-aged peers, while a criterion-referenced test would simply indicate that a student has mastered all of their current grade-level mathematics standards.

38. C: Erikson suggests that children begin to associate with either industry or inferiority in early adolescence. Industry refers to a person's ability to succeed and feel worthy. Typically, healthy children who receive the appropriate support and encouragement at home and at school will feel a sense of industry. This identification is important, as it can be the basis of future educational, social, and coping skills. For example, a child who has a strong sense of industry will be more likely to cope with a low grade on a test. He will understand that he may need to study harder for the next test or seek assistance. On the other hand, a child with a poor school, family, or peer support system may experience feelings of inferiority. In this case, he is likely to have insufficient coping mechanisms and not perform well in school.

39. B: This example describes collaboration and could also be considered an example of "leaderless" collaboration, where all parties in the collaborative effort have equal leadership status. Co-counselors within the same school may also conduct each of the other roles listed independently or together. For example, counselors may frequently consult with one another on particularly difficult cases, ethical dilemmas, or areas of individual expertise. Effective counselors will also likely conduct an evaluation of their programming together. Although likely less common in a school setting due to availability of time, counselors may also at times conduct counseling together, particularly in groups.

40. D: A well-designed needs assessment can be a powerful tool for school counselors in identifying areas of need, defining goals, and planning programming. Needs assessments can also identify areas where there may be equity gaps, individual student concerns, or common student concerns that may be addressed by small-group counseling. While it may be tempting to use a needs assessment to track changes in data from year to year as a form of program evaluation, this is not the purpose for which they are designed and are unlikely to be effective for program evaluation due to changes in student enrollment or staffing from year to year and a lack of specificity within the questions to evaluate individual programs.

41. C: School counselors support the implementation of MTSS by providing a standards-based curriculum to all students (the intervener role). It is not appropriate for school counselors to lead the implementation of MTSS as a whole because MTSS is a team approach. Even within an MTSS framework, it is still inappropriate for a school counselor to coordinate a testing program or to provide standard individual counseling to all students in a certain tier of MTSS.

42. A: A statistical trend is a method of measuring a change over time. There are a variety of methods and tests which can be utilized to analyze statistical trends. If a statistically significant trend exists within a set of data (such as graduation rates over the course of multiple years), then that trend could be understood as the overall direction of data. In the example described, there could be a trend toward increasing or decreasing graduation rates. It is also possible to have no trend within a data set. The mean is the average of the data, which is not helpful in analyzing changes over time in this example. The mode is the most common value within the data, and the standard deviation has to do with distribution along a bell curve, neither of which are helpful pieces of information for the example given.

43. A: Elementary School is the time when children are learning the most and developing important motor skills and mental functions. Counselors must be able to recognize developmental delays, as well as advanced learners. School counselors will be major advocates for students who may experience developmental delays. While the other options may be important, these issues are more likely seen at the junior high and high school levels. Knowledge in continued education will be important for high school students who wish to pursue a college education; counselors with students in these age groups will need to educate students and offer assistance in applying to colleges and obtaining financial aid and scholarships. Additionally, relationship building, adjustment, and coping mechanisms are issues most often seen in junior high school, as these years are a time of many changes physically, emotionally, and educationally.

44. C: Small group counseling can be very beneficial for students with various anxiety disorders, and there are multiple programs and curricula available for counselors to use for this purpose. There are several benefits for both the students and the counselor in utilizing small group counseling for this purpose. A busy school counselor with a large caseload can see more students at one time in a small group setting, potentially increasing their effectiveness in reaching all students. Students in a group also benefit from peer exposure, learning from others' experiences, practicing new skills together, and having a level of social exposure that can help build confidence in social situations. However, group members should be carefully considered because not all students with anxiety can immediately function in a small group setting. Some students with severe social anxiety may need preparatory individual counseling to be able to benefit from small group counseling. Therefore, answer choice C is correct because not all students are less likely to be anxious in a group setting.

45. D: The system support component of the comprehensive school counseling program utilizes a counselor's leadership skills to support the total school environment and promote systemic change. System support activities such as professional development, committee work, and program management all provide opportunities for school counselors to demonstrate leadership and advocacy at the school level. While there could be some components of counseling curriculum, individual student planning, and responsive services that allow a counselor to demonstrate leadership, the system support or indirect services component is more strongly related to leadership roles.

46. B: Alfred Adler's theory of individual psychology focused on feelings of inferiority vs. superiority and Adlerian therapy investigates the effect of the client's birth order on behavior. Adler was once a colleague of Sigmund Freud, but he eventually separated from Freud's circles.

47. B: The ASCA Mindsets & Behaviors for Student Success outline skills and mindsets essential for student success in college and beyond. Counselors planning a classroom guidance curriculum should utilize the Mindsets & Behaviors to begin to outline learning objectives for their lessons.

48. B: Development of the mission and vision statements for the counseling program establish program focus and define student outcomes, which are part of the Manage component of the ASCA

National Model. While collaboration with a building principal is often part of the Define component, in this case, the task is being completed in collaboration with the principal as part of the Manage component.

49. D: The program evaluation is designed to serve each of the listed purposes except for advocating for a pay raise. While school counselors advocate in general for the profession, and that may include advocating for adequate professional compensation, the individual program evaluation is not designed to serve this purpose.

50. C: In the industry vs. inferiority stage of development, an individual begins to compare their personal accomplishments (academic, relational, athletic, etc.) to their peers and as a result, develops either a sense of pride or a sense of inferiority in comparison to others. The autonomy vs. shame stage focuses on a developing the senses of independence and autonomy in a child who is given the opportunity to make basic decisions about their lives, or a sense of shame when the child is not given such input. In the initiative vs. guilt stage, a child learns a sense of pride when allowed to work toward a goal and practice responsibility, or a sense of guilt when they are unsuccessful in this task. Identity vs. role confusion is the stage in which adolescents grapple with the question, "Who am I?".

51. D: Criterion-referenced assessments measure the test-taker's mastery of specific skills or objectives; results can typically be expressed in terms such as "passing" or "proficient." Students taking criterion-referenced assessments have either mastered the objectives or not; the abilities of other students taking the assessment have no impact on their score or test result. Norm-referenced assessments, however, compare the individual test-taker to their peers. These results are typically expressed as a percentile rank, rather than "passing" or "proficient."

52. D: Counseling is a direct student service, while consulting, collaborating, and evaluating are all indirect services. Specifically, counseling is a responsive, direct service. Consultation and collaboration can be easily confused for direct services because they involve working directly with other professionals or stakeholders, often in "direct" response to a student need. However, direct services are defined as services provided to students.

53. C: Personality assessments, such as the Myers-Briggs Type Indicator, can be useful tools for a variety of purposes, including self-reflection, learning coping skills, and identifying areas of academic or career interest. They are not, however, diagnostic assessments to be used for diagnosing personality disorders, evaluating for learning disabilities, or determining placement in special education or honors coursework. Personality assessments like the MBTI require an individual to be able to accurately reflect on and interpret their own thoughts, feelings, and behaviors and rate them accurately and therefore should never be utilized as a sole data point in decision making.

54. B: When it comes to providing equal access to the curriculum via a Section 504 plan or IEP, the most common terms used are "accommodation" and "modification." While counselors will frequently hear and use these terms in conjunction with each other, they refer to different types of strategies. Accommodations are those strategies that change the environment, time, type of output, or size of the task at hand without fundamentally changing the task, instructional level, or content that the student is learning. Accommodations allow students to access the curriculum as well as their non-disabled peers and perform the same learning tasks as their peers. Preferential seating (such as seating away from distractions or close to the teacher) is an example of environmental accommodation. Extended time is an accommodation that changes the length of time given to complete a task without changing the task itself. Modifications, however, change the task or content

159

itself based on a child's needs. Modifications may lower or change the learning standards expected of the student. An example of a modification would be giving a child an alternate reading passage on their reading level. Interventions are instructional strategies used to help a child learn content; an example would be small group instruction.

55. B: Researchers have studied the effects of providing social skills training to gifted and special needs students. These trainings often take a cognitive-behavioral approach to learning new behaviors. The results of these studies show that these students demonstrate a significant increase in their sociability. This includes their willingness to participate in social situations, such as on the playground. Social skills trainings often focus on listening skills, empathy, building rapport, self-disclosure, and appropriate eye contact. This training typically does not affect a student's self-esteem or other school related issues, such as attendance or grades.

56. D: Each of the first three options describes a typical, appropriate goal for the initial or "forming" stage of group counseling, which typically takes place in the first or second session. Conflict between group members typically develops in the transition or "storming" stage of the group. Later stages include working or "norming," and termination or "adjourning."

57. A: This example most directly demonstrates the idea of "installation of hope," whereby group members can see others' successes and feel hopeful about their own prospects for growth and improvement. The concept of universality describes the understanding that what group members are experiencing is not unusual and they are not alone in their experiences. Group cohesiveness explains the sense of belonging that group members feel when working toward a common group goal. "Imparting information" could be a tricky answer choice in this scenario. Jim is sharing his experience with the group, but not necessarily sharing new information that they could learn from. "Installation of hope" is a better fit for this situation because the information Jim shared could inspire other group members in their progress.

58. A: Restlessness, difficulty concentrating, irritability, difficulty sleeping, headaches, and stomachaches persisting for more than six months are all symptoms of generalized anxiety disorder. None of the symptoms described are consistent with autism spectrum disorder. Although irritability and inability to focus could be symptoms of oppositional defiant disorder and attention-deficit hyperactivity disorder, the other symptoms described are not consistent with those disorders.

59. B: Formative assessments are used to determine the effectiveness of an intervention and can be used to modify the treatment. This is an important step in the intervention process, as a student's rate of learning is not always apparent. This type of assessment can be in the form of informal questions to determine if the student understands the topic. The goal of a formative assessment is to provide the best possible setting for the student in order to increase learning and understanding. When done at regular intervals, the counselor can determine if the goals of the intervention are being met in a timely manner. A formative assessment will also provide an indication of an ineffective intervention strategy.

60. A: Cognitive behavioral therapy focuses on changing irrational thoughts that lead to unwanted or negative feelings. In this scenario, the counselor would challenge the student's belief that they received a failing grade on their math test because there is something inherently wrong with them or their intelligence. Instead, the counselor may help the student reframe their difficulty, such as by saying, "I received a failing grade on my math test because I did not prepare and study effectively." Meanwhile, answer choice B would be a problem-focused approach, and answer choice C reflects a more solution-focused approach. Answer choice D represents a person-centered approach.

61. B: The ecological model consists of the microsystem, macrosystem, and excosystem. The microsystem encompasses the students' immediate family and support systems. This will include parents, siblings, extended family, and friends. The macrosystem is defined by the students' culture. This will vary from student to student and often may include various subcultures. The exosystem refers to students' social support systems, such as their community. Understanding these three aspects of students' support systems will assist in developing appropriate programs and interventions, as the counselor will be able to incorporate the students' beliefs, morals, and values into counseling programs.

62. C: As with most brief solution-focused counseling, the process of termination is similarly guided by the client's understanding of their own goal and picturing their desired outcomes. Asking the client how they will know when they are done with their counseling sessions allows the client to visualize their desired outcome and articulate the specifics of their goal. While there is not a limit to the number of sessions in this type of therapy, the number of sessions is typically limited because clients make progress quickly. Goal progress and readiness for termination are measured by the client's perception, not the counselor's observation. The client may not have completely met their goal by the time they are ready to terminate their counseling sessions, but rather may have made a great deal of progress toward that goal and feel confident in their ability to continue to make progress.

63. A: Students may benefit from speaking to representatives from all of these organizations. However, a representative from the local police department would be the best option. These individuals are usually trained in drug education for school-aged children. Additionally, most police departments have drug prevention programs in place that have been proven to have positive outcomes. By bringing in individuals from the community, students get a different perspective of the issue at hand. Students will be able to ask questions and receive life experience answers from the presenter. This helps to show students the reality of the problem, as well as its consequences.

64. C: ASCA does not support school counselors in taking on the role of schoolwide testing coordinator because this task detracts from the role of a counselor in providing academic, social/emotional, and career support to students.

65. C: Closing-the-gap action plan documents are used to develop plans to address discrepancies between groups of students. In the situation described, there appears to be a discrepancy between students with disabilities and nondisabled students in the rate of high school graduation, so a closing-the-gap action plan would be appropriate. Within that plan, a counselor may identify activities for classroom guidance lessons or small group counseling, but the overall plan to address the discrepancy is the closing-the-gap action plan. In addition, the documentation of activities and evaluation methods takes place within the closing-the-gap action plan template.

66. B: Making a broad announcement about the student's arrival is likely to embarrass the student and possibly create more alienation from the general student body. As this student does not necessarily have a problem, direct counseling and education may not beneficial. School counselors who offer the student, as well as her family, supportive services will be the most beneficial in easing the transition from one school to the next. Counselors can enlist the support and assistance from other students by providing the new student a peer guide for the first couple of days. The guide will show them around the school and make sure the student knows where her classes are. This guide can also provide information about the school, such as the various clubs and sports available and upcoming events. Additional support from the school and the community will provide the student and her family with important information about the school and the new area.

67. B: The gatekeeper of a group is the member who tries to keep everyone else on task and ensure they are participating in the group. The scapegoat is the group member whom everyone else tries to blame when things go wrong. The energizer is the group member who attempts to get others excited and enthusiastic about the group, and the interrogator asks a lot of questions of the group.

68. A: Counselors can be responsible for more than just the mental and emotional well-being of students. When a school offers various career development programs, students who participate gain valuable skills for the future. On-the-job training programs are an excellent way to increase job skills. Additionally, these programs often help students decide what career path to follow. These programs allow students to go to school and work while earning school credits and gaining practical business experience. Counselors must understand that cooperation and communication with the community and leaders in the business community can be the key to success for these types of programs.

69. D: MST is an evidence-based practice (EBP) for adolescent substance abuse and associated issues. MST addresses severe behavioral issues, including community influences, school issues, and family factors. Family involvement is a critical element for adolescent substance use disorder treatment. The Incredible Years is an early childhood EBP for children with challenging behaviors, including symptoms of ADHD and ODD. The parent-implemented intervention is an EBP for children with ASD. Finally, self-help groups, including Alcoholics Anonymous and Narcotics Anonymous, are not EBPs for adolescent substance use and antisocial behaviors.

70. B: Role conflict refers to unrealistic demands on the counselor. This often occurs when counselors do not establish appropriate boundaries between themselves and the students. In addition, not establishing boundaries with teachers can lead to unrealistic expectations of the counselor. Role conflict often leads to counselor burnout because the counselor tries to help everyone. On the other hand, role ambiguity occurs when an individual is unclear about his role within a particular occupation. Role mutations occur when counselors serve in roles not intended for those in the counseling profession, which often leads to inconsistent counseling practices and programs. Schools and counselors must be clear on the expectations and responsibilities of the school counselor in order to provide effective programs for the students.

71. A: In this situation, Mrs. Johnson primarily was advocating for her student's legal rights under Section 504. Typically, the leadership role applies to the development and delivery of a comprehensive school counseling program, while the consultant role usually involves a third party. Convening a team meeting may involve collaboration, but the counselor's role in that process was as an advocate for the rights of her student.

72. A: A reinforcement is an operant that increases the likelihood of the target behavior happening again. Reinforcements can be positive or negative. Positive reinforcements reward the target behavior with something pleasant or enjoyable, while negative reinforcements reward the target behavior with the removal of something unpleasant or undesirable. B.F. Skinner's famous experiment involved rats who escaped a painful electric current by pushing a lever, which was a negative reinforcement. Punishment is the opposite of reinforcement as it decreases the likelihood of the behavior happening again. Neutral operants do not affect the frequency of the target behavior.

73. D: Keeping parents informed about their students' academic progress is one important factor in the success of a student. These reports are useful in tracking a student's progress and identifying when intervention is necessary. By including the parents in these reports, counselors can take a step in gaining the parents' participation and cooperation if problems do arise. These reports also allow parents to send comments to the teachers, as well as request conferences. Additionally, providing parents with information about school events and activities will allow parents opportunities to volunteer with the school and stay up-to-date on the extracurricular programs offered at a school.

74. B: Trauma-informed practices would be the most reasonable place for this counselor to start when working with this family. The children experienced a traumatic event and are demonstrating classic effects of trauma. Family systems therapy would be conducted in a mental health setting with a trained therapist. Multi-tiered systems of support and positive behavior intervention and support may be somewhat helpful for the children, but trauma-informed practices are the best support for recovery from a traumatic experience.

75. D: Social bullying is bullying that focuses on damaging or reducing a victim's social relationships, including exclusion or spreading rumors. Social bullying is most common in female students. While middle school boys are more likely to experience or participate in physical bullying, such as hitting, kicking, or fighting, they are not immune to social bullying. Cyberbullying can be a form of social or verbal bullying, including name-calling, spreading rumors, making threats, exclusion, and other types of harassment; cyberbullying is common at the middle school level. Finally, many bullying prevention programs identify various roles students play in bullying, including the role of "bystander" or "onlooker," a student who witnesses bullying but does nothing to stop the bully or support the victim; a student in this role is considered to be supporting the bullying behavior.

76. A: In this situation, the counselor is serving as the "resident expert" to provide information to the classroom teacher, who is seeking information to support his student. They are not working together to come up with a solution, which would be an example of collaboration; it is a one-way exchange of information. Consultation could be a method by which counselors provide professional development, such as by providing information to a large group of teachers. Although this consultation could result in an outside referral, as in choice D, the consultation itself is the best description for the meeting in this scenario.

77. D: The ASCA Ethical Standards for School Counselors indicate that counselors have a duty to refer when students need a higher level of support than a counselor can adequately provide. In making referrals, counselors should be careful not to endorse any specific provider and, when possible, should provide parents with a vetted list of possible counselors that is approved by the district. The duty to refer does not apply to counselors who feel that they cannot provide services to a student based on their personal or religious beliefs and, in those scenarios, counselors should seek additional training and development.

78. C: Assisting students with course selections to help students make choices that are rigorous and align with their post-secondary plans is an appropriate activity for a school counselor. Understanding appropriate and inappropriate counseling tasks is a major focus of the Management section of the ASCA National Model; this is an area that school counselors should be very familiar with in order to plan their use of time and advocate for appropriate duties. A comprehensive school counseling program designed with the ASCA National Model will focus on prevention, intervention, and advocacy, not clerical or administrative tasks. When it comes to assisting students with post-secondary plans, there are many tasks that school counselors may have done historically or may still do in some schools that are not considered appropriate activities. These include tasks such as calculating class rank or grade point average, coordinating schoolwide SAT testing, copying student records for college applications, or doing other clerical tasks related to college applications.

79. C: Programs addressing teen pregnancy are designed to offer students education and support for various issues. As a counselor, regardless of your personal beliefs, you must be sensitive to the needs and views of your students. Prevention programs can provide education about safe sex, as well as information about the reality of being pregnant and a teenage parent. These prevention programs should be geared toward those who are not pregnant but may currently be or thinking about being sexually active. Intervention programs should be geared toward those who are currently pregnant or recently had a child. These programs should provide supportive services along with education about being a teenage parent. Whenever possible, involving the student's parents in the programs will help increase the student's support system.

80. C: Process data focuses on the implementation of an intervention, such as the number of students who participated or the evidence of the intervention itself. Perception data describes what the participants of an intervention believe or think they have gained as a result of the intervention. Outcome data describes the measurable impact of an intervention, such as a gain in skills or abilities or improvements toward a specific goal. Answer choice C describes process data, not outcome data.

81. B: While students may not be identified for an IEP based on their language needs, it is possible for a student who is identified as an English language learner to also have a disability that qualifies them for an IEP. Each of the other statements about ELLs is true and is an important consideration for school counselors in considering the needs of their students.

82. B: Pavlov's theory of conditioning responses states that when an action is repeatedly followed by a response, the one performing the action will either continue or stop doing so depending on the response. In this case, the child continually receives a negative response from his peers. Theoretically, the child would begin to relate his actions to this negative response and cease the action. However, this is not occurring and may be an indication of developmental delays. As seen in the vignette, the child has little social support at home, and there is a clear indication of other interpersonal issues with his parents. To help this child, a counselor could explore social development delays he has and propose some type of intervention.

83. B: Peer mediation programs train student mediators to guide their peers through a collaborative conflict resolution process. Described as a "win-win" style, this conflict resolution style attempts to find a common solution that both parties can agree on. Other styles of conflict resolution may result in both parties not agreeing on the outcome. The competing style forces one member of the conflict to "win" at the expense of others, while the accommodating style sees one member of the conflict give in to the needs of the other member over their own. The avoiding style is exactly what it sounds like, and the conflict is ignored or postponed rather than addressed.

84. D: Skill practice is typically not a stated goal of a support group and would not be appropriate in this situation. Skill practice would be more appropriate for an educational or therapy group.

85. C: Perception data is data that measures what participants think they know, believe, or can do. This type of data is typically measured in the form of feedback surveys or pre- and post-tests. This is not the only type of data that can be analyzed to determine the effectiveness of a classroom guidance curriculum and identify areas for improvement. Answer choices A and D represent process data, and answer choice B represents outcome data. A thorough evaluation of the classroom guidance curriculum would include each of these types of data to identify both the effectiveness of the program and any potential areas of improvement.

86. B: Mentor-mentee programs are a well-researched intervention for students at-risk. Tier I interventions are school-wide programs designed to provide quality instruction and support for all students. "At-risk" students, such as those who are failing courses, have chronic absenteeism, were retained in the previous grade level, or who have various other risk factors would most likely require a tier II or tier III intervention, typically in a small group or one-on-one setting. Therefore, a mentor-mentee program designed for at-risk students would not be a tier I intervention. Research supports mentor-mentee programs as having positive impacts on student outcomes, both academic and behavioral. Mentor-mentee programs can be found both in the community and within schools. School counselors wishing to implement mentor-mentee programs could design and manage their own program or seek out a community resource for their students; regardless of where the program is managed, counselors should ensure parent permission for students to participate, especially when volunteers from the community are serving as mentors or when mentors may seek information about their mentees' progress in school.

87. B: Students have the right to seek confidential counseling. Counselors should inform parents of this confidentiality, as well as the roles, responsibilities, and expectations of the counselor and the student being counseled. Counselors should also work to provide parents with objective information regarding their children within the scope of confidentiality. At times, it may be necessary to inform the parents of certain issues pertaining to safety. This information will be provided only after the counselor has made a professional judgment that the client is in danger or intends to inflict harm on another and after telling the client of their intention to inform their parents. Finally, the counselor also has a responsibility to keep conversations he has with the parents confidential.

88. D: When developing a counseling program, the counselor should take a number of factors into consideration, including what the students would like to gain from the programs. One factor that students often consider is academic counseling. This type of counseling provides students with additional support as they progress through their courses, as well as support during transitional periods such as moving from high school to college. In addition to this, students are often interested in counseling programs pertaining to career and self-awareness. Many students would also like to know the availability of counselors and the frequency of planning sessions they have with the counselor. Finally, visibility of counselors and their ability and availability to answer questions and assist with problems is often listed as a student concern for counseling programs.

89. A: The school data profile is an important tool provided within the ASCA National Model to assist counselors in disaggregating student data. This data can be collected both short- and long-term and in a variety of areas, including achievement and behavioral data. The school data profile can be used to both manage the school counseling program (by identifying areas of focus for closing-the-gap action plans or advocating for equity issues) and evaluate the school counseling program (by analyzing long-term data to understand the impact of the program). Attainment of competencies and needs assessment data are types of perception data that can be difficult to represent in a spreadsheet, especially if the data is more qualitative in nature. Attainment of competencies data is process data that could be prepared in a spreadsheet but is not the focus of the school data profile.

90. B: An educational group is one that is designed to teach information and develop skills, regardless of the topic. Therefore, a group that teaches parenting skills would be considered an educational group. A group that focuses on processing a common experience of grief and loss would be an example of a support group, while the group planning a school event would be a task group. Finally, the group focused on overcoming test anxiety would be considered a counseling or therapy group.

91. C: Cognitive behavioral therapy is rooted in the belief that a client's emotional state is directly related to their beliefs or thoughts about their problems. Much of a client's time within cognitive behavioral therapy is spent challenging cognitions and changing self-talk, which in turn results in changing the client's emotional state. Don't confuse the ABC model in cognitive behavioral therapy with the ABC behavior model often used in schools when developing behavior interventions.

92. C: The School Counselor Performance Appraisal is a part of the Accountability component of an ASCA National Model program. The specifics of the tools used to complete the appraisal are based on school, district, or state guidelines and processes. ASCA recommends that School Counselor Performance Appraisals include a self-evaluation component in addition to an administrative evaluation and assessment of goal attainment. Like all program evaluation tools, the School Counselor Performance Appraisal should be based on a variety of data. This tool can be utilized by the school counselor and school administrators to make program decisions and adjustments.

93. B: Brief solution-focused counseling always focuses on the exception to the problem, improvements since the previous session, and progress toward the goal. Therefore, most subsequent sessions will begin with the counselor asking the client about what has improved since the previous session.

94. B: Standardized tests are a common experience and data point for schools across the country, and many schools and districts have used the results of these tests in all of the ways described in the answer choices. However, ASCA warns against placing too strong of an emphasis on individual test scores. Standardized tests provide only one data point in making decisions about curriculum, instruction, and the education of individual students. School counselors advocate for the use of multiple measures of student progress in making decisions about advanced or remedial coursework, intervention services, promotion, and retention. School counselors also advocate for the use of multiple measures in guiding school improvement, curriculum development, or instructional coaching. Standardized test scores can provide valuable information about academic achievement or school improvement, especially when the data is disaggregated by subgroup or compared to a norm-referenced group. However, this data should not be the sole or even primary data point in making decisions about students.

95. C: According to the ASCA Ethical Standards for School Counselors, counselors should evaluate any personal biases that may prevent them from providing comprehensive services to all students. When school counselors identify biases that interfere with providing comprehensive services to all students, they should seek additional training and development rather than deny counseling services to these students based on their personal biases. School counselors should work to promote an environment that respects diversity.

96. B: There are three types of action plans that can be created as part of a comprehensive school counseling program: curriculum action plan, small-group action plan, and closing-the-gap action plan. Therefore, the three corresponding results reports to analyze the effectiveness of these action plans are the curriculum results report, small-group results report, and closing-the-gap results report. There is not an individual counseling action plan or results report.

97. C: While students with educated parents are not a risk factor, this is not considered a type of parent involvement. Involvement begins at the parenting level. Schools cannot tell individuals how to parent; however, they can provide information for parents about encouraging good academic practices while at home. For example, informing parents about the appropriate amount of time their child should spend on homework is one strategy. Communication is the next level of participation. Sending home progress reports and holding conferences both increase communication between schools and parents. The third level involves volunteering, which can include one-time projects or long-term participation. The last three levels include learning at home. Examples of this are providing information on the skills their children will learn throughout the school year, decision-making by encouraging participating on a school advisory board, and collaboration with the community.

98. B: Discussion groups are effective ways to get parents and students involved in learning about cultural diversity. These discussion groups can offer participants the opportunity to talk about their particular cultures. Additionally, these groups offer a nonthreatening venue for others to ask questions and work out misunderstandings about various cultures that have been perpetuated by stereotypes. These groups also offer parents and students the chance to celebrate different cultures though activities. In addition to group discussions about participants' cultures, discussions about various types of families and lifestyles are beneficial. For example, biracial families, families with adopted or foster children, and families with stepparents are increasingly common in American society, and education about these various types of families is just as important as learning about other cultures.

99. D: Regardless of the type of abuse a girl may experience, there will be deep psychological effects that may last much longer than the actual abuse. Oftentimes, these girls will have low self-esteem and look for ways to make themselves feel better. Additionally, those children who are abused may turn to drugs and alcohol to numb the effects of the abuse. Teenage girls who experience abuse are also more likely to become pregnant than those girls who do not experience abuse. Finally, those experiencing abuse will often lose interest in school and their futures, and counselors will see a decline in their grades. Since the idea of abuse if often thought of taboo and embarrassing, counselors should be aware of these risk factors and outcomes when assessing students.

100. D: Counselors must respect the cultural identity of their students. Since the student is not seeing the counselor because of cultural identity issues, it would be considered professionally unethical for the counselor to address her Chinese heritage. It is, however, the counselor's responsibility to understand this student's cultural identity in order to develop effective interventions for this student's presenting problem. The counselor must also have a clear understanding of her own beliefs and stereotypes in this situation that may cause bias when treating this student. Counselors who are unaware of these issues may inadvertently treat a student of another culture with negativity or less support than she would a student of her own culture.

101. A: Thorough data analysis, including disaggregating data by subgroup, is typically used for either creating a closing-the-gap action plan or completing a school data profile. This type of data analysis is helpful for identifying potential achievement gaps or equity issues within the school or district that the counselor can plan to address with a closing-the-gap action plan. This type of detailed, schoolwide data analysis is typically not used for creating a small-group action plan, although a small group may be utilized as a strategy within a closing-the-gap action plan. The annual agreement is a document created between a counselor and an administrator to plan for and establish goals for the upcoming school year and is focused on the counseling program itself; a needs assessment is usually in the form of a survey completed by students, staff, and/or parents to identify strengths and areas of concern in the school.

102. C: With programs aimed at increasing graduation rates, outcome data such as the four-year graduation rate is often the primary piece of data that is highlighted; an effective counselor examines graduation rates even further by disaggregating data into student subgroups in order to identify gaps in achievement. Changes in this rate over time are also important in identifying areas of need or improvements made as a result of school counseling programs. School counselors also impact student mindsets and behaviors through their interventions, and perception data is an important method of measuring how students feel, what they think they know, and what they believe. Answer choice C represents a piece of perception data gathered through a student survey, possibly in a pre- and post-test format, that provides the counselor with information about the effectiveness of their intervention on their students' beliefs. Answer choices A and B represent process data, which is another important type of data to evaluate when evaluating program effectiveness.

103. A: Teacher advisors cooperate with school counselors to provide students with all-around support. These advisors help students adjust to a new school by offering orientation and support. Additionally, teacher advisors provide students with a sounding board when resolving disputes or misunderstandings with faculty members or other students. Oftentimes, advisors will initiate student work groups for various issues students may experience. These groups may focus on communication, conflict resolution, or general adjustment strategies. Overall, teacher advisors serve as advocates for students in order to make school and the educational experience both pleasant and rewarding.

104. B: Problem-centered, structured counseling groups allow students to share their experiences and hear similar experiences from their peers in a safe environment. This type of group setting also allows students to gain the support of their peers as well as receive feedback. Counselors conducting these groups should focus on changing deviant behaviors and encouraging participants to try out new behaviors during the week. These exercises can be discussed during sessions, and students can learn how to brainstorm appropriate behaviors together by sharing their experiences. While it is possible to conduct a problem-centered group for a number of different issues, topics such as self-actualization, safety, and physiological issues are typically the focus of primary prevention groups.

105. C: Typically, a counselor will conduct a student survey in order to gain an overall view of the student body. By collecting demographic information, the counselor can determine important differences in the student body. This information will assist in developing additional programs, activities, or interventions. When conducted as a formative assessment, demographic information can provide an indication of whether different groups of students are finding more benefit in a particular program or intervention. Again, this information will allow the counselor to modify a program or add programs to better fit the needs of all students involved.

106. A: The ASCA National Model states the question to be answered by the program evaluation as "How are students different as a result of the school counseling program?" Within the program evaluation, data about academic achievement, progress toward stated goals and objectives, counselor use of time, and the effectiveness of program components is collected and evaluated, but the impact on students is the focus of the evaluation process. Measuring student impact allows the school counselor to understand their progress toward stated goals and to identify areas for improvement or adjustments to their counseling program.

107. D: The use-of-time assessment is an ASCA National Model document, but it is not an action plan. The use-of-time assessment analyzes the counselor's activities over the course of the school year and is typically done twice per year; as an assessment, it is a look backward over activities already conducted rather than a data-driven plan for future actions. Curriculum action plans, small-group action plans, and closing-the-gap action plans are all data-driven planning documents that help the counselor design interventions for the future. The curriculum action plan helps counselors create an effective plan for implementing the school counseling curriculum, and the small-group action plan is a similar document for planning small-group interventions. Closing-the-gap action plans help counselors design interventions focused on addressing discrepancies in academic or behavioral outcome data between student groups.

108. C: Teacher advisors serve as advocates for students. They are respected adults whom students can turn to for support when problems arise. Therefore, it is important for students to be comfortable with their teacher advisors. While it is not practical to allow students to make a final decision on the advisor, schools should include students in the decision-making process. It is suggested that students be able to choose three to five teachers they would like to work with. Based on this information, counselors and teachers can then assign teacher advisors while keeping the student's wishes in mind.

109. A: Particularly with a group focused on social skills with students who struggle with appropriate social behavior, the individual interview is an extremely important part of the group selection process. Since all of the identified students are already known to struggle with social skills, it is necessary to interview each student to determine their current level of functioning with the skills necessary for group participation, such as active listening and turn-taking. Answer D, conducting an individual counseling session to practice group skills, may be appropriate for some group members after determining the final makeup of the group.

110. A: The recommended and most commonly used practice for academic intervention plans is a strengths-based focus. Most students needing an academic intervention plan are already aware (or their parents and teachers are aware) of the problems they are facing. The school counselor's role in the academic intervention process is to identify the strengths the student has that may be supported in order to increase academic outcomes. The interventions designed in this type of plan are typically focused on either utilizing existing strengths or overcoming barriers. Cognitive behavioral therapy describes a method of one-on-one counseling, which at times may be a part of the plan, but it would not be the approach used to actually develop the plan. Family factors are often considered in developing academic intervention plans, but family therapy is not part of a school counselor's duties and should not be used to develop an academic intervention plan.

111. C: Denial occurs when individuals experience shock and disbelief over the loss of a loved one. The experience is so overwhelming that it cannot be experienced all at once. Denial serves as a protective or coping mechanism during the initial stage of grief and loss. Elizabeth Kubler-Ross's five stages of grief are denial, anger, bargaining, depression, and acceptance. Individuals in the anger stage of grief may blame others or believe that the circumstances surrounding the death were unfair, whereas individuals in the bargaining stage may try to make a deal with a higher power to have a better or different outcome. The depression stage of grief involves profound sadness and loss before finally reaching the acceptance stage in which the individual accepts the permanently altered reality and readjusts to live life beyond the loss.

112. B: Although using this type of assessment may result in more neutral responses, most individuals will provide their true thoughts. Receiving an assessment with all neutral responses should be considered as an outlier. Depending on the purpose of the assessment, the counselor may consider disregarding it in the results and providing an explanation in any required report. Depending on the nature of the assessment, the counselor can conduct additional assessments with the student to determine any difficulties this student may be having. Regardless, when giving students surveys, it must be indicated that all responses are confidential, and the students should respond as honestly as possible.

113. A: IDEA, the Individuals with Disabilities Education Act, provides for the education of children with disabilities by requiring schools to provide a free, appropriate public instruction through an individualized education plan (IEP) to children with disabilities in one of thirteen categories. These categories include: autism, deaf-blind, developmental delay, emotional disturbance, hearing impairments (including deafness), intellectual disability, multiple disabilities, orthopedic impairments, other health impairments, specific learning disabilities, speech or language impairments, traumatic brain injury, and visual impairments (including blindness). Therefore, the school counselor would refer to the provisions of this law as well as school policies under IDEA to provide information to Hanna's parents. The other laws named in answer choices include Section 504, Family Educational Rights and Privacy Act (FERPA), and Every Student Succeeds Act (ESSA). Section 504 is also a disability-related law, but Section 504 addresses how a school will provide accommodations and modifications to remove the barriers a child's disability may create for accessing curriculum; an IEP outlines a specific educational plan including specialized instruction. FERPA has to do with the privacy of student records, and ESSA is a federal law guiding K-12 public education policy.

114. B: Psychological career theory, also known as personality career theory, focuses on an individual's personality type and the types of careers that best fit that personality type. A psychological or personality approach will always begin with a Self-Directed Search to determine the individual's personality type. Researching careers that students are already interested in or learning about the skills and abilities needed in those careers are common activities in many schools, but these do not fit the psychological career theory whereby individuals are matched to potential careers based on their personality type. Before researching careers, students would need to take the personality survey to determine which types of careers are best suited for their personality type. A field trip to visit a real-life work setting would be more aligned with a social learning career theory, such as the approach developed by John Krumboltz. A social learning career theory is based on the concept that interests are learned, so exposure to a variety of careers and work sites gives an individual more learning and experiences from which to develop their interests.

115. B: Although FERPA permits sharing academic information within the school for staff with a "legitimate educational interest," outside agencies do not qualify for this permission. Although sharing this information with the case manager would probably directly benefit the student by assisting the tutoring program with identifying areas of need, the counselor must have parental consent to share this information with any outside agency. Having the student choose whether to provide this information is not appropriate, especially if they are a minor.

116. A: Generally speaking, the mean is less than the median in distributions with data skewed to the left. The mean, median, and mode (i.e., measures of central tendency) are all the same values in a normal distribution. When distributions are skewed to the right, the mode is the lowest value. In distributions skewed right (i.e., positive distributions), the mode is less than the median and the median is less than the mean.

117. B: Any form of electronic communication between the school counselor and other school officials can create an official school record that needs to be treated appropriately under FERPA, even if student names are not used. All forms of electronic communication should adhere to the ethical standards, and special care should be taken to protect confidentiality by utilizing accepted security standards. The ASCA Ethical Standards encourage counselors to take care in purging electronic sole-possession case notes, similar to hard-copy sole possession case notes.

118. A: Generally speaking, classroom guidance is a preventative activity; it is systematically delivered to all students. Intervention activities take place when an issue or problem is identified, therefore an activity that is systematically delivered to all students is not an intervention activity. Outreach involves literally "reaching out" of the school and into the community, and classroom guidance obviously does not fit this description. While classroom guidance may be focused on academic topics, "academic" is not a type of counseling activity.

119. D: Thinking, feeling, and relating are considered a modern model of human development. Thinking begins at home and consists of the values, thoughts, and beliefs imposed by parents. These thoughts are further supported by social interactions. Cognitive skills training assists students in further developing these abilities. Feelings can also be associated with the development of self-concept and self-esteem. Emotional literacy skills training and programs help students become more aware of their own feelings. Finally, relating involves an individual's interpersonal skills. Social literacy skills programs will assist students in relating to other students and adults.

120. D: Program outcome data provides information on the direct impacts of the school counseling program on student outcomes. When combined with program process and perception data, outcome data helps a school counselor create a clear picture of their program over the course of a school year. The school data profile, closing-the-gap action plan, and state testing results can all help clarify goals for the next school year, but the outcome data provides information that is most directly related to the school counseling program to identify areas for improvement.

Praxis Practice Tests #2 and #3

To take these additional Praxis practice tests, visit our bonus page:
mometrix.com/bonus948/praxsccoun5442

How to Overcome Test Anxiety

Just the thought of taking a test is enough to make most people a little nervous. A test is an important event that can have a long-term impact on your future, so it's important to take it seriously and it's natural to feel anxious about performing well. But just because anxiety is normal, that doesn't mean that it's helpful in test taking, or that you should simply accept it as part of your life. Anxiety can have a variety of effects. These effects can be mild, like making you feel slightly nervous, or severe, like blocking your ability to focus or remember even a simple detail.

If you experience test anxiety—whether severe or mild—it's important to know how to beat it. To discover this, first you need to understand what causes test anxiety.

Causes of Test Anxiety

While we often think of anxiety as an uncontrollable emotional state, it can actually be caused by simple, practical things. One of the most common causes of test anxiety is that a person does not feel adequately prepared for their test. This feeling can be the result of many different issues such as poor study habits or lack of organization, but the most common culprit is time management. Starting to study too late, failing to organize your study time to cover all of the material, or being distracted while you study will mean that you're not well prepared for the test. This may lead to cramming the night before, which will cause you to be physically and mentally exhausted for the test. Poor time management also contributes to feelings of stress, fear, and hopelessness as you realize you are not well prepared but don't know what to do about it.

Other times, test anxiety is not related to your preparation for the test but comes from unresolved fear. This may be a past failure on a test, or poor performance on tests in general. It may come from comparing yourself to others who seem to be performing better or from the stress of living up to expectations. Anxiety may be driven by fears of the future—how failure on this test would affect your educational and career goals. These fears are often completely irrational, but they can still negatively impact your test performance.

Elements of Test Anxiety

As mentioned earlier, test anxiety is considered to be an emotional state, but it has physical and mental components as well. Sometimes you may not even realize that you are suffering from test anxiety until you notice the physical symptoms. These can include trembling hands, rapid heartbeat, sweating, nausea, and tense muscles. Extreme anxiety may lead to fainting or vomiting. Obviously, any of these symptoms can have a negative impact on testing. It is important to recognize them as soon as they begin to occur so that you can address the problem before it damages your performance.

The mental components of test anxiety include trouble focusing and inability to remember learned information. During a test, your mind is on high alert, which can help you recall information and stay focused for an extended period of time. However, anxiety interferes with your mind's natural processes, causing you to blank out, even on the questions you know well. The strain of testing during anxiety makes it difficult to stay focused, especially on a test that may take several hours. Extreme anxiety can take a huge mental toll, making it difficult not only to recall test information but even to understand the test questions or pull your thoughts together.

Effects of Test Anxiety

Test anxiety is like a disease—if left untreated, it will get progressively worse. Anxiety leads to poor performance, and this reinforces the feelings of fear and failure, which in turn lead to poor performances on subsequent tests. It can grow from a mild nervousness to a crippling condition. If allowed to progress, test anxiety can have a big impact on your schooling, and consequently on your future.

Test anxiety can spread to other parts of your life. Anxiety on tests can become anxiety in any stressful situation, and blanking on a test can turn into panicking in a job situation. But fortunately, you don't have to let anxiety rule your testing and determine your grades. There are a number of relatively simple steps you can take to move past anxiety and function normally on a test and in the rest of life.

Physical Steps for Beating Test Anxiety

While test anxiety is a serious problem, the good news is that it can be overcome. It doesn't have to control your ability to think and remember information. While it may take time, you can begin taking steps today to beat anxiety.

Just as your first hint that you may be struggling with anxiety comes from the physical symptoms, the first step to treating it is also physical. Rest is crucial for having a clear, strong mind. If you are tired, it is much easier to give in to anxiety. But if you establish good sleep habits, your body and mind will be ready to perform optimally, without the strain of exhaustion. Additionally, sleeping well helps you to retain information better, so you're more likely to recall the answers when you see the test questions.

Getting good sleep means more than going to bed on time. It's important to allow your brain time to relax. Take study breaks from time to time so it doesn't get overworked, and don't study right before bed. Take time to rest your mind before trying to rest your body, or you may find it difficult to fall asleep.

Along with sleep, other aspects of physical health are important in preparing for a test. Good nutrition is vital for good brain function. Sugary foods and drinks may give a burst of energy but this burst is followed by a crash, both physically and emotionally. Instead, fuel your body with protein and vitamin-rich foods.

Also, drink plenty of water. Dehydration can lead to headaches and exhaustion, especially if your brain is already under stress from the rigors of the test. Particularly if your test is a long one, drink water during the breaks. And if possible, take an energy-boosting snack to eat between sections.

Along with sleep and diet, a third important part of physical health is exercise. Maintaining a steady workout schedule is helpful, but even taking 5-minute study breaks to walk can help get your blood pumping faster and clear your head. Exercise also releases endorphins, which contribute to a positive feeling and can help combat test anxiety.

When you nurture your physical health, you are also contributing to your mental health. If your body is healthy, your mind is much more likely to be healthy as well. So take time to rest, nourish your body with healthy food and water, and get moving as much as possible. Taking these physical steps will make you stronger and more able to take the mental steps necessary to overcome test anxiety.

Mental Steps for Beating Test Anxiety

Working on the mental side of test anxiety can be more challenging, but as with the physical side, there are clear steps you can take to overcome it. As mentioned earlier, test anxiety often stems from lack of preparation, so the obvious solution is to prepare for the test. Effective studying may be the most important weapon you have for beating test anxiety, but you can and should employ several other mental tools to combat fear.

First, boost your confidence by reminding yourself of past success—tests or projects that you aced. If you're putting as much effort into preparing for this test as you did for those, there's no reason you should expect to fail here. Work hard to prepare; then trust your preparation.

Second, surround yourself with encouraging people. It can be helpful to find a study group, but be sure that the people you're around will encourage a positive attitude. If you spend time with others who are anxious or cynical, this will only contribute to your own anxiety. Look for others who are motivated to study hard from a desire to succeed, not from a fear of failure.

Third, reward yourself. A test is physically and mentally tiring, even without anxiety, and it can be helpful to have something to look forward to. Plan an activity following the test, regardless of the outcome, such as going to a movie or getting ice cream.

When you are taking the test, if you find yourself beginning to feel anxious, remind yourself that you know the material. Visualize successfully completing the test. Then take a few deep, relaxing breaths and return to it. Work through the questions carefully but with confidence, knowing that you are capable of succeeding.

Developing a healthy mental approach to test taking will also aid in other areas of life. Test anxiety affects more than just the actual test—it can be damaging to your mental health and even contribute to depression. It's important to beat test anxiety before it becomes a problem for more than testing.

Study Strategy

Being prepared for the test is necessary to combat anxiety, but what does being prepared look like? You may study for hours on end and still not feel prepared. What you need is a strategy for test prep. The next few pages outline our recommended steps to help you plan out and conquer the challenge of preparation.

STEP 1: SCOPE OUT THE TEST

Learn everything you can about the format (multiple choice, essay, etc.) and what will be on the test. Gather any study materials, course outlines, or sample exams that may be available. Not only will this help you to prepare, but knowing what to expect can help to alleviate test anxiety.

STEP 2: MAP OUT THE MATERIAL

Look through the textbook or study guide and make note of how many chapters or sections it has. Then divide these over the time you have. For example, if a book has 15 chapters and you have five days to study, you need to cover three chapters each day. Even better, if you have the time, leave an extra day at the end for overall review after you have gone through the material in depth.

If time is limited, you may need to prioritize the material. Look through it and make note of which sections you think you already have a good grasp on, and which need review. While you are studying, skim quickly through the familiar sections and take more time on the challenging parts.

Write out your plan so you don't get lost as you go. Having a written plan also helps you feel more in control of the study, so anxiety is less likely to arise from feeling overwhelmed at the amount to cover.

STEP 3: GATHER YOUR TOOLS

Decide what study method works best for you. Do you prefer to highlight in the book as you study and then go back over the highlighted portions? Or do you type out notes of the important information? Or is it helpful to make flashcards that you can carry with you? Assemble the pens, index cards, highlighters, post-it notes, and any other materials you may need so you won't be distracted by getting up to find things while you study.

If you're having a hard time retaining the information or organizing your notes, experiment with different methods. For example, try color-coding by subject with colored pens, highlighters, or post-it notes. If you learn better by hearing, try recording yourself reading your notes so you can listen while in the car, working out, or simply sitting at your desk. Ask a friend to quiz you from your flashcards, or try teaching someone the material to solidify it in your mind.

STEP 4: CREATE YOUR ENVIRONMENT

It's important to avoid distractions while you study. This includes both the obvious distractions like visitors and the subtle distractions like an uncomfortable chair (or a too-comfortable couch that makes you want to fall asleep). Set up the best study environment possible: good lighting and a comfortable work area. If background music helps you focus, you may want to turn it on, but otherwise keep the room quiet. If you are using a computer to take notes, be sure you don't have any other windows open, especially applications like social media, games, or anything else that could distract you. Silence your phone and turn off notifications. Be sure to keep water close by so you stay hydrated while you study (but avoid unhealthy drinks and snacks).

Also, take into account the best time of day to study. Are you freshest first thing in the morning? Try to set aside some time then to work through the material. Is your mind clearer in the afternoon or evening? Schedule your study session then. Another method is to study at the same time of day that you will take the test, so that your brain gets used to working on the material at that time and will be ready to focus at test time.

STEP 5: STUDY!

Once you have done all the study preparation, it's time to settle into the actual studying. Sit down, take a few moments to settle your mind so you can focus, and begin to follow your study plan. Don't give in to distractions or let yourself procrastinate. This is your time to prepare so you'll be ready to fearlessly approach the test. Make the most of the time and stay focused.

Of course, you don't want to burn out. If you study too long you may find that you're not retaining the information very well. Take regular study breaks. For example, taking five minutes out of every hour to walk briskly, breathing deeply and swinging your arms, can help your mind stay fresh.

As you get to the end of each chapter or section, it's a good idea to do a quick review. Remind yourself of what you learned and work on any difficult parts. When you feel that you've mastered the material, move on to the next part. At the end of your study session, briefly skim through your notes again.

But while review is helpful, cramming last minute is NOT. If at all possible, work ahead so that you won't need to fit all your study into the last day. Cramming overloads your brain with more information than it can process and retain, and your tired mind may struggle to recall even previously learned information when it is overwhelmed with last-minute study. Also, the urgent nature of cramming and the stress placed on your brain contribute to anxiety. You'll be more likely to go to the test feeling unprepared and having trouble thinking clearly.

So don't cram, and don't stay up late before the test, even just to review your notes at a leisurely pace. Your brain needs rest more than it needs to go over the information again. In fact, plan to finish your studies by noon or early afternoon the day before the test. Give your brain the rest of the day to relax or focus on other things, and get a good night's sleep. Then you will be fresh for the test and better able to recall what you've studied.

STEP 6: TAKE A PRACTICE TEST

Many courses offer sample tests, either online or in the study materials. This is an excellent resource to check whether you have mastered the material, as well as to prepare for the test format and environment.

Check the test format ahead of time: the number of questions, the type (multiple choice, free response, etc.), and the time limit. Then create a plan for working through them. For example, if you have 30 minutes to take a 60-question test, your limit is 30 seconds per question. Spend less time on the questions you know well so that you can take more time on the difficult ones.

If you have time to take several practice tests, take the first one open book, with no time limit. Work through the questions at your own pace and make sure you fully understand them. Gradually work up to taking a test under test conditions: sit at a desk with all study materials put away and set a timer. Pace yourself to make sure you finish the test with time to spare and go back to check your answers if you have time.

After each test, check your answers. On the questions you missed, be sure you understand why you missed them. Did you misread the question (tests can use tricky wording)? Did you forget the information? Or was it something you hadn't learned? Go back and study any shaky areas that the practice tests reveal.

Taking these tests not only helps with your grade, but also aids in combating test anxiety. If you're already used to the test conditions, you're less likely to worry about it, and working through tests until you're scoring well gives you a confidence boost. Go through the practice tests until you feel comfortable, and then you can go into the test knowing that you're ready for it.

Test Tips

On test day, you should be confident, knowing that you've prepared well and are ready to answer the questions. But aside from preparation, there are several test day strategies you can employ to maximize your performance.

First, as stated before, get a good night's sleep the night before the test (and for several nights before that, if possible). Go into the test with a fresh, alert mind rather than staying up late to study.

Try not to change too much about your normal routine on the day of the test. It's important to eat a nutritious breakfast, but if you normally don't eat breakfast at all, consider eating just a protein bar. If you're a coffee drinker, go ahead and have your normal coffee. Just make sure you time it so that the caffeine doesn't wear off right in the middle of your test. Avoid sugary beverages, and drink enough water to stay hydrated but not so much that you need a restroom break 10 minutes into the test. If your test isn't first thing in the morning, consider going for a walk or doing a light workout before the test to get your blood flowing.

Allow yourself enough time to get ready, and leave for the test with plenty of time to spare so you won't have the anxiety of scrambling to arrive in time. Another reason to be early is to select a good seat. It's helpful to sit away from doors and windows, which can be distracting. Find a good seat, get out your supplies, and settle your mind before the test begins.

When the test begins, start by going over the instructions carefully, even if you already know what to expect. Make sure you avoid any careless mistakes by following the directions.

Then begin working through the questions, pacing yourself as you've practiced. If you're not sure on an answer, don't spend too much time on it, and don't let it shake your confidence. Either skip it and come back later, or eliminate as many wrong answers as possible and guess among the remaining ones. Don't dwell on these questions as you continue—put them out of your mind and focus on what lies ahead.

Be sure to read all of the answer choices, even if you're sure the first one is the right answer. Sometimes you'll find a better one if you keep reading. But don't second-guess yourself if you do immediately know the answer. Your gut instinct is usually right. Don't let test anxiety rob you of the information you know.

If you have time at the end of the test (and if the test format allows), go back and review your answers. Be cautious about changing any, since your first instinct tends to be correct, but make sure you didn't misread any of the questions or accidentally mark the wrong answer choice. Look over any you skipped and make an educated guess.

At the end, leave the test feeling confident. You've done your best, so don't waste time worrying about your performance or wishing you could change anything. Instead, celebrate the successful completion of this test. And finally, use this test to learn how to deal with anxiety even better next time.

> **Review Video: Test Anxiety**
> Visit mometrix.com/academy and enter code: 100340

Important Qualification

Not all anxiety is created equal. If your test anxiety is causing major issues in your life beyond the classroom or testing center, or if you are experiencing troubling physical symptoms related to your anxiety, it may be a sign of a serious physiological or psychological condition. If this sounds like your situation, we strongly encourage you to seek professional help.

Additional Bonus Material

Due to our efforts to try to keep this book to a manageable length, we've created a link that will give you access to all of your additional bonus material:

mometrix.com/bonus948/praxsccoun5422